Guerrillas in the Bureaucracy

WILEY SERIES IN URBAN RESEARCH

TERRY N. CLARK, EDITOR

Guerrillas in the Bureaucracy

The Community Planning Experiment
in the United States

MARTIN L. NEEDLEMAN

CAROLYN EMERSON NEEDLEMAN

A WILEY-INTERSCIENCE PUBLICATION

JOHN WILEY & SONS, New York · London · Sydney · Toronto

HT
167
.N38

Library of Congress Cataloging in Publication Data:
Needleman, Martin L.   1936–
     Guerrillas in the bureaucracy.

     (Wiley series in urban research)
     "A Wiley-Interscience publication."
     Bibliography: p.
     1. Cities and towns—Planning—United States.
I. Needleman, Carolyn Emerson, 1941–   joint
author. II. Title.

HT167.N38   309.2′62′0973   73-19806
ISBN 0-471-63099-3

For Ed and Mark

Planners who don't fight the system get trapped into impossible moral dilemmas. As long as they accept the low level of federal commitment to the cities and try to plan rationally within that framework, they're forced to act inhumanely. It's like having one life raft for a hundred drowning people. . . . That's why some of us feel we have to go outside the system.

COMMUNITY PLANNER

Cities, especially American cities, are attracting more public attention and scholarly concern than at perhaps any other time in history. Traditional structures have been seriously questioned and sweeping changes proposed; simultaneously, efforts are being made to penetrate the fundamental processes by which cities operate. This effort calls for marshaling knowledge from a number of substantive areas. Sociologists, political scientists, economists, geographers, planners, historians, anthropologists, and others have turned to urban questions; interdisciplinary projects involving scholars and activists are groping with fundamental issues.

The Wiley Series in Urban Research has been created to encourage the publication of works bearing on urban questions. It seeks to publish studies from different fields that help to illuminate urban processes. It is addressed to scholars as well as to planners, administrators, and others concerned with a more analytical understanding of things urban.

TERRY N. CLARK

Acknowledgments

We would like to extend our sincere and heartfelt thanks to all the planners who gave so generously of their time and insights while we were interviewing in their cities. Although they must remain anonymous in the study, we feel a personal and individual debt to each of them, as well as respect and admiration for their commitment to America's troubled cities. We are particularly grateful to the directors of the city planning departments we visited for their cooperation in granting us permission to interview their staffs, their assistance in pulling together information about their departments' activities, and especially their patience with our disruption of departmental routine. In addition, we owe much to two old and dear friends: Elwin H. Powell, without whose unfailing support this study would never have been completed, and Mark C. Kennedy, who gave needed encouragement in the early stages of the project and made invaluable comments on an early draft. The research was facilitated by a grant from the National Science Foundation, which we gratefully acknowledge. We would also like to thank some others who have helped in various ways—some indirect but all deeply appreciated—to make the publication of this book possible: Lars Rydell and Charlene Becker Rydell for helpful criticisms and even more for their warm and constant friendship, which sustained us through some dark moments; John Sirjamaki and Lionel Lewis for their support and encouragement; Robert Lynch for drawing our attention to some very useful concepts in the work of F. G. Bailey; Terry N. Clark, Eric Valentine, and the editorial staff at John Wiley & Sons for their assistance; and Sadie Needleman, Virginia Williams Emerson, George A. Emerson, and Bernice Emerson for their faith.

The first author, on whose doctoral dissertation this book is based, bears major responsibility for the overall conceptualization and analysis presented here. The second author shares responsibility for collecting and codifying the data and bears major responsibility for modifying the dissertation into book form.

MARTIN L. NEEDLEMAN

CAROLYN EMERSON NEEDLEMAN

Vassar College
Poughkeepsie, New York
September 1973

Contents

Part Three: The Planner and His Department

Part Four: The Planner and City Hall

Part Five: The Planner and His Role

Part Six: Conclusions

Guerrillas in the Bureaucracy

Introduction

This study of community planning began as a sociological stab in the dark, for city planning is a profession about which very little is known. When a particular occupation exists in a society over a long period of time, so that people hear about it and encounter those working in it, a general familiarity with the occupation's content develops. Most of us have some idea of what a teacher or a doctor does. Our knowledge may be incomplete or perhaps inaccurate in detail, but the rough outline of the occupation has become part of our shared culture. Supplementing this informal acquaintance, the systematic study of occupations and professions by social scientists has given us intricate analyses of a wide range of jobs and the people who work in them—nurses, policemen, doctors, lawyers, academicians, miners, factory workers. Even those in marginal or illegal occupations—such as confidence men, jazz musicians, and call girls—have served as the subjects of research. The profession of city planning, however, remains relatively unexplored.

Despite its relevance to some of the most serious problems and deepest concerns of contemporary society in the United States, city planning has attracted little attention from either the general public or social scientists (1). Its emergence as a definable occupational category is recent and the visibility of its activities low. Most people, if they have heard of city planning at all, have only the foggiest idea of what city planners do.

Accordingly, our original intent in undertaking this research was broad and general: to gain some insight, through systematic organizational analysis, into the present operations of city planning agencies in the United States. Our interest was partly academic but also deeply personal. Like many people concerned with the increasing difficulty of living in cities, we were and remain convinced that planning must play a greater role if urban decline is to be halted. In designing the original study, we noted that many interest groups agree that seemingly discrete urban problems are interrelated and require planning for their solution. Yet it is clear from the literature available on planning, as well as from the state of American cities, that city planning's impact has so far been minimal. As Edward C. Banfield observes, urban planning is presently little more than an exercise in futility:

> American cities . . . seldom make and never carry out comprehensive plans. Plan making is with us an idle exercise, for we neither agree upon the content of a "public interest" that ought to override private ones nor permit the centralization of authority needed to carry a plan into effect if one were made (2).

The failure of city planning, it seemed to us, pointed up a major contradiction in contemporary society in the United States. Public planning assumes order, coordination, and rational use of resources to maximize equity among the various sectors that make up the social order. However, public planning must operate within the environment created by the two major institutions that have historically shaped the social fabric of American life: capitalism and democracy. These institutions, which together make up what could be called the "liberal society," encourage freedom of action on the part of individuals and organized groups in pursuit of their interests, permitting a wide variety of experiments but also waste, disorder, and extreme inequity. Both capitalism and democracy thrive in a social context of creative disorder quite contrary to the requirements of planning. Because of this inconsistency, city planning—so desperately needed and so desperately resisted—presents a new American dilemma, which seems to be moving no closer to resolution as cities continue to decay. Thus not only to examine an obscure profession but also to illuminate a major and agonizing source of strain in society, we set out to explore the point where the contradictory pressures of public planning and private interest intersect: the city planning agency.

The Logic of Exploratory Studies

The narrowing of focus from this original general investigation of city planning agencies to a detailed analysis of community planning programs is a direct outcome of the methodology used, and it merits some discussion because it illustrates a valuable but still underrated approach in sociology. Exploratory research has long occupied a kind of second-class status among sociologists because the research design often changes from week to week and the methods of data collection seem haphazard and lacking in rigor. To call a study "exploratory" faintly but unmistakeably impugns its claim to scientific legitimacy. Some regard it as an informal and sloppy preliminary stage of investigation, interesting mainly because it paves the way for "real" research on pre-

viously unfamiliar subjects. However, by now a number of
exploratory studies have gained wide recognition as classics in
sociology, giving the field some of its more useful concepts
and theories. Thus it seems clear that such research can have
a value beyond mere introduction of new subjects, and that it
is not necessarily lacking in methodological and theoretical
sophistication.

Exploratory studies do, however, have a logic all their
own, different from research based on a groundwork of prior
information. Their methodology is tailored to their special
purpose, which is to collect information about an unknown
phenomenon, develop categories of thought where none existed before, and generate new ideas—not to test preestab-
lished hypotheses. At the start of an exploratory study, the
researcher is in no position to foresee what aspects of his subject will prove most interesting or important. Elaborate hypotheses developed out of sketchy information can quickly
become a Procrustean bed into which the researcher forces
his findings no matter how ill the fit. Precision research meth-
odologies become traps rather than tools, because they assume
a stability in the basic categories of the research rarely found
in exploratory studies. Researchers investigating subjects
about which little is known—Italian gangs, gypsum miners,
black streetcorner men—have often found the final product of their analyses only distantly related to the ideas they
started out with. Indeed, such studies often begin with a deliberate vagueness and crudity of design and methodology, to
allow for maximum flexibility to follow up and develop seren-
dipitous observations and fragmentary ideas that come up in
the course of the research. The basic strategy of exploratory
research is to start by spreading as wide a net as possible,
sweeping in not only the particular elements that initially
seem most interesting but also data and ideas that at first may
seem irrelevant or trivial. The resulting mass of material may
be untidy, but it nurtures insights that would be aborted by a

more elegant approach. As the study progresses, the researcher will gradually discover where he is headed and which data or ideas he will use; he cannot know in advance.

We feel we owe a debt to those sociologists who have included in their published exploratory studies a frank account of the methods they used in gathering and analyzing their data—writers such as Peter Blau, Ely Chinoy, Herbert Gans, Alvin Gouldner, Elliot Liebow, Arthur Vidich and Joseph Bensman, William Foote Whyte, and Harold Wilensky (3). These notes gave us not only many helpful practical hints but also the faith that our research approach was not as illogical as it sometimes seemed and would eventually yield worthwhile results. We hope that the account which follows, describing the stages this study passed through, will lend some encouragement to others floundering in the initial confusion of an exploratory study.

Collecting the Data

In beginning this study, we made an early commitment to the personal interview technique for collecting basic data. We were interested not only in city planners' attitudes and social-psychological responses to their conflict-ridden occupational status, but also in the information they could give us concerning the operations and organization of the city planning department. We hoped to use them both as subjects and as expert informants about the system they worked in. Open-ended personal interviews seemed to us to be the only way to tap into this full range of data. Although we later supplemented the interview data with documents and participant observation, as well as a brief biographical questionnaire that each planner filled out and mailed back to us, we found that these lengthy informal interview sessions yielded information that probably could have been gained in no other way.

To guide the interview and ensure comparability, we constructed an interview schedule on the basis of the available planning literature. We went over the few available studies of American city planning and the major planning journals dating back over a twenty-year period, making notes of all topics and issues that seemed remotely likely to get planners talking about the problems, satisfactions, and nature of their work. These notes, converted into a manageable number of general questions, formed the bulk of the interview schedule. We clustered the questions roughly into topics that seemed promising sociologically—role orientations and role transformations, the fit between the department's formal and informal structure, degree of professional identification, interaction with other departments, definition of planning, attitude toward the past and present role of planning in urban development, and reactions to proposals for innovations in the role of planning currently being discussed in professional journals.

We then carried out a pretest in the planning departments of two nearby cities—a disillusioning experience that led to the drastic revision of the interview schedule. The original had been too long with too many closed-ended specific questions that overlapped. It didn't fit the rhythm of the planners' responses. Although still lengthy, the revised version consisted of simpler questions, designed to start the planner on a train of thought rather than forcing a structured response. (Appendix A is a sample of the schedule.)

The pretest also convinced us that the study would be far more fruitful as a multicity study than as a depth analysis of one planning department. In that way common themes and problems would show up that we might otherwise miss or fail to recognize. To ensure rough comparability, we decided to focus on medium to large sized cities, each with a long history as the primary metropolitan center in its geographic region. The nine cities selected (Boston, Philadelphia, Detroit, Providence, Cincinnati, Cleveland, Buffalo, Baltimore, and St.

Louis) represent the full range of problems afflicting established urban centers across the country—housing shortage, traffic congestion, pollution, scarce recreational facilities, overtaxed municipal services and inadequate revenues, high crime rates, ethnic and racial agitation, and physical urban decay.

Because our purpose was exploration rather than hypothesis testing, we did not take a random sample. Instead we aimed at interviewing every member of the management and staff of each city's planning department who carried the official designation of city planner. Initially records were also kept of informal conversations with some members of the department's nonplanning staff, such as drafting personnel and secretaries, but these staff members showed such caution in their comments on internal department affairs and unfamiliarity with the department's external activities and relationships that we soon dropped the effort and concentrated only on the planners themselves. The nine departments in the study included a total of 173 planners. Of these, we were able to interview 155. The refusal rate was very low, with only four planners turning down the request for an interview; most of the planners missed were unavailable because of leaves or illness.

Interviews typically lasted about two hours, with many over four hours and a few as long as seven hours. Only three were shorter than 45 minutes. Since one or both of us were around each department every day for at least several weeks, contact with the planners was not limited to the interview itself. We sometimes attended department and planning commission meetings with them, went out with those who were speaking to community groups, and talked with them over lunches and dinners. Some volunteered to take us on "grand tours" of the city or to show us the city's night life. A few we visited in their homes and corresponded with after leaving the city. Besides providing additional information about their professional activities, these informal contacts lent fullness and intimacy to the interview data. Our research notes began to recall to us not a series of impersonal, anonymous "respondents" but unique and memorable individuals, whose struggles and feelings took on the vividness of recounted adventures from thoughtful autobiographies or the lives of well-defined characters in an absorbing novel.

As the interviews accumulated, we constantly discussed them, reread them, and searched them for signs of patterns emerging. About halfway through the research we began to notice a convergence in the data. Many of the internal tensions in the planning department, the personal frustrations of individual planners, and the frictions with other city departments seemed related to a common source: an innovative program called *community planning*, in which planners are assigned to work with the residents of specific areas of the city. We had known of this new development in planning from our initial contacts with planners and review of planning literature, and we had included a number of questions concerning advocacy and community contacts in the interview schedule. But we had not anticipated the extent of experimentation with community planning.

Of the nine departments we investigated, six had established community planning programs. In two of the larger departments as much as half the planning staff was involved in work with assigned districts rather than comprehensive planning or city-wide concerns. In two others the program encompassed only a few special areas of the city; a handful of planners would be assigned to work with active community groups in these districts. But even where the program was relatively limited in scope, it seemed uniquely problematic for both the department and the planners who worked in it. Reactions to the community planning programs pervaded the interviews, cropping up in responses to questions aimed at different issues entirely. Bitter antagonisms between those involved in the community planning programs and the rest of the planning staff showed up frequently, both factions viewing the other as an obstruction or irrelevant to "real" planning. Those directly involved in the community planning programs—a total of 70 out of the 155 planners we interviewed—were themselves often disturbed over the conflict-filled situations their new role created for them. It seemed that the dilemmas of balancing public planning and private interest that we had set out to investigate had spilled over from the city planning department's external relations into the structure of the department itself, and even into the actions of individual planners.

As we shall see, community planning in many ways represents the antithesis of the type of planning traditionally carried out by the city planning department. With the contradictions, frictions, and accommodations between the two different planning approaches looming larger with each interview, we decided to focus on these issues. While still using the same interview schedule and still contacting all planners rather than just those directly working in community planning, we began relating all our material to the development and special problems of this troubled and troublesome innovation that is becoming a major battlefield for competing values and priorities in city planning in the United States.

Gaining Departmental Cooperation

In some ways the most critical step in the development of this study was gaining the cooperation of the department's management. Without this support we would have been denied access to the planners during working hours. Planners probably would have granted much shorter interviews if the sessions with us represented lost leisure time rather than a part of their job. Similarly, their attitude toward the study probably would have been different if we had lacked the director's sponsorship, since this support legitimated our status as bona fide researchers. Moreover, we wanted not only interviews but access to department documents and the opportunity to observe the planners at work. For this we had to be present and accepted in the department office.

Therefore, the initial contact with the planning department's director in each city was a tense moment. Various approaches were tried. In most cases the first step was a letter, on university stationery, describing the study briefly and mentioning that one of us would be in the city in the near future and would like to discuss the possible participation of the planning department. This was followed by a phone call arranging an appointment. These initial meetings tended to be similar, so that it was soon possible to anticipate and prepare for the directors' reservations about sponsoring the study. Their questions typically revolved around three concerns: the legitimacy of the research, the time it would take, and the protection of department secrets.

Although no department we approached had ever been the subject of a full-scale sociological study, most were constantly being bombarded by requests for interviews by graduate planning students, university undergraduates, and high school students. Groups of observers frequently asked to visit the department. Although the directors felt it their civic duty to allow some public contact of this sort, they were also defensive, showing signs of "interview fatigue." If we wanted to do extensive interviewing, they implied, the research had better be serious and important—not a pointless drain on the planners' energy. This objection was usually dropped once the study was fully explained.

Worries about the time we would need presented a greater problem. We were, after all, asking for at least an hour, maybe more, with each staff member. In one large department the business manager, horrified at the idea of having to justify such a time loss to the city administration, kept muttering, "That's 30 hours! Maybe 60!" By this point in the conversation, however, the directors were usually intrigued by the study and curious about what we would find. We assured them that each department included would be sent a copy of the research findings when the study was completed. This made it possible for them to interpret the time loss as an investment in a free professional analysis and evaluation of city planning rather than a waste of the taxpayers' money. As we went along, the time-loss problem became easier to solve; since planning departments in other cities had agreed, each subsequent department we contacted more readily cooperated. Once the study gained official sanction, the department personnel, both staff and management, were extremely generous in their contribution of time. Even though we inevitably needed much more time than originally anticipated, practically no objections were raised.

The directors were understandably worried about information gathered for our study coming back in some unpleasant way to haunt the department, aggravating its sometimes strained relations with the city administration and the public, or fueling internal disputes among staff members. We assured each that his department's privacy would be respected, that the activities of specific departments and individuals would be thoroughly disguised in any published version of the study, and that no gossip or damaging information would be spread either within the department or to others. Such promises would probably have been useless if the directors had not already decided we were trustworthy. The description of the study at the beginning of the meeting apparently had the side benefits of conveying a sense of research responsibility and sympathy for city planning, inclining the director to accept our promise of anonymity at face value. Again, once commitment to the study was made, cooperation was extremely good. Both management and staff discussed potentially embarrassing departmental problems and mistakes with remarkable frankness and showed us many "in-house" documents, including a few kept secret even from other members of the department.

Analyzing the Data

While collecting the data, we discussed the interviews and our observations continually, noting in a running log any patterns or generalizations that occurred to us. Thus when we began the analysis, some of the major themes and concepts used in the study were already sketched in a primitive form. We found, however, that a great many important linkages were impossible to detect as we went along. They could be uncovered only by reading and rereading the data—the transcribed interviews, notes on our observations in the departments we visited, department documents, and the idea file we had kept while reviewing planning literature and carrying out the interviews. As we went over and over this material, we matched up similar situations. Planner X's reported experiences would call to mind something mentioned by Planner Y, and this in turn would remind us of a comment by someone else or an observation we had made in one of the departments. We would then formulate a tentative concept, typology, or category and go searching through the data to see if, with this clue, we could find evidence of a general pattern. Sometimes what seemed at first a promising lead proved idiosyncratic to a few planners or limited to one department, and had to be dropped. Other concepts, stimulated by a single interview, turned out to be crucial in directing us to something we might otherwise have missed in the comments of planners who shared the behavior pattern but spoke about it briefly or indirectly. At this point the serendipity value of the "shotgun" approach we had used, taking down notes on everything no matter how peripheral it seemed to community planning at the time, became apparent. Once bits of data fell together, they seemed so obviously related that we wondered how we could have overlooked the connection while interviewing. Yet often the connection had not been clear at the time and involved data that might have been discarded as irrelevant if we had been more selective.

This method of data treatment—qualitative content analysis—differs considerably from the numerical approaches often used in formal attitude surveys or structural analyses. The planners' responses to individual questions in the interview schedule are not easily reduced to precise enumerations or scales. Some talked about similar things in different parts of the interview; some spent most of the interview talking about one particular issue that intrigued or disturbed them and answered other questions perfunctorily. The responses are also very uneven because some planners were far more articulate, reflective, and insightful about their work than others. It would have been useless to try to quantify all responses to any particular question. Instead, we shuttled back and forth, stitching together bits of experience that seemed related, trying to capture elusive social-psychological variables such as the planners' definition of their situation, the feel and texture of their interaction with each other, their sense of excitement and frustration as they deal with community residents and other city agencies.

The hazards of this method are obvious. Tough questions confront the researchers using it. Are the patterns they see "really" there? Without numerical guideposts, can they make any claim to typicality for their findings? The method is clearly open to abuse if employed irresponsibly. This is also true, however, of more rigorous research methods. The ultimate test of any method must be the utility and replicability of its findings. We believe that the patterns we describe in this study are important to understanding what is happening

in actual working city planning departments today, and that
they can be confirmed by anyone who examines the problematic course of the community planning experiment in the
United States.

Plan of the Book

The study's aim is a simple one: to provide a close look at
community planning programs in a number of major American cities, showing how they affect people, cities, and the nature of planning by their presence. Rather than comparing ,
each of the community planning programs to each other or
analyzing the differences in departments that have undertaken the experiment and those that have not, we present
here a composite picture of how community planning fits
into the city planning enterprise. This approach protects our
subjects' anonymity, which would be jeopardized in a city-
by-city comparison. Moreover, detailed comparison of these
fledgling programs seems to us premature and less useful than
an overall view, as the community planning programs we observed are strikingly similar, sharing common problems and
consequences despite their differences in geographic, economic, and political setting.

The analysis, organized around major points of tension,
falls into six parts. The first part, The Community Planning
Experiment, sets the scene. Chapter One explains why community planning has emerged at this point in the development of professional city planning, and how it differs from
the type of planning traditionally practiced in city planning
departments. The incompatibility between the assumptions of
community planning and those of its parent bureaucracy, analyzed in Chapter Two, suggests a stormy career for the innovative program.

Part Two, The Planner and His Community, focuses on

common problems of the community planner in establishing and maintaining links with the citizens living in his assigned community. Some of these typical difficulties are administrative in nature: how, for instance, the city is to be divided into districts with any credibility as coherent communities, and whom within these districts the planner should treat as community representatives. These issues are dealt with in Chapter Three, which examines how the community planner searches out a target area and target population in the confused and conflict-riddled urban social setting. Other common problems, analyzed in Chapter Four, involve the dilemmas the planner typically faces as a representative of the city planning department charged with responsibility for dealing with a specific community's problems. Chapter Five examines the strategies and tactics community planners resort to in coping with these dilemmas, as they struggle to make their way through the network of conflicting demands that we call the "community planning pressure system." As we shall see, the usual effect of this pressure system is to transform community planners into "administrative guerrillas."

Part Three, The Planner and His Department, deals with the relationship between the staff of the community planning program and the rest of the planning department: that is, the department's management and the staff of other sections within the department. Chapter Six describes some unusual organizational characteristics of the planning department that make it what we call a "counter-irrational" bureaucracy; these organizational features frustrate community planning but they also function to protect the new program from the usual dismal fate of innovations in bureaucracies. Chapter Seven analyzes the sources of friction between community planners and their colleagues, showing how a gulf typically develops between "old" and "new" planners with the community planning program forming a distinct and often embattled faction within the department. In Chapter Eight we see how the department management tries to control the disruptive activities of planners acting as administrative guerrillas, and how community planners evade these controls.

Part Four, The Planner and City Hall, concentrates on the relationship of community planning to other power units in city government, particularly the operating agencies that control city services affecting the planner's target area. As community planners seek to expand their contacts and influence with operating agencies, they meet with immediate and powerful opposition. We analyze in Chapter Nine why contact between community planners and the operating agencies inevitably takes such bitter forms. In Chapter Ten we explore what actually happens when community planners challenge the operating agencies' jurisdictional boundaries. We shall see why some of the planners' methods succeed while others fail, and why in some cases the attempt proves fatal for the community planning experiment.

In Part Five the focus shifts from the planner's relationships with others to the planner himself. In The Planner and His Role we delve into the community planners' feelings about their work, analyzing the social psychology of the administrative guerrilla role. We shall see how planners deal with the high personal demands, high level of frustration, and disillusionment built into this "volatile role." We shall also suggest some parallels with similar roles in other organizational settings.

Part Six presents some conclusions. Here we sum up the predicament of community planning in its present social context and return to the basic questions posed in the introduction: What does the appearance of this experiment signify for city planning, and what does it contribute to the struggle to make American cities habitable?

Throughout the book all names of cities, neighborhoods, and individuals in the quoted material are disguised. We have done this not only to protect those who gave us information so freely but also to underscore our conviction that the community planning experiment transcends local peculiarities and idiosyncrasies, and that it must be assessed as a movement which, once launched, may not easily be reversed.

Notes

1. Two major analyses of the operations, personnel, and political context of city planning departments are Alan Altshuler, *The City Planning Process* (Ithaca, N.Y.: Cornell University Press, 1965) and Francine F. Rabinovitz, *City Politics and Planning* (New York: Atherton Press, 1969).

2. Edward C. Banfield as quoted in John W. Dyckman, "What Makes Planners Plan?" *Journal of the American Institute of Planners, XXVII* (1961), p. 165.

3. Peter Blau, *Dynamics of Bureaucracy* (Chicago: University of Chicago Press, 1955); Ely Chinoy, *Automobile Workers and the American Dream* (Garden City, N.Y.: Doubleday, 1955); Herbert Gans, *The Urban Villagers* (New York: The Free Press, 1962); Alvin Gouldner, *Patterns of Industrial Bureaucracy* (Glencoe, Ill.; The Free Press, 1954); Elliot Liebow, *Tally's Corner* (Boston: Little, Brown & Company, 1967); Joseph Bensman and Arthur Vidich, "Social Theory in Field Research," in *Sociology on Trial*, Maurice Stein and Arthur J. Vidich, Eds. (Englewood Cliffs, N.J.: Prentice-Hall, 1963), pp. 162–172; William Foote Whyte, *Street Corner Society* (Chicago: University of Chicago Press, 1955);

21

Harold Wilensky, *Intellectuals in Labor Unions* (Glencoe, Ill.: The Free Press, 1956). See also Arthur J. Vidich, Joseph Bensman, and Maurice R. Stein, Eds., *Reflections on Community Studies* (New York: Harper & Row, Harper Torchbook edition, 1971).

ONE

THE COMMUNITY
PLANNING EXPERIMENT

One

The Rise of Community Planning

A new element has entered city planning in America. Virtually unnoticed by the general public, an experiment is taking place, one with profound implications for the future of American cities. The experiment is *community planning*—the opening of city planning to citizen participation on a decentralized basis. Planning departments in a number of major cities have undertaken programs in this innovative type of planning, for the first time encouraging citizens to take a direct and active role in shaping the planned development of their own neighborhoods. Community planning has become a fad. But community planning represents much more than a fad, for these experimental programs, still in an almost embryonic stage, already show potential for restructuring in basic ways the relationship between city residents and those who govern them.

We aim in this book to analyze the community planning experiment: what it is, what it does, and what it means. Our findings, based on a multicity interview study described in the Introduction, suggest an unanticipated and possibly irreversible pattern of events and relationships which, at least in broad outline, comes into play wherever community planning is tried.

To understand the forces that have brought community planning into being, we must look briefly at the history of American city planning (1). As a profession, city planning has "arrived," but its grip on legitimacy is both recent and hard won. Through most of the country's history, the shape and tone of urban life have been the accidental products of contests in which unregulated special interests vied for advantage. The cities were left to grow and decay haphazardly, almost totally without planning. Although city governments occasionally commissioned architects and engineers to design municipal buildings, public parks, or major city thoroughfares, most decisions were based on political considerations or left to chance and the marketplace. The civic reform movements of the 1890s—born of revulsion against cities' sprawling, festering immigrant slums and corrupt political machines—inspired many private civic organizations to develop their own plans for improving the physical and social conditions of urban life. The impact of these private plans on the city governments' policies proved generally negligible. It was not until well into the twentieth century that the idea of systematic planning began to filter into city government itself. Political pressure mounted during the early decades of the century for municipal governments to assume responsibility for city planning, urged on by a motley crew of social reformers, businessmen, and property owners who differed on the ends they considered desirable but agreed on the need for some means of regulating city growth. By the end of World War I, most large cities had responded by establishing city planning commissions headed by lay boards of prominent civic leaders, usually businessmen, to oversee the city's development.

The concerns of these early city planning boards were primarily esthetic and cultural. They defined urban improvement as the building of art galleries and museums, impressive civic centers, beautiful parks, and dramatic boulevards. Accordingly, the commissions were staffed with architects and engineers who were assigned the task of developing grand designs for the physical, visual aspects of the city—creating the City Beautiful.

City planning rapidly began to develop a professional identity of its own, independent of architecture and engineering. In 1917 a national professional association, the American Institute of Planners, was established. In the 1920s many universities set up departments of city planning to train specialists in the new field. Publications on city planning began to appear. With this increase in professional activity, the prevailing concept of planning began to shift from its early aristocratic emphasis on civic adornment to a more "scientific" approach emphasizing the interrelations among different aspects of the city's physical structure. The newly professionalized city planners concerned themselves with balancing land use, locating public facilities rationally, maintaining the economic viability of the city. Their basic tool in this effort was the long-range, comprehensive "master plan," a kind of blueprint for achieving the ideal city (2). Preparation of a master plan soon became the *raison d'être* of professional city planners; it remains a primary function of city planning agencies today. Turned out by the hundreds by city planning agencies and private planning consultants hired by city governments, master plans display such similarity that standard formats appear in planning literature. Here is one such description:

> The typical master plan is a portrait of the future condition of the city. It begins with a demographic and economic analysis of the city, including a projection of future growth. . . . Then there are chapters and maps which describe the present deficiencies. . . . The planning chapters outline the future ideal, a city without

> slums, divided into zones for each major land use, com-
> mercial, industrial, and residential; efficient highway and
> mass transit systems; and properly distributed open space
> and public facilities. . . . In the final section, the propos-
> als for individual municipal functions and land uses are
> synthesized into a master-plan map, with recommenda-
> tions for its implementation. These include a zoning ordi-
> nance to order land use as prescribed in the master plan;
> building codes to discourage slums; subdivision ordi-
> nances to regulate the building of new areas; a list of the
> needed facilities; proposals for governmental reorganiza-
> tion to coordinate development activities; and a rhetorical
> appeal to citizens and politicians to participate in and
> support the realization of the plan so as to achieve an or-
> derly, efficient, and attractive community (3).

These master plans are far more comprehensive and sophisticated than the original City Beautiful concept of city planning, but the dream remains the same: creation of an orderly,
beautiful, coordinated, economically thriving, and structur-
ally sound physical environment for the city's residents.

The trends of urban life in recent years, however, have
dealt harshly with this dream. Unsolved social problems, ac-
companied by growing physical blight in the city's core and
increasingly inadequate municipal services, have undermined
the cultural and economic vitality that the planners hoped to
promote. Affluent residents, industry, commercial interests
—exactly those for whom the planners sought to make the
city an attractive environment—are disengaging from their
urban locations of the past and relocating in suburbs, shrink-
ing the city's tax base. Services and facilities for those who remain in the city continue to decline in quality. Clearly, something has gone wrong, both with urban development and
with city planning (4).

At first glance, the social problems and physical decay of
cities have simple explanations. For one thing, cities lack
money. The outdated revenue-collecting mechanisms of local

government have left cities financially unable to implement the planners' recommendations. The cures for urban decay laid out in the master plan are unlikely to be applied without new sources of revenue such as massive federal subsidies to cities. A second obvious explanation is that planners lack power. Their role is advisory at best. The implementation of the master plan depends on a political decision-making process that grants no greater weight to the recommendations of planners than to other special interests. Therefore, the planners' proposed solutions for urban problems may be simply ignored. These two resource deficiencies loom so large that they tend to obscure other possible causes for the failure of planning to improve urban life (5).

Many city planners, however, no longer comfort themselves with these one-dimensional explanations. The failure of urban renewal has made that impossible. Urban renewal was a shattering experience for the city planning profession. The program represented the greatest opportunity in United States urban history for rational, comprehensive land use planning. The "necessary" conditions were present— money, increased authority, planning talent. The "right" things were done—ugly slums cleared, downtown areas rebuilt from the ground up, attractive sites for new private investment created. Yet in city after city, the hoped-for renaissance of urban life failed to occur. Cleared sites went begging, spurned by private investors; shoppers proclaimed the new downtowns sterile; displaced city residents damned the program that had cost them their homes and in no tangible way improved their lives. The general malaise continued unabated, and the exodus from the city actually accelerated. Physical urban renewal, it became clear, was a cosmetic. By itself, it could not touch the city's deeper problems (6).

Their confidence in traditional planning practices badly shaken, many city planners began to question the profession's basic assumptions. In graduate schools and planning journals the profession turned inward, embarking on a voyage of self-exploration, and in some cases self-annihilation, that has not yet ended. The proper goals, role, and organization of city planning, no longer taken for granted, have become central issues in the profession's most passionate debates as planners struggle to regain a sense of relevance to urban development (7). Out of this push and pull of intellectual pressures, two major positions on reorientation of city planning are emerging. Unfortunately for the profession's solidarity, the two are radically different and seemingly contradictory.

The first position is manifested in calls for regional and national planning. Many planners have come to doubt the value and even the possibility of planning for cities as isolated entities. Urban renewal and any similar programs, they argue, are doomed to founder if they include no control over development outside city limits. The city is an unrealistic unit, carved arbitrarily out of a web of interconnections involving suburbs, other cities, rural areas, and national facilities and resources. Supplies and people flow back and forth between the city and the surrounding region, and distant parts of the country as well. The services and facilities of the city have regional and often national significance. Thus the causes of many urban problems lie outside the city itself, and the actions proposed by planners will affect areas outside the city limits. It makes no more sense for a planner to restrict his attention to the city, following this argument, than for a doctor to limit his medical examination and treatment to his patient's big toe. Accordingly, planners taking this position wish to fix responsibility for city planning at the national level, so that arbitrary boundaries such as city limits and state lines can be disregarded and urban centers planned rationally on a regional basis (8).

For other planners, however, the deficiencies of past planning suggest a different reorientation for the profession: greater decentralization of planning. For them, urban renewal marked an end of innocence for city planning. The casualties of urban renewal included not only the poor and the minorities whose needs were deferred and homes demolished, but also the planners' concept of the "general public interest." The program had purported to improve the city as a whole, but its benefits and burdens were clearly distributed very unevenly among those who lived in and used the city. Perhaps, some planners reasoned, such an outcome is and always has been inevitable in planning. Any planning decision has more favorable consequences for some interest groups than for others. Once stripped of the mask of "serving the public interest," all the activities of city planners can be seen as service to a particular set of clients, with other potential clients losing out. The planner-client relationship is obscured somewhat by the fact that the publicly employed planner receives no direct payment for services from those whose special interests he furthers. But with or without conscious recognition, the city planner cannot avoid acting as an advocate for special interest groups of some kind. The traditional beneficiaries of city planning have been the city's white, affluent, business elite. Therefore, according to this argument, planning departments should try to balance the profession's activities by extending advocacy services to those groups neglected in the past— the city's residents, especially the poor and the minorities. In this way the conflicting interests of all groups will be represented in contests over specific planning proposals. Although some must lose, at least the outcome is less certain. There is less chance that the interests of any one group will be sacrificed completely or consistently. Planners taking this position wish to see planning become a self-consciously client-oriented profession, much like law, providing technical assistance as advocates for neighborhoods and special interest groups in a competitive, pluralistic system of planning decision making (9).

In city planning agencies faced with urgent urban problems, these contradictory recommendations by the profession's intellectual elite are necessarily tempered by practical considerations. The proposed centralization of planning, in a nation that has prided itself on its laissez-faire ideology for centuries, seems unlikely to gain public acceptance without major alterations in attitudes toward democracy, private enterprise, individual civil rights, and social responsibilities. Moreover, the few examples of regional planning in the United States familiar to city planners hardly inspire confidence. For many, their often rancorous experiences with federal highway programs and regional planning authorities have only strengthened the suspicion that in the United States, national planning either would be ineffectual or would reflect power rather than justice. They fear their particular city stands to lose more than it would gain. Moreover, such a massive reorganization of planning would threaten the survival of their city agency, perhaps the existence of their individual jobs. In any case, centralization is not applicable to their immediate situation. However desirable or undesirable in the abstract, regional and national planning requires federal initiative, money, and commitment and thus lies outside the direct control of the city planning department.

Decentralization, on the other hand, has an unmistakable appeal for embattled city planning departments, for reasons that may have more to do with urban politics than planning theory. City planners, often used as scapegoats or disregarded by the city's political leaders, have always chafed at their lack of influence in city government. They would like to be taken more seriously, to gain the ear of the mayor, to be consulted by councilmen. One strategy for increasing the department's influence is to prove the political value of planning to the political leaders who possess the formal authority to implement plans. If the planners could suddenly provide an administrative reform that would placate the angry citizens' groups besieging city hall without costing the city government much money, they feel, political leaders would be more inclined to respect the planners' recommendations in the future. Thus decentralization—just this kind of inexpensive popular reform—represents a means of strengthening the planning department.

Another practical appeal of decentralization is that it involves primarily internal reorganization and thus can be undertaken at the department's own initiative without waiting for action at the federal and state level. Many socially concerned planners—even those who favor greater centralization in planning—feel that in the context of present American institutions, city residents need advocate planners to safeguard their interests. In the absence of a massive overhaul in the organization of planning, decentralization represents to many planners the most constructive step a department can take in coping with urban problems.

For these reasons, many city planning departments under pressure to "do something" about urban decline have turned, with mixed feelings, to decentralized community planning as the only promising response within their reach. The new programs being established (called area planning, district planning, or community planning) involve assignment of individual planning staff members to specific areas within the city. Each community planner takes responsibility for analyzing and developing a plan for his district, working closely with the residents. He makes sure the needs of his area's residents are pointed out in discussion of any planning decision that would impinge on their neighborhood. Once the individual area plans are completed, they are all to be integrated into the planning department's recommendations for the master plan, which covers the entire city. The following statements of purpose, typical of the rhetoric with which these programs are launched, give an idea of the role community planning is expected to play (10):

Community Planning in Metropolis

We have established an Area Planning Division to bolster our ties with community organizations and to assist them in planning for the improvement of their neighborhoods. Increasingly in the coming years, citizen participation in *all* governmental processes will become a more insistent phenomenon; and the Metropolis City Planning Commission must expect to devote ever greater resources to this effort, in order to

– assure that the government-citizen dialogue is maintained and expanded,
– improve the knowledge and skills of community personnel in their working cooperatively with their government, and
– support the citizens' abilities to make optimum use of governmental and private programs for community improvement.

Definition of Citizen Participation in Planning in Steeltown

Citizen participation in planning is the development of the interests of nongovernmental individuals or groups and the communication of these interests to the government in such a manner that they are given serious consideration in the planning activities of the governing body.

Where different groups hold divergent interests, they are ordinarily resolved through negotiation in the political forum. Where negotiation and compromise are impossible either one interest group submerges the other or there is a division in the political body. Serious divisions have historically resulted in civil war or secession.

City planning, therefore, is an integral part of the political process. A great deal of planning is based on value judgments. These value judgments cannot be responsibly made by planning technicians; they can be made only by *The People* through responsible political action but it must be understood that a competent professional planner has much to contribute in the process of reaching meaningful value judgments.

Such statements, some of them quite detailed and lengthy, occasionally include cautions that working with the community will not be easy. But their dominant tone is optimistic and idealistic; they fairly bristle with hopeful references to "a better tomorrow," the "Young Great Society," and "the voice of The People."

The new commitment to decentralization is highly tentative and limited, however. The planning department, reluctant to divert much in the way of manpower or resources to an untested approach, continues to concentrate on its traditional activities—preparing and updating parts of the city-wide master plan, writing policy statements on city-wide development, and responding to informational requests from the city's political leaders. As an experimental program, community planning generally operates on a shoestring with few support facilities such as secretarial assistance. The community planners form a distinct unit separated from the rest of the department, often occupying offices on a different floor or even in a different building. Their approach and manner and the nature of their work, so different from traditional city planning, are by no means accepted as legitimate by all officials in city government or even by all members of the planning department staff. They are on trial, constantly reminded that the main virtue of community planning is its necessity—and a questionable necessity at that (11).

Little is known about the nature and development of these experiments in decentralized planning. Even those who design and work in community planning programs have questions about the habits of their new creature. How does community planning fit in with other activities of the planning department? What happens to the structure and goals of the new programs over time? What does the program accomplish? How do community planners deal with the unfamiliar demands of citizen participation? Most important, what does community planning in its present form imply for the future course of urban planning in the United States? Is it a tool for finally rendering planning responsive to those who live in cities rather than those who own them, or is it a Frankenstein's monster that will so fragment the planning effort that all hope of rational urban development is lost?

Notes

1. The brief summary of the development of American city planning presented here is based primarily on the comprehensive history commissioned to commemorate the fiftieth anniversary of the founding of the American Institute of Planners, Mel Scott's *American City Planning Since 1890* (Berkeley: University of California Press, 1969). See also John T. Howard, "City Planning as a Social Movement," in *Planning and the Urban Community*, Harvey S. Perloff, Ed. (Pittsburgh: University of Pittsburgh Press, 1961), pp. 151–155.

2. Herbert J. Gans, *People and Plans: Essays on Urban Problems and Solutions* (New York: Basic Books, 1968), pp. 57–75.

3. *Ibid.*, p. 60.

4. Henry Fagin, "Advancing the 'State of the Art'"; Peter A. Lewis, "The Uncertain Future of the Planning Profession"; and Theodore E. Hollander, "How Encompassing Can the Profession Be?"; in *Urban Planning in Transition*, Ernest Erber, Ed. (New York: Grossman, 1970), pp. 125–151. See also Robert L. Williams, "The Planner and His Profession"; Joseph M. Heikoff, "The Planning Profession in Search of Itself"; and Ladislas

39

Segoe, "The Planning Profession: Its Progress and Some Problems"; in *Planning 1964* (Chicago: American Society of Planning Officials [ASPO], 1964), pp. 93–109.

5. Planners may defend themselves against critics by pointing out their resource deficiencies, implying that if these obstacles were removed, planners could solve the city's problems. For instance, John T. Mauro, Pittsburgh's former Director of Planning and Development, writes: "Well, I've got news for this erudite audience: You can't build or change a thing without land and money.

"Give me funds to acquire land and money to improve our urban ghettos—block by block—and on a continuing basis, and I'll help to solve some of the frustrations that come from big concepts and no immediate payoffs.

"Give me land in the suburbs—without restrictions as to its use—and we will build housing for the low and moderate-income families, setting in motion the horizontal mobility needed to achieve an integrated society and the ultimate disappearance of the ghetto itself.

"Let me tie together cheap mass transportation and reasonable cost housing over the metropolitan area and I'll accelerate the entire process.

"Give me public works programs, including urban renewal, and we'll beef up the construction industry to the point where it must turn to the hard-core unemployed and underemployed for the mass manpower needed to get the job done quickly.

"Give me land and tax incentives for private industry to build new plants to employ the poor Negroes and poor whites, and this nation will provide the long-term income security needed to hold together families, neighborhoods, and cities.

"Give me funds to convert our educational plants into comprehensive community social service centers and we can save millions in duplicating and often conflicting facilities and programs.

"The greatest contribution the city planning field can make today is to learn how to manage land and money.

"Without these fundamental ingredients, you can't create jobs, housing, educational facilities, modern transportation systems, parks, playgrounds, or help resolve the city's desperate financial plight or fulfill the great American dream.

"And even more important, baby, without land and money,

you're never going to cool it!" [*Planning 1968* (Chicago: ASPO, 1968), pp. 66–67]. See also John W. Reps, "The Future of American Planning," *Planning 1967* (Chicago: ASPO, 1967), pp. 48–49.

6. Several classic criticisms of urban renewal are Herbert J. Gans, "The Failure of Urban Renewal: A Critique and Some Proposals" and George M. Raymond, Malcolm D. Rivkin, and Herbert J. Gans, "Urban Renewal: Controversy," in *Urban Renewal: People, Politics and Planning*, Jewel Bellush and Murry Hausknecht, Eds. (Garden City, N.Y.: Anchor Books, 1967); Charles Abrams, *The City Is the Frontier* (New York: Harper Colophon Books, 1965); Herbert J. Gans, *The Urban Villagers* (New York: The Free Press, 1962); and Fred Powledge, *Model City* (New York: Simon and Schuster, 1970).

7. See John R. Seeley, "What Is Planning? Definition and Strategy," *Journal of the American Institute of Planners* [JAIP], *XXVIII* (1962), pp. 92–93. Even the former executive director of the American Society of Planning Officials, Israel Stollman, voices this uncertainty: "There is another stylish crisis that has invaded us, the crisis of identity. It afflicts not only our young people but all of our sister professions. Even venerable institutions such as the churches and the universities are asking for fresh answers to the questions: What are we? What is our role? For planners, these questions have been raised in a number of issues: the relation of physical to social and economic planning; advocacy planning; to whom is the planner accountable? When is the planner's scope so broad that he loses professional competence? When is his scope so narrow that he loses social responsibility? Or, is planning so feeble that we would do better to transform ourselves into a society of improvising officials, of specialists in muddling-through?" [*Planning 1968* (Chicago: ASPO, 1968), p. 316.

8. Scott, *op. cit.*, Chapters 5 and 8. See also H. Wentworth Eldredge, "Toward a National Policy for Planning the Environment" and William R. Ewald, Jr., "National Planning Cannot Wait for an Elite," in Erber, *op. cit.*, pp. 3–26. A good example of the linking up of urban problems with regional conditions is Niles M. Hansen's *Rural Poverty and the Urban Crisis: A Strategy for Regional Development* (Bloomington: Indiana University Press, 1970).

9. This position is identified with the work of Paul Davidoff, a

major proponent of advocacy planning. See Davidoff and Thomas Reiner, "A Choice Theory of Planning." *JAIP*, *XXV* (1959), p. 108, and Davidoff, "Advocacy and Pluralism in Planning," *JAIP*, *XXXI* (1965), pp. 331–338. See also Walter W. Safford and Joyce Ladner, "Comprehensive Planning and Racism," *JAIP*, *XXXV* (1969), pp. 68–74; Bernard J. Frieden, "Toward Equality of Urban Opportunity," *JAIP*, *XXXI* (1965), pp. 320–330; Gordon Fellman, "Neighborhood Protest of an Urban Highway," *JAIP*, *XXXIV* (1968), pp. 118–122; William L. C. Wheaton and Margaret F. Wheaton, "Identifying the Public Interest: Values and Goals," with accompanying comments by C. David Loeks and Charles R. Ross, in Erber, *op. cit.*, pp. 152–173.

10. These typical statements of purpose are taken from documents provided by city planning departments which asked to remain anonymous.

11. These observations concerning the limited commitment of city planning departments to decentralization are based on interviews with city planners, to be discussed at length in the following chapters.

Two

Tradition and Innovation
in the Planning Department

From an administrative point of view, the course of the community planning experiment seems unlikely to run smoothly. Introducing this kind of innovation into the already existing city planning agency means juxtaposing within one bureaucratic system two very dissimilar planning approaches, based on fundamentally incompatible assumptions. The planning department has traditionally assumed that planning is best done by trained professionals with a minimum of participation by amateurs. Community planning, on the other hand, assumes that meaningful planning requires the participation of those affected by the plan, however unsophisticated their views may be.

Elite Council Versus Arena Council

The differences between the two planning approaches come into sharper focus with the help of a useful pair of concepts developed by F. G. Bailey. Bailey describes two ideal types of decision-making bodies, which he calls the *elite council* and the *arena council*. In his words:

> Elite councils are those which are, or consider themselves to be (whether they admit it openly or not), a ruling oligarchy. The dominant cleavage in such a group is between the elite council (including, where appropriate, the minority from which it is recruited) and the public; that is to say, the dominant cleavage is horizontal. The opposite kind of council is the arena council. These exist in groups in which the dominant cleavages are vertical. The council is not so much a corporate body with interests against its public, but an arena in which the representatives of segments in the public come into conflict with one another (1).

In these terms, the traditional planning department is organized as an elite council, and the community planning effort represents an arena council.

The two types of councils, Bailey continues, handle their internal disagreements in radically different ways:

> Other things being equal, arena councils will not damp down dispute and will come reluctantly and with difficulty to compromise, if they do so at all, because each councillor (or each group of councillors) is steered by the heavy rudder of those whose interests he represents, and to whom he is answerable. But the elite councillors have no such rudder; they are likely to come into conflict, but they have a strong incentive to present a front of consensus and keep their ranks closed in the face of their public (2).

Thus in traditional elite council planning, planners may disagree over the specific proposals that would benefit the city most, but all agree that the planning department should maintain a united front in presenting its recommendations. In the community planning program, however, the cleavage between professional planners and the public breaks down. The community planner, assigned to represent the interests of a particular group of citizens, develops allegiances to his community that set him at odds with any fellow staff member whose proposals are inimical to those interests. For him, the planning department is an arena in which disputes can properly become both bitter and open.

For elite councils to voluntarily establish arena councils in their midst, provoking the internal rifts they find so distasteful, is not as remarkable as it might seem. It is, in fact, a common tactic for coopting critics without expending extra resources. In times of public unrest, the United States government has not infrequently responded by expanding the political franchise, the most recent examples being federal reinforcements for the legal voting rights of racial minorities and the extension of the vote to eighteen-year-olds. The groups in question may be too small or too disorganized to use their newly won rights effectively, but the symbolic victory of gaining access to the decision-making machinery substitutes, at least temporarily, for material gains. The chance to fight over cutting the loaf is more important than the bread itself.

When the movement from elite to arena council occurs in a bureaucratic setting, it may be seen as a kind of *bureaucratic enfranchisement*, analogous to extension of political suffrage to previously unrepresented groups, through which the bureaucracy under fire hopes to pacify a public dissatisfied with its services. Sophisticated citizens' groups, recognizing that in contemporary American society their fate is decided as much in bureaucracies as in political forums, increasingly have set bureaucratic enfranchisement as a major goal. From their perspective, increased citizen involvement in local institutions represents a means of advancing their particular interests. But in many cases the increased citizen participation also serves as a substitute for increased financial investment—for example, community control of schools that remain underfunded; creation of federally financed volunteer service programs in place of massive federal aid to cities; and acceptance of welfare rights activities without commitment to higher spending on public assistance. City planning is by no means alone among resource-short bureaucracies in establishing an arena council subunit in response to social tensions.

Encapsulation Versus Expansionism

A second fundamental difference between traditional city planning and the new community planning programs revolves around the proper scope and authority of the planning department in the city's administrative machinery. Planning departments are limited by the city charter to an advisory staff position. The actual administration of city services falls to a battery of line departments with delegated executive authority, usually including departments of public works, education, sanitation, public health, housing, parks and recreation, and traffic. Additional line departments funded primarily by federal grants, such as Model Cities and urban renewal, may also be present. Called operating agencies, these line departments oversee the city's day-to-day activities and design their own policies and procedures independently both of each other and of the planning department. Figure 1 is a diagram of the most common position of the planning department. Occasionally, the planning department will be responsible directly to the chief executive without an intervening planning commission, or it may be attached to one of the operating agencies such as housing or urban renewal. In all of these organizational arrangements, however, the position of the planning department is marginal to actual city administration.

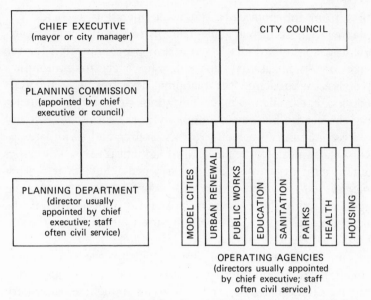

Figure 1. Position of the planning department in city administration. (Only part of the city bureaucracy is represented here).

With this structure, most city governments come to resemble a collection of feudal principalities, each operating agency jealously guarding its jurisdictional boundaries and vigorously resisting any interference with its autonomy from city planners. Federally funded agencies may be required by the provisions of their grants to maintain some contact with the planning department, but they resist conceding any real control. The other operating agencies generally strive to avoid the city's planners entirely, preferring to do their own planning or hire private planning consultants.

The planning department has traditionally adapted to this "baronial" administrative system through a process of *departmental encapsulation,* voluntarily restricting the scope of planning activities so as not to provoke resentment or retaliation from the politically powerful operating agencies. For planners whose primary allegiance is to the planning department as an elite council, such a response is indicated for the sake of organizational survival. However, to community planners, who define the planning department as an arena council, encapsulation is self-defeating. Responsible for meeting the needs of a specific community, they feel compelled to trace community problems to their source and formulate operational solutions, regardless of administrative boundaries among city departments. In other words, they favor *departmental expansionism:* increased coordination of operating agencies with the planning department functioning as the central control unit and involving itself intimately in the operational details of the city's administration.

Thus we have a collision. In the midst of the elite-council, encapsulated planning department, a group of community planners undertakes to carry out arena-council, expansionary planning activities. As we shall see, the staff members in the new program find they have little choice but to reject the department's traditional approach. The demands of representing and working closely with a specific community force them to break ranks with their colleagues and to invade the jurisdictions of operating agencies. As we shall also see, the community planning program becomes increasingly disruptive for the rest of the planning department as it grows.

The Fate of Innovations in Bureaucracies

Judging from theories concerning the fate of innovative special units in bureaucracies, the chances that such a troublesome new program will survive intact are slim indeed. One classic (and pessimistic) model, formulated by Anthony Downs, has particular applicability to community planning (3). The course of developments Downs describes, called the "rigidity cycle," runs as follows. First, because of increase in size and/or insulation from client complaints, the parent bureau begins to manifest an "ossification syndrome." It becomes increasingly incapable of fast or novel action. At this point the organization can respond to new demands only by means of a bureaucratic "breakout":

> The bureau or one of its parts is suddenly instructed by its sovereign to undertake an urgent task. . . . Based upon their experience with the bureau, top-level officials realize that it is incapable of carrying out this task. Its cumbersome machinery cannot produce results fast enough, and its anti-novelty bias may block the necessary innovation. Therefore, a new organization is set up for this task outside the normal operations of the bureau, . . . much smaller than the bureau as a whole, . . . exempt from almost all existing controls, regulations, and procedures, . . . [and characterized by] extraordinarily high morale and zeal (4).

Translating this process to the context of city planning, we can see the creation of the community planning program as just this kind of bureaucratic "breakout," by means of which the city government hopes to accomplish the "urgent tasks" of blunting attacks from outraged citizens' groups, halting urban decay, and forestalling riots. The community planning program, organized as a small, isolated unit within the planning department, is exempt initially from many of the department's rules and procedures. For example, community planners are much freer than most city planners in determining their own hours, and they spend a good deal of their time outside the office away from any supervision. The high morale and zeal characteristic of breakouts—similar to that of volunteer service programs like VISTA or the Peace Corps —are hallmarks of community planning. At its inception, community planning fits the Downs model almost perfectly.

Before long, according to Downs, special organizations of

this kind begin to degenerate, "rarely [maintaining] their high productivity for more than a few years, if that long" (5). This degeneration occurs primarily because the new program's effectiveness and cohesion derive from its isolation, which cannot be maintained once the program begins to operate. Its success undermines the conditions for its survival. To accomplish its special task, it must eventually deal with the more ossified portions of its own parent bureau and also with other bureaus; to gain the cooperation of these organizations, it must compromise its autonomy. Moreover, events relevant to the new organization's assignment occur outside its purview, which may lead to redefinition of the assignment or divert the staff into working to expand its scope so as to control these events. As time passes, the parent bureau's top-level officials may begin to focus their attention on other matters, losing interest and patience with the breakout unit; this jeopardizes any special privileges the new program initially enjoyed. "As a result of these factors," Downs writes, "the high-productivity phase in the special organization's life gradually comes to an end. It loses its 'special' nature and merely becomes another section of the bureau struggling under the normal weight of rules, regulations, and agonizingly slow decision-making procedures" (6). These late stages in Downs' theory fit the development of community planning programs only partially, as we shall see.

Social scientists are well acquainted with the idea that bureaucratic innovations pass through a life cycle, in the course of which the parent bureaucracy defends itself from internal challenge by developing ever tighter controls over the innovation, compelling its modification, sometimes crushing it entirely. Sociological literature on bureaucracy abounds with studies of cases in which innovations have been stifled (7). The combined weight of these sociological analyses indicates, at the very least, a gloomy prognosis for the survival of the new community planning programs. The difficulties of many recent experiments in citizen participation within elite-council bureaucracies—from civilian police review boards to community action programs—do little to dispel the sense of preordained mutation or untimely death for the community planning programs' original democratic goals and structure.

However, caution is needed here. As Alvin Gouldner observes, social theories are not merely the cold products of rational, logical thought. They carry about them an emotional halo, or perhaps shadow, of sentiment which plays an important part in attracting adherents to the theory. This mood is the theory's "metaphysical pathos" (8). Gouldner, noting that "the metaphysical pathos of much of the modern theory of group organization is that of pessimism and fatalism," asks:

> Why is it that "unanticipated consequences" are always tacitly assumed to be destructive of democratic values and "bad"; why can't they sometimes be "good"? Are there no constraints which *force* men to adhere valorously to their democratic beliefs, which *compel* them to be intelligent rather than blind, which leave them *no choice* but to be men of good will rather than predators? (9)

"It is the pathos of pessimism," he suggests, "rather than the compulsions of rigorous analysis, that leads to the assumption that organizational constraints have stacked the deck against democracy. . . . It is only in the light of such a pessimistic pathos that the defeat of democratic values can be assumed to be probable, while their victory is seen as a slender thing, delicately constituted and precariously balanced" (10). Analyses emphasizing the failures in introducing democratic innovations into bureaucracies may not be wrong, but they are incomplete.

In examining current community planning experiments,

we find that some have indeed been limited or discontinued. But others appear to be thriving, and in some cases forcing accommodations in their parent bureaucratic system. Unexpected allies have emerged in support of the new programs, as their client groups mobilize into quasi-political constituencies. The approach of the new programs shows more compatibility than does centralized city planning with expressed (if seldom realized) American values of democracy and free enterprise; therefore the legitimacy of community planning may be less "precarious" than that of the social controls applied by the parent bureaucracy to curb its activities. Moreover, some unusual characteristics of the new program and those who staff it create an organizational setting in which the routinization and ritualism that typically undermine new programs may not easily take hold. Most important, the community planners themselves are developing an unanticipated adaptive role that allows them to move among the contradictions that surround them. In tracing the clash of tradition and innovation in the planning department, we will—mindful of Gouldner's admonition—be analyzing not only how and why community planning programs change and wither, but also how and why they survive and may prevail.

Notes

1. F. G. Bailey, "Decisions by Consensus in Councils and Committees," *Political Systems and the Distribution of Power*, Michael Banton, Ed. (London: Tavistock Press, 1966), p. 10.

2. *Ibid.*

3. Anthony Downs, *Inside Bureaucracy* (Boston: Little, Brown and Company, 1967), pp. 158–166.

4. *Ibid.*, pp. 160–161.

5. *Ibid.*, p. 161.

6. *Ibid.*, p. 162.

7. For example, Philip Selznick's classic study of the Tennessee Valley Authority (*TVA and the Grass Roots*, New York: Harper and Row, 1949) details the gradual displacement of that new program's goals as it struggled for legitimacy in a hostile social environment. Through the compromises involved in the TVA's attempts to coopt its opposition, its instrumental goals were converted into terminal goals. The well-known work of Robert Michels (*Political Parties*, Glencoe, Ill.: The Free Press, 1949) suggests that innovations involving democratic procedures in their internal affairs will inevitably succumb to the "iron law of

oligarchy," moving inexorably to an elitist internal structure as skills and information concentrate in the hands of a few due to the personal ambition of the leaders and the apathy of the rank and file. Burton Clark, examining the difficulties of adult education in California ("Ogranizational Adaptation and Precarious Values," in *Complex Organizations,* Amitai Etzioni, Ed., New York: Holt, Rinehart and Winston, 1961, pp. 159–167), proposes that this innovative program owes its marginality to "value insecurity." Values are "precarious," he suggests, when they are (1) undefined, (2) held by functionaries whose position is not fully legitimized, and (3) unacceptable to a "host" population. These conditions, being "identifiable in a wide range of situations," help account for the failure of innovations in bureaucracies.

On the social-psychological level, strangulation of innovation has commonly been linked to the inevitable dulling effect bureaucracies are thought to have on professionals and intellectuals that enter them. Robert K. Merton suggests that "bureaucracies provoke gradual transformations of the alienated intellectual into the a-political technician, whose role is to serve whatever strata happen to be in power" (*Social Theory and Social Structure,* Glencoe, Ill.: The Free Press, 1957, p. 214). He further observes that bureaucrats develop a "trained incapacity" to adapt to new conditions and procedures, creating an unfavorable climate for innovative programs (*ibid.,* pp. 197–198). Similarly, Philip Selznick observes that professionals in bureaucratic organizations may shift their commitment from professional values to professional techniques—a process he calls the "retreat into technology" (*Leadership in Administration,* Evanston, Ill.: Row, Peterson, 1957, pp. 77 ff). Describing the transforming effect of organizational pressures on professional orientations, C. Wright Mills (*White Collar,* New York: Oxford University Press, 1951) points out: "Much professional work has become divided and standardized and fitted into the new hierarchical organization of educated skill and service; intensive and narrow specialization has replaced self-cultivation and wide knowledge; assistants and sub-professionals perform routine, although often intricate, tasks, while successful professional men become more and more the managerial type" (p. 112). The intellectual, Mills claims, "is becoming a technician, an idea-man, rather than one who resists the environment . . . and defends himself from death-by-adaptation" (p. 157).

In the same vein, Harold L. Wilensky discusses in intricate empirical detail the changes wrought by organizational pressures in the initial role orientations of intellectuals entering labor organizations (*Intellectuals in Labor Unions*, Glencoe, Ill.: The Free Press, 1956): "The overall pattern can be seen as a movement away from ideas and toward jobs: the Missionary abandons ideology and moves to professional service, an immersion in the political process, or careerism; the Program Professional loses interest in program promotion and shifts to a preoccupation with technical and administrative detail. Quitting aside, the final resting places for all types beset with severe role conflicts are (1) Technician Professional; (2) Politico. Cases of every type end up in the Technician Professional slot. The Politicos are likewise an outgrowth of all main types, although the principal source is the Party Missionary" (p. 166).

In an analysis of relations between the political party in power and the civil service in Saskatchewan, Canada, Seymour Martin Lipset shows how bureaucrats, having developed value commitments to the programs they administer and the clients they traditionally serve, can subvert innovative programs initiated by political leaders by engaging in "administrative sabotage" with the purpose of "stopping hair-brained radical schemes" ("Bureaucracy and Social Reform," in Etzioni, *op. cit.*, pp. 260–267).

8.   Alvin W. Gouldner, "Metaphysical Pathos and the Theory of Bureaucracy," in Etzioni, *op. cit.*, pp. 71–81.

9.   *Ibid.*, p. 73.

10.   *Ibid.*, p. 80.

TWO

THE PLANNER
AND HIS COMMUNITY

Three

The Planner in Search
of Community

The duties assigned to community planners are varied and often vague, leaving much to the discretion of the planners themselves. Research on the area of the city assigned to them usually forms part of the work. The community planners carry out "windshield surveys" of the condition of housing, map out vacant land in the area, try to assess the community's recreational needs, and so on. With the help of the area's residents, they try to locate and evaluate such important but obscure community facilities as "jive corners" for youth to congregate and pass the time of day, or the system of pedestrian short cuts used by those who live in the area.

The information planners gather may be used for a number of purposes—drawing up community development plans, acquainting community residents with problems or possibilities they were previously unaware of, helping community groups bring pressure to bear to get a needed service or stop an unwanted development, or preparing grant applications

for state or federal development programs. Most of these endeavors involve the planners in community education and organization work. They usually attend numerous community
meetings, ranging from formal speaking engagements to informal evening sessions with small groups in private homes.
Depending on the circumstances, the planner may serve as a
target for community hostility, a guide through the government bureaucracy, or a trusted ally in protecting the community from some threatening city policy.

As community planners gain in experience and exposure,
they usually develop extremely demanding schedules of community contact work, rushing from meeting to meeting as
they juggle such efforts as a fight against a highway here, a
drive to get rat control there, advising one community group
on how to incorporate and apply for housing funds, helping
another community group plan a playground, running interference for neighborhoods that have problems with other city
agencies, and working with a community council to draw up
a development plan for the area. The depth of the community planners' involvement and the specific direction their
work takes are left up to them. Their most substantial guide-
line is that in all their efforts, they should work with the
community.

"Working with the community" sounds reasonably simple, but when a planning department sets out to do this, the
elusiveness of the concept of "community" in an urban setting becomes apparent. Before the community planning program can get off the ground, some basic questions must be
settled. How is the city to be divided into areas, and how are
community planners to be distributed among them? In mixed,
rapidly changing, and highly factionalized areas, what part of
the resident population is the community planner going to
work with? How can he determine who represents the community? What about the other professionals who may already be working for communities on a paid or volunteer

basis as private advocate planners? To work with his community, the community planner must first find it.

The Community Planner as a Scarce Resource

In setting up a community planning program, the planning department immediately confronts the problem of defining appropriate areas. How large and how homogeneous should they be? How much consciousness of themselves as distinctive communities should they have? Must they include active community organizations that can work with the planner? There is little consensus on the most useful criteria for setting area boundaries, and even if a set of criteria were settled on, the information necessary to apply the system is usually not available. The planning department, chronically overburdened with routine work, lacks the staff to conduct preliminary surveys. Available city population data are often outdated or of doubtful accuracy, and no current listing of the city's community organizations exists.

In this situation, the division of the city into areas is done by guesswork, intuition, and tradition. "Natural boundaries" such as highways and railroad tracks provide some area borders, and institutional complexes such as hospitals and universities usually are placed within an area rather than being split up. The central business district, the one area most likely to be already designated, is generally used as is. If the department has previously divided the city into areas for some other purpose, the old maps will be resurrected and used. For example, districts set up in the past for hearings on zoning ordinance changes may become the basis for the new community planning program. As we shall see, the arbitrariness and irrationality of the resulting area boundaries, although perhaps unavoidable, come back to haunt the community planner as soon as he tries to deal with his area as a meaningful unit.

Although community planning programs are designed to provide a planner for each area, they are never launched with enough planners to go around. The staff shortage is usually serious, as shown by the following complaints from community planning section chiefs:

> I supervise the district planners in the department. We have four now; hopefully, we might get as many as eight sometime soon. But we'd need a dozen people to cover all sections of the city.

> Our problem is that there are approximately 200 neighborhoods with community organizations and only five community current planners and six community planners.

> We have requests for planning assistance from 60 neighborhoods, but right now our staff's so short we can only provide service to 20. Altogether, there's a possible 150 neighborhoods that could use planners, and only seven planners on our staff.

Sometimes one planner is given responsibility for as many as three or four districts. However, this solution vitiates the stated intent of the program, which is to provide an area of the city with a planner attuned to its special needs as distinguished from the interests of other areas or the city as a whole. If a community planner cannot direct his attention to one definable area, why depart from the traditional model of comprehensive city planning at all?

A more common way to allocate the scarce supply of planners among numerous areas is simply to leave some areas out. The areas to be included are selected by the head of the community planning section, sometimes in consultation with the director of the planning department. These administrators have their own priorities as planners, but they are also concerned with the new program's vulnerability, correctly seeing its survival linked to its utility for the mayor and city council. Thus the selection of areas also reflects two basically political (and contradictory) considerations: on the one hand, a bias toward picking "easy" areas which will justify the program through examples of smoothly operating successes; on the other hand, a desire to prove the program's relevance as a mediator in the city's conflicts with "difficult" communities.

Highly organized communities are most likely to ask for planning assistance, especially if they feel threatened by some impending development that could be affected by city government policy. For example, communities that lie in the path of a highway, hospital or university expansion, or a proposed railroad spur often approach the department for help. So do communities that have formed protective organizations in response to threatened invasion by unesthetic buildings, public housing, or poor blacks. Since these requests come from strong community organizations with high trouble potential for the city government, the areas they represent usually are assigned planners. As a community planning section chief said, "I don't turn away calls. I pick up neighborhoods on a sporadic basis, in response to crises." It is generally acknowledged that "area planners go to the squeaky wheel," with some planners adding sentiments like "it's a dirty deal that some neighborhoods [that need community planners more] don't get them."

In assigning planners to areas that have *not* requested planning assistance on their own, priorities reflect anticipated crisis. Where riots have made the city government aware of tensions in the inner city, these explosive areas are included in the new program even though they are likely to be difficult to work with and to show little improvement. Neglecting these riot-prone areas, and thus making the community planners seem unresponsive to a serious problem, would undermine the new program's credibility more than including such areas, even if this meant being able to establish only a tense and problematic relationship. One particularly riot-torn city concentrated its community planners heavily in the inner city.

As a planner in this program explained, "besides those neighborhoods where citizens demanded assistance, we're working
with those areas we felt acutely needed our help. It's our
response to civil unrest. We don't want to see another
blow-up."

In cities that have not experienced major riots, the planning department's tendency is to concentrate on "safer bets,"
the ring of transition areas on the city's outer edge. These
outer areas are viewed as more salvageable than the inner
city, and probably better able to make use of the planner's
special skills. Even though the new program purports to provide a necessary and unique service, neglect of the more
blighted areas may be rationalized by pointing to the presence of other city or federal agencies in the inner cities, while
the outer areas are being "forgotten." As the chief of one
community planning program put it:

> We are concentrating on the outer fringe of the city, be-
> cause it just takes too much to do the inner city. Besides,
> there are other agencies working in the inner city—the
> housing department, Model Cities, and so on. I'd stay
> away from the Model Cities area unless we had a lot
> more staff. Community organizations outside of the inner
> city are more competent and more effective than those in
> the inner city—easier for the planner to work with.

In general, then, planners are distributed according to an
area's potential to cause trouble for the city government, not
according to severity of planning-related problems. Some of
the areas that get planners will be relatively affluent and
problem free, but well organized. Some moving toward the
brink of social and physical collapse steadily but quietly—a
common situation in low-income white ethnic areas—will
be left out. Those surest to be included are the decaying, em-
bittered inner city communities whose residents have expressed their desperation in violence.

Competing Communities

Once assigned an area, the planner usually confronts not one but several distinct populations, each with a claim to be the community whose interests he should further. Divisions are common, for example, between area residents concerned with stable housing on the one hand and the area's expansion-minded institutions, such as hospitals and universities, on the other. Often the area is partially industrial and partially residential and polarized as to the direction that future land use should take. The area's residents frequently split along ethnic, racial, and income lines and do not regard themselves as parts of the same community. To complicate the situation further, in areas of high population turnover the residents available for the planner to work with may be replaced, before any plans can be implemented, by a new population with different demands.

Community planners react to these mixed, warring, and transient populations within their assigned areas in two ways. A few, finding no consensus in community demands, become immobilized. For example, after listing a number of class and generational conflicts in his area, one planner added, "I haven't come to the conclusion yet that it's unworkable. I try to avoid the underlying conflict and postpone action." Most planners, however, solve the problem by redefining their assignment. They choose to view "the community" as that part of the area's population they personally feel is most deserving or most in need of planning assistance. The responses of two planners, working in similar areas bordering on the same expansion-oriented university, show how differently planners can define the same kind of population mix:

> My area is predominantly white upper middle class—
> about 40 percent. The rest is 40 percent working-class

white, less than 20 percent black. If Buildmore University takes a wrong step, the area will rapidly decline and become all black. We're working to make the university understand that by building dorms on campus, they would create a housing vacuum and bring the whole neighborhood down.

My community is made up of rich whites—a tight Jewish community, a lot of professors—and poor blacks. There's no communication. . . . The blacks need help, the whites don't, so I devote most of my time to the blacks.

In a different city a planner, noting that the Italians who had once predominated in his area were rapidly moving out as blacks moved in, decided to ignore the present population completely in favor of the probable future population:

They're afraid of Negroes and change, they want to protect their neighborhood. But the way they're moving out, I don't know what's so fucking attractive about their neighborhood in the first place. They ought to wake up to the problems here. I'm going to go around them for a while, just not pay any attention to them. In another four years they will not be speaking for anyone—because they'll all be gone!

Thus in most cases the nature of the community is ultimately defined by the personal priorities and prejudices of the community planner himself. The assignment of large heterogeneous areas to a single planner with limited time and resources precludes any other outcome. But, as we will see, the result is to move the community planning process one step further away from rational planning and toward representative politics.

Community Representation

"Working with the community" in a direct sense is impossible. The areas assigned are far too large for personal contact between planner and residents, ranging in population from 20,000 to 200,000 with a few even larger. "There's an area in this city that has one planner for 400,000 people," a planner told us, adding, "I try to help him, but I'm overloaded too." At occasional meetings involving the areas' total population, the turnout is small and those who attend come to make specific, urgent demands for action, not to participate in drawing up community plans. Open community meetings are sometimes held to comply with federal grant regulations. However, planners speak of these meetings as futile and often painful formalities; the following remark is typical:

> Sure, we have a community council open to all; we have
> to have it as part of the program. At our last meeting
> only 40 showed up. That's out of 22,000 residents. They
> were mainly making demands about implementing short-
> range objectives. They were polite and reasonable
> enough, but we could only disappoint them.

Most of the planner's contacts therefore involve not "the community" but community representatives. To say that those claiming to represent the community may not have full community support is true, but it misses the point. In the highly complex, heterogeneous collectivities arbitrarily called communities and assigned to planners, there is no way that any particular community leader *could* represent the total community, even under the best circumstances. And community planning, as a hastily designed institutional experiment, hardly provides the best conditions for local democracy. No adequate formal mechanism exists for selecting individuals that represent even a majority of the community's residents, and the residents would not be prepared to use such a mechanism if it were available. We observed several attempts to establish elections for local planning committees, inspired sometimes by federal grant requirements and sometimes by democratic impulses within the planning department. Without exception, they were smothered by community apathy. The committees "elected" by a few hundred votes became primary community contacts for the planners, but without any valid claim to representativeness.

In the absence of any institutional means for achieving democratic participation, the planner can only fall back on the multitude of self-appointed community representatives with narrow goals and limited support. These individual leaders and community organizations are usually in conflict with each other, each having the feeling, as one planner put it, that "their group *is* the neighborhood and has the right to override everybody else." The comments that follow indicate the discomfort of many planners working with community contacts they know to be unrepresentative:

> One problem I've had as an area planner is that my section of the city has 150,000 people in it. What people do you work with in the limited time you have? Maybe it's not the ideal solution, but I feel you have to try to pick the winners. Our program is geared to communities with a high degree of organization. Areas with no community organizations or with warring factions are just not ready to go. We're not geared up—not staffed up —to be community organizers. That's another job. I just work with the strongest groups and hope they're somewhat representative.

> We're trying to do a real job of citizen participation, not eyewash. We want to keep citizen participation open and democratic. But you know, citizen groups don't necessarily want it open. In my local area most citizens don't

know what they want, and those that do operate in a
jungle of political activity. But you must work with these
community groups as they are. This may leave a lot of
people out of citizen participation, but it's the best we
can do right now.

Usually my relations are with the leaders of the most important organizations. I deal with them and try to get
them to understand planning issues. I know the organizations' rank and file will most probably accept the viewpoint of their leaders. I use this, but it bothers me and I
criticize it. I feel I should try to get the rank and file to
understand too. Once in a while I'll write a long letter to
the organization about housing programs, what redevelopment is, and so forth, free of jargon. I don't know if it
gets to the rank and file.

In working with existing community groups, the planners
we talked to quickly find themselves deep in community politics. Although their community contacts presumably all
share a common interest in getting more city services and facilities for their area, planners spend much of their time em-
broiled in local conflicts that have little to do with planning
issues. Having gained a vehicle for making their views known
in the city planning department, community leaders seem
ready to throw it away in petty squabbling among themselves. This apparently irrational behavior becomes perfectly
intelligible, however, once it is recognized that influencing
the planning department is not the primary goal of most
community leaders. They see the survival and expansion of
their own organizations as far more important, both to the
area's development and to their personal status positions, than
the uncertain benefits that might or might not flow from city
hall at some distant future time. Their participation in community planning meetings is therefore geared to increasing
their power in local politics. One frustrated planner explained
how his work was affected:

Every community has more than one group that represents one part of the community. There are reasons for
these groups to be independent; they can't just merge for
our benefit. But most of them have hidden agendas. No
matter what we are working on, they're always bringing
up issues outside the issue we came together for. They
take positions on every issue that reflect the personal
power struggles in the community. They may be against
something we are discussing not because they oppose it
on its merits, but just because another individual favors it
and it's someone they don't want to cooperate with. Or if
it will help another group, they'll be damned if they'll
support the suggestion—even if it's an idea they like.

Much to their dismay, planners find themselves used as scapegoats by community leaders. A typical complaint ran:

The major neighborhood group in the area isn't cooper-
ating with me at all. The neighborhood leader demanded
that I produce money in advance for his group's project
once it was approved. He knows the project has to be
programmed in detail first. I can't just get money in advance, it's illegal. But we had a big fight over it and a lot
of bad publicity. I feel that the neighborhood leader is
trying to discredit me and the planning commission for
his own political reasons.

How do the planners cope with this situation? Two reactions seem to be common. Some planners feel obligated to
preserve political aloofness, acting as neutral technical aides
to all community groups on an equal basis. "In each neighborhood there are many rival groups; you can't fraternize
with some and ignore others," we were told. Planners taking
this approach struggle to tug and stretch the community into
a rational mode of behavior. They encourage organizations to
operate "efficiently," in a "more businesslike manner," to see
themselves as "part of a system," and to develop interest and
skills in long-range planning. Also, they spend considerable

effort trying to combat what might be called the "mini-area outlook" of most community groups. This problem was described by a planner with a large area:

> All neighborhoods have narrow outlooks. Each little neighborhood refuses to look at things across the street from their boundary lines; they'll consider only what's inside of what is theirs alone. They won't recognize any connection with the rest of the area. A hospital across the street from their boundary won't be counted as part of the neighborhood. The people want the hospital in *their* neighborhood.

With a note of despair, another planner remarked, "I'll be lucky if I can get the people in my area to look at their whole neighborhood, not just their block!"

However valiant the attempts to depoliticize the community's input into planning, they usually end in failure. The outcome can be the total elimination of community input, with the planner rejecting all citizen participation as infeasible in his area. After cataloging the conflicts and power struggles among the groups in his area, one planner voiced the conclusion of many: "Their disagreements lie outside of planning and can't be resolved by us. You end up sometimes having to disregard them all—you just make decisions on a technical basis and let it happen."

The second approach planners take in coping with disunity among their community contacts also involves a compromise of the community planning program's original democratic aims. Instead of trying to draw together all the competing community organizations into a coalition, some planners themselves become active participants in local political conflicts. They single out one or two groups to work with, usually those most willing to accept their own views of the community's best interests, and ignore or subvert all rival groups.

Some see this approach as inevitable but undesirable. Trying to work with all competing groups accomplishes nothing, they reason, and working with one or two groups is better than planning with no community contact at all. One planner, after discussing in detail a strategy he was working on with "the community," revealed that he was really referring to just one group in the area:

> There is another group, also making demands if the highway goes through their area. I don't know how they feel. I don't know which group has greater needs. . . . This other group is putting a lot of political pressure behind a project I don't think will solve their problems. It's up to me to determine how this project rates with others in the area. I won't exactly try to defeat it, but I can't avoid hurting its chances. My very allocation of time affects the priority the project is given.

Other planners, less reluctant, throw themselves into the local political fray with zest. "Intrigue is rewarding," one said. He was working actively with one strong group, keeping others at bay by playing them off against each other and by skillful public relations. Explaining that this was the only realistic approach a concerned, competent planner could take, he described his relationship with some of the various community organizations in his area:

> The community [i.e., the community organization he was working closely with] feels I'm their man on the inside. The community youth, especially the young babes, work with me.

> I didn't like the Model Cities leadership when I came here, but I need their cooperation. I operate on enlightened self interest . . . we stay friendly.

> The mammies are a problem. They're hung up in fighting the black woman/white man issue. The black politi-

cians operating now aren't worth a shit. Their power base is the mammies.

The Panthers here deal with me. They came on tough, but it doesn't work with me. I have links to the Mafia, you might say. . . . So I could make a few phone calls and use them against the Panthers. Scared the shit out of them. By now we get along. I teach in a soul school and so forth.

Those planners dealing selectively with the community in this way naturally risk alienating some groups entirely. They accept this as an unavoidable hazard—"the name of the game," as one put it. Occasionally they find themselves blocked by opposition from some group whose strength they underestimated. "You win some and lose some," is the general feeling. Defeats are taken as an indication that change is needed in tactics, not in the partisan approach itself. The planner quoted above described his reaction when one of his neighborhoods voted down a bond issue he supported:

I did have one defeat. It was an uptown area where we could have brought clout; we had a black plurality. I traded promises of some capital improvements for support on a bond issue, and then the mammies double-crossed us. I should have predicted it. I usually don't go into areas in the first place where there's already something going, a political organization—because it's usually all mammies.

Another planner miscalculated the strength of the Model Cities organization in his area and failed to establish contacts with them, with disastrous results for the major project in his area. He explained what happened this way:

The Model Cities area overlaps a portion of my area. There's always been poor communication between the planning department and Model Cities. The policy was

not to go into the Model Cities area. I never went to
Model City meetings. I didn't work with them at all in
developing plans for the community center I was trying
to get for the area. When we finally got it set up, it was
located in the overlap area because the Catholic Church
donated space there. We allowed ourselves to be swayed
by Kate Ryan, a leader in my area, to exclude Model Cities people. Now I see that this was a tactical error. Model
Cities set up a competitive community center and worked
against us. They had the support of the people—Model
Cities funding is important for the area, they do drug
help and run an alcohol halfway house, and the people
rallied to them, not to us.

When one group is clearly stronger than its rivals, or when
conflict among various groups is minimal, the problem of
which to work with is not acute. But in those much more
common situations where strong community groups are at
war with each other, the planner is trapped in a dilemma—
immobilized if he tries to work with all groups, and out on a
partisan limb if he doesn't.

The Special Problem
of the Private Advocate

Besides community organizations and active residents, the
"voice of the community" often includes a number of private
professional advocates. These come from various sources, a
primary one being the private planning or architecture firm.
As discussed in Chapter One, most professional planners and
architects are familiar with the concept of advocacy planning
and design from the debates of recent years within these professions. Advocacy planning is used as shorthand for the position associated with Paul Davidoff, that there is no neutral
public interest and that planning inherently involves serving a
specific client. Better planning will result, this argument runs,

if the special interest nature of planning is recognized and all planners become self-conscious advocates for their clients, much as lawyers serve the neutral ideal of justice by acting as partisans for their clients. Institutions, developers, and business enterprises have long hired private planners not only to develop plans but also to act as liaison with city government agencies and further the specific interests of their employers wherever possible—in other words, to act as advocates. In recent years, communities as well have begun to retain the services of private planning firms to work in their behalf. Strong community organizations, especially those that are legally incorporated and well funded, may hire private planners and architects to represent their interests long before their area is included in any city-sponsored community planning program. Or, after inclusion in a city's program, community organizations may still want to employ a private consultant to negotiate with the city's community planner and monitor his work.

In addition to the paid professional advocate, communities may get free advocate planning services from professionals who volunteer their time. Planners and architects from private firms may consider it a civic duty to provide technical aid to community groups that lack funds to hire private advocates. Some socially concerned local chapters of professional organizations such as the American Institute of Planners and the American Institute of Architects encourage their members to donate services to community groups. VISTA workers and church group members with professional training may act as advocates without pay. One planner, who had worked in a private architecture firm before entering the city planning department, described some of the differing motivations and methods of volunteer advocates:

> My own volunteer advocate efforts weren't very effective. I was working in a private firm then. Three of us

architects got together and gave design advice to a non-
profit housing corporation. We designed a whole neighborhood near a park. We had a lot of enthusiasm. Some
25 people finally got involved professionally. But there is
a chapter of the American Institute of Architects here
that also wanted to lend its services and we found ourselves in conflict with them. They could solicit more funds
than we could and provide better service, and eventually
they took over our group. But their organization killed
the pleasure of it. The people involved in our group were
doing it because they were frustrated in their architecture
firms—they wanted to make decisions, to help people,
feel gratified by their work. The American Institute of
Architects was so bureaucratic, it was the same bag as the
firm in the first place. Most of us dropped out. One project is continuing, a community center. It has some
VISTA workers who are architects spearheading it,
young and dedicated types.

In cities with major universities, planning students are another source of private advocates. Working on behalf of a
community group, especially in the inner city, appeals to
many socially concerned planning students who offer their
services in their spare time. In addition, training programs
with a community planning emphasis sometimes require students to participate in workshops or special projects involving work with community groups. Some students choose the-
sis topics that take them into the community as volunteer
advocates. "My area," a community planner told us, "is so
close to the university that it's overstudied. The community
is thoroughly worked over by 'social action projects.' Young
people are crawling all over the place."

We asked the community planners working for the city
how they felt about these private advocates. Do they see
them as allies? Is there a sense of rivalry with them? Do they
think the private advocates' activities help the community's
development, or retard it?

Some confusion over the definition of private advocate

planner was apparent. "Sometimes the term advocate planner baffles me," a planner said. "It gets used for anybody with planning ideas in the community, but you can't just have untrained residents coming in and acting as planners." Another planner, after indicating he was very favorably inclined to the concept of advocacy, added: "I hate the word advocate planner though. It's overused. It's come to mean nothing but a shaggy-haired guy who lives with the folks."

Once the issue was limited to qualified professionals acting in an advocate capacity, the community planners divided sharply in their feelings. A few saw private advocacy as a useful supplement to the city's planning efforts: "I look on it as an extension of our staff. We can't do it all. Let the advocate planner do some of it." A common observation was that community groups were at a disadvantage, lacking the professional training to judge whether the city planner's proposals were in their best interests. Without advocate planners to act as a check and balance mechanism, to point out flaws and unconsidered alternatives, the city planner could "get away with murder." "There could be other points of view that are as valid as my plan, but I'm either ignorant of the facts or biased against them," one planner remarked. "Without some technical help from an advocate planner, the community can't formulate the problems and solutions that I don't see or don't agree with." Another planner explained:

> Advocates should play a major role in community planning. I wouldn't have said this not so long ago. But I've seen what an evil situation it is with city planners and communities that are completely dependent on them. People in general don't understand the problems of their neighborhood or even their block. The city planner can mislead the people badly. Myself, I'd like to be called to account by the citizens of a neighborhood. I'd much rather have an advocate out there than just citizens who I can snow.

Other community planners showed antagonism to private advocates. Some of this feeling was based on personal experience and rooted in recent conflicts over the community's allegiance within the planners' assigned areas, as the following comments illustrate:

> Private community planning consultants are phonies and opportunists.

> Advocate planners stir up the community against city planning by accusing us of being pro-business. They assume the position of crusaders. They mold themselves to citizen views temporarily, but they don't really mean it. They're motivated to improve their political images or to make a buck, that's all.

> Listen, I've seen a lot of advocate planners who didn't speak for the community, but they enjoyed the power and position.

> A private consultant has to plan in terms of local politics so that he won't get fired and so the next community will hear he's "good" and hire him. They'll say anything. Some guy, a private advocate planner, did four presentations to the planning commission recently. In each presentation he said he was raised in that area!

> Community leaders in my area are hiring people— social planners—to protect their neighborhoods. These advocates train the people to be sneaky. They get lawyers who think they can bulldoze through street closings and so forth.

Most planners, including some of those who expressed the deepest concern for adequate community representation in the planning process, had qualms about the private advocacy they had observed. Some of their reservations are illustrated in the quotes below:

> There are problems with each community having its own advocate planners. There aren't enough planners in the

first place, certainly not enough good ones. Communities don't have a lot of loot. They'd just end up hiring neophytes and getting into trouble. . . . "Advocate planners" are mostly schoolboys—you need experience to guide people.

I'm not against private advocate planners, but most communities can't afford to get a good one. I'd prefer our area planners to some hack local architect.

I've done advocacy planning as a student. It was exciting. I enjoyed it tremendously. But it tends to bring everything to a complete stop. We made the blacks in the city plenty aware of their community and its needs, but in the process we broke all connection with the city government. Most of the leaders we worked with are now in jail.

Advocacy divides the community, polarizes people. The idea of it sounds good, like a lawyer in a courtroom. But it isn't a courtroom. There's no impartial jury, and no way to bring the case to a conclusion that all will accept.

In general, the presence of private advocate planners is accepted by the community planner as a fact of life, something he can't ignore and might as well make the best of. They represent just one additional complication in the planner's already confusing search for his community.

Four

Community Planning Dilemmas

Thus far we have considered only the complexities of defining boundaries and legitimate representation for the community planner's target area. These definitions are basically administrative in nature. Although they may change later under pressure, they must be at least tentatively established before planning begins.

Only after the planner enters his area, makes contact with community leaders, and begins work do the more serious dilemmas and contradictions inherent in community planning become fully apparent. As discussed earlier, community planning is an experimental program, grafted onto a parent planning system based on very different assumptions. The community is unprepared for this new kind of planning, much of the structure of city government and finance is antagonistic to it, and the community planners themselves are confused as to their mandate. Community planning fits into the community's expectations and the city's institutional structure like a heretic in church.

In this chapter we examine five of the major problems that plague planners in their dealings with community residents. Each planner we talked to had a unique story to tell. We have tried here to isolate difficulties shared by large numbers of planners, problems that seem rooted in the fabric of the community planning program rather than the idiosyncrasies of individual planners. The problems considered include (1) distrust of city officials by community residents, (2) the paradox of role restriction, (3) social versus physical planning priorities, (4) conflicts of interest between the area and the city as a whole, and (5) the significance and limits of citizen participation.

The Stigma of City Hall

Community residents usually consider the history of their contact with city government a dismal succession of unheard grievances and deteriorating services (1). Thus any representative of city hall meets with initial coolness and perhaps contempt. City employees are seen as insensitive, incompetent, owing their positions to political patronage rather than merit, and unlikely to have any concern for or influence in improving the community. Community planners enter the community carrying the lead weight of this city hall image. "People in the neighborhood think of me as a bureaucrat," a planner said. "They don't view planning as a profession with ethics and concern—I'm just another civil servant." "It's not that the community distrusts us, exactly," another explained. "They just don't think of us at all. They don't contact the planning department that much. They don't think of us as here to help them."

Where residents do know of the planning department, they usually associate it with the city's economic growth, especially development of the downtown area—concerns seen as irrelevant or antithetical to the immediate interests of residential communities. This leads them to suspect the community planner's motives. As one planner put it:

> The citizens don't believe what we say. They think that the city planner works for industry and corporate business, that the planners are drawing up plans for economic growth. You tell them that X land is not good for residential development for XYZ reasons. They say, "Oh no, we know your game. It's because you have some kind of plot to stop us in favor of industry." They do have some justification for their suspicions. We do get asked to promote programs for business and industrial development for the city's economic health. These programs end in someone's personal profit; they have to, in a free enterprise economy. Thus people start suspecting we are helping business for some sinister reason.

The block clearance excesses of past urban renewal projects also stigmatize the planner. Although the planning department's involvement in urban renewal is often peripheral, as we shall see later, residents tend to view the planner's entry into their community as the first step toward massive demolition. "Past experience has made citizens wary," we were told. "They fear any planning in their area is a scheme to get urban renewal in through the back door." Another planner who had responsibility for a well-heeled historical residential area said, "They feel safer if they do their own planning with private consultants. Past experience makes them think anything we get involved in eventually gets hit by urban renewal—the mass clearance type. So they want nothing to do with our agency. They want their neighborhood preserved, not leveled."

Where the planner's community is a racial ghetto, particularly one with strong community organizations, distrust of city hall assumes the nature of a rallying battle cry for community residents. Even in the rare cases where the city gov-

ernment has significant minority group representation, public
officials are viewed as flunkies of a white power structure
whose interests never coincide with those of ghetto residents.
White planners constantly complained about the wall of suspicion they confront in ghetto areas, saying such things as,
"I've got two strikes against me, I'm from the city and I'm
white," and "With blacks my problem was being white, and
even more, working for the city." A white planner working
in a Chinese area said, "I may never be fully accepted here.
The people here suspect the city wants to get rid of China-
town. They think I'm just here to placate them." One black
planner whose staff was white explained, "There's a real
problem getting the community to have confidence in my
cats. The main community group I deal with has had a long
tradition of working with stupid whites from the city. We've
had to overcome this image." Even black planners working in
black areas may find association with a white-dominated city
government to be an obstacle to community trust. A black
planner described the suspicious reaction of residents in his
area to one of his suggestions:

> We told our group to try for an urban renewal program.
> Now, I'm black—I could understand their fears about
> urban renewal. But I could also understand that this par-
> ticular program could help the community grow and
> prosper. They remain undecided as to whether to accept
> our recommendation. The Urban League's against it, also
> people from other neighborhoods who went through
> urban renewal elsewhere. I tell them this program is dif-
> ferent. They're not sure. Can they really trust me? I
> work for an agency that's all white except for me. Maybe
> I'm not on their side.

Some community planners are unable to comprehend the
hostile reception they receive in ghetto areas. One remarked, for example, "I don't understand the black minority.

They treat me with suspicion. Why? I'm friendly and know what city hall can and can't do; I could help them if they'd work with me." Others attribute the lack of rapport with the community to their own deficiencies: "I was young, without technical experience or skill in dealing with people, especially those whose education, goals, and aspirations differed from mine. The distrust was mutual." One white planner, who had worked for a year in a black area with such intensity that he had ruined his health, acknowledged sadly that he still had not achieved genuine acceptance. His interpretation left little hope that the distrust of ghetto residents could be overcome by the individual efforts of the community planners:

> They still don't really believe they'll get anything, even though they have accomplished some things. You know, lots of urban blacks are screwed up mentally. They think there's always a trick, a white man's joke on them. It's one of the tragedies of racism, that it has produced people too paranoid to work effectively for their own interests. These are the shipwrecks of our society. Some are really sick. This has to be kept in mind—it's not a rational scene.

The Paradox of Role Restriction

The community bases its antagonism on a double misunderstanding: (1) planners are intimately connected with all city government activities and therefore culpable for all unpopular acts by other city agencies and officials; and (2) planners have full control over investment in the city and therefore withholding of funds can be attributed to their insensitivity to community needs. The irony of these common misunderstandings is fully appreciated by the community planners we talked to. Many of them, as we shall see, desire more influence over both the activities of other city agencies and the determination of the city's financial policies. However, the role they are currently authorized to play in city government is extremely limited. To be denied the authority they feel is necessary and then be blamed for acts they have no control over is a "Catch-22" frustration they wish to avoid at all costs. Therefore even those who chafe most at their role restrictions are constantly trying to convince the community that the planner's influence on city government is minimal.

Communicating that their role is highly specific and independent of other agencies is not easy. One planner told us:

> It takes a lot of talking to let people know, in my district, that we are not representing the redevelopment authority but the planning function. Actually, the redevelopment authority and the planning board have been centralized under one director. This is almost impossible to explain to people. We say our agency is really two agencies rolled up into one—that we are acting not as the renewal authority but as the city planning agency. We're struggling for a new identity, especially since people hate the redevelopment authority. We're always saying, "We're *not* redevelopment, we're *planning*." Sometimes we make sick jokes about having a bulldozer parked outside.

As the most accessible city official, the community planner becomes a target for accumulated grievances against the city. A planner working in the inner city described this scapegoating process:

> One thing that does bother me is that I represent the city. When there is a meeting with the community, they will take out all their anger with the city on me. I catch hell every time something happens—like maybe Licensing and Inspection has come in and condemned or pointed out violations that homeowners can't afford to fix, and there's no home and loan program to correct the problems. It's basically out of my hands but I'm the one who's available, so they raise hell with me.

Only by disassociating himself from other offending city agencies can the planner escape the community's wrath. "The community people look upon us as a savior," said one planner whose attempts to do this had succeeded. "By now they know it's not planning that plagues them when they have problems with garbage, street pavings, and so on. They're mad, but not at us."

Similarly, planners have trouble shedding responsibility for delays in implementation of plans. As one commented sadly:

> The citizen feels that planners have supreme power in city hall. But the real situation is the extreme opposite. We are powerless. [Do you tell them that?] Oh, sure. They never believe you.

Some, like this planner, try to convey that the planning role has nothing to do with implementation—that once the plan is completed, their job is done:

> I go to community meetings representing the city. At the last one I gave a definition of the planning commission's role. The community had it confused with the political process. I told them that the planning commission's role was to make recommendations of allocation of scarce resources. But any complaints about the implementation or adequacy of the actual programs should go through political channels. We are planners and architects, not politicians.

Others who define planning more broadly emphasize, in their dealings with the community, the obstacles they face in trying to get their plans carried out. One planner, whose community was currently blaming him for not getting federal funds to put a detested railroad underground, said, "I'd like the community people to come to Washington with us so we could let them hear directly from the people in Washington why this project is being rejected. I'd approve the

funds, but I don't have the power." If the planners can communicate their powerlessness, they feel, any delays or perver-
sions in their plans will not be viewed as their fault. Planners
who have done this successfully seem relieved. "For the most
part my community recognizes that we're there to assist
them," one said. "They realize that we are only one body of
city government and after plans have been drawn up our
hands are tied by the city bureaucracy." Another commented, "We do plans but then it's taken out of our hands.
Like urban renewal going wrong—even people in the
neighborhoods know it's not the fault of the city planners."

Thus to gain community trust, planners try to convince
the community that their role in city government is both limited and powerless. By doing so, however, they raise the
community's skepticism about their potential usefulness. If
the planner is not the influential individual the community
has supposed, why bother with him? Community residents
view planning as valuable only if it affects actual development. Faith in the planner's ability to deliver is perhaps even
more crucial to gaining community cooperation than over-
coming the community's distrust of city hall. Hence the planner finds himself walking into an unavoidable paradox. By disassociating himself from the city's power structure, he casts
doubt on his capacity to perform meaningful services. But by
claiming to have influence on city policy, he indirectly assumes responsibility for all the shortcomings in those policies
and thus jeopardizes community trust. Without basic changes
in the role of planning in urban development, the community
planner has two equally unattractive choices in presenting
himself to the residents in his area: he can seem influential but
relatively untrustworthy, or trustworthy but relatively useless.

Physical Solutions to Social Problems

The deepest concerns of community residents are usually social: crime, idle youth, employment, rat control, air pollution, changes in the area's racial composition, getting streets cleaned and garbage collected regularly. If the planner can convince residents he is really there to help plan for neighborhood improvement, these are the problems they direct the planner toward—not the physical structures and land use patterns in the area. Unfortunately, as we have already pointed out, the planning department has no formal control over provision of city services. Although planners can sometimes influence the location of schools, they have little to say about whether the schools function as multipurpose centers, provide adult education in the evening, open their recreation facilities during the summer vacation, or bus children for racial balance. Once a health care facility has been decided on planners may help place it, but they do not participate in basic decisions on how the city's health care delivery system should operate—whether, for instance, storefront clinics and mobile health care vehicles should supplement centralized hospitals, or whether community immunization programs and birth control education should be undertaken. Planners can design a recreation center or a park into their plans; but even if they succeed in getting the physical facility, they have no control over the facility's hours, programs, maintenance, and supervision. Job training, street sweeping, garbage collection, drug abuse programs, and placing traffic lights at dangerous corners are all out of the planner's hands. The operational aspects of city government are the jurisdiction of other city agencies: departments of education, streets and roads, parks and recreation, sanitation, public health, the city police.

Most of the community planners we talked to agree with

their areas' residents that community social problems are serious, sometimes appalling. But without the authority to plan
for social services directly, how does the community planner
deal with the social service needs of his area? We found four
common adaptations to this problem.

A few planners meet the problem with *denial*. They define
social planning as something already being done by the planning department, denying that any change in planning policy
would be helpful. Usually this means social planning must be
absorbed into the concept of physical planning. They will
say, for instance, "Definitely we do social planning. How can
you do one without the other? The idea of a special 'social
planner' is ridiculous"; or "Of course we have social planning
here. Any planner shouldn't have to think twice about including social factors. They come in naturally whatever he
does." In a few cases, social planning independent of physical
planning is viewed as valid but given a lower priority. For
example, one planner explained his indifference to social planning this way:

> Sure, you have to consider social factors like family struc-
> ture, the values of a particular ethnic group, and so on.
> But the real priority is the physical disease of the city—
> not social problems like crime or health. Housing, the
> physical structure, is the real priority. The other things
> are symptoms of physical urban decay. They might im-
> prove if people had decent shelter.

For the planners relying on denial, the social problems of
their areas are not the kind of issues that can be solved
through planning at all.

Other planners deal with their community's social needs
through *referral*. They define social planning as a necessary
city function, but one that should be carried on outside the
planning department. Some point out that the present staff of
the planning department is untrained for anything but physi-

cal planning. "Social planning is needed, all right," said one, "but we shouldn't do it here. Let someone else do it. I'd like us to do a first-class job of physical planning rather than dabbling in economic and social planning areas that we don't know much about." These planners refer all questions about social services in their areas to the "appropriate" departments of city government—that is, the operating agencies.

The operating agencies unfortunately are typically ill equipped for the task and unresponsive to citizen complaints. This consideration leads some of the planners to speak of a vaguely defined agency that "ought to be set up" and "coordinated somehow" with the planning department. "Much of any necessary social planning should be done by other agencies," we were told, "but if they can't do it, there should be a department of health and welfare with social planners in it. We should be concerned with them and in contact with such planners—but not have them here in the planning department." The fact that a new city agency specializing in social planning shows no sign of materializing in the foreseeable future seems unimportant to planners taking this position. By removing the social planning function to another agency, even an imaginary one, they protect themselves from feeling helpless in the face of the unsolved social problems in their areas. If social planning can be passed on to "someone else," these planners can continue mapping out the physical development of their areas without asking whether their efforts might be in vain.

Others, dissatisfied with the incompleteness of the referral approach, urge *transformation* of the institutional limitations on community planning. They want to involve the planning department not only in the social aspects of physical land use but also in social planning independent of physical planning. "We have control of the capital improvements program, but we need to have more control of the operating budget," said one, voicing a commonly expressed opinion. "We need it to do real planning; we must have control of programming as well as capital improvements." As we shall see in Part Four, planners with this attitude are disinclined to respect the formal divisions of city administration and often find themselves in conflict with officials in the operating agencies.

Most of the community planners we talked with, however, have chosen another approach. They reject denial and referral as ineffective, and they regard transformation—the attempt to expand their formal authority—as futile and possibly suicidal. The strategy they fall back on is one we call *translation*, which consists of redefining the community's social problems so that they do fall within the planning department's sphere of authority. These planners consider the social needs in their areas too urgent to go totally unmet. If the city's operating agencies are "failing the people," as one planner put it, they feel the planning department should try to deal, however inadequately, with the community's social problems. But since the only tools directly at the disposal of the planning department are oriented to the physical structures and layout of the area, these planners find themselves searching for ways to translate each social problem into a physical problem. If the residents feel their children are not being taught to read in school, the planner cannot intervene directly in teaching policies; so he will try to increase the number of school buildings in his area, hoping to solve the education problem with physical structures. If the residents are worried about teenage vandalism, the planner cannot set up gang control programs or alter police practices; so he will work to get a park or recreation center for his area, hoping to solve juvenile delinquency problems with physical facilities. "For citizen involvement we need people with sociological background," we were told, "people who can communicate with the citizens and translate their wants into physical plans we can do something about."

Many of the planners we talked to feel pressured into taking this approach. In an outburst of frustration, one complained:

> There's a tendency here to "solve" social problems by working through their physical manifestations. We get pushed into it. We should be doing more, but the director here puts tremendous pressure on the physical side of things. It's his downfall. Draw him a pretty picture and he'll love it!

Others point out, with equal frustration, that community residents themselves often translate concerns that are basically social into physical demands. "Community groups are as guilty as planners in their desire for physical solutions," one said. "Community groups want buildings," explained another, adding:

> The most tangible evidence of their own power is to get some kind of public facility. And, you guessed it, it's usually a recreation center. They see it as a way of controlling juvenile delinquency. The leaders of the community are more sophisticated than that—they know parks don't necessarily keep kids off streets—but they want support and the community thinks a park will do the job. It's hard for them not to fall back on the same old rhetoric.

Once the community residents have decided that a physical structure will solve a social problem, the planner rarely can persuade them otherwise. He may back their proposal, knowing it to be misdirected in terms of their real concerns, simply because he would lose all community cooperation if he tried to stand in the way. A planner described such a situation in his area:

> Community people are concerned with immediate community facilities. In my area the key thing around which they are organized is getting a recreation center. They

think this would reduce teenage acts against property.
The white teenagers around here are like marauders—
they go through a neighborhood breaking windows in
the houses. I don't think a park is going to stop this by
itself! But there's a lot of political pressure behind the
project now. There's no point at this stage to even raise
the issue of whether the park will solve the juvenile delinquency problem. Nobody would listen.

Although most planners rely heavily on translation as a
strategy for dealing with their community's social needs, it is
not an approach they feel comfortable with. Even when they
describe cases in which both the planning department and the
community residents applaud their efforts to solve social
problems with physical solutions, a shadowy sense of futility
seems to lie behind their words. A planner told us:

Sometimes I feel that whatever I do in the community,
it's peripheral to the most pressing community problems.
What the people here really need are jobs, or higher income. This is very frustrating! I feel guilty getting them
to deal with general planning matters, like getting a recreation facility. These things won't affect their worst
problems.

The feeling that the planners' best efforts are foredoomed to
failure, which we will explore further in Chapter Eleven,
runs like a dark thread through the fabric of their daily activities, lending a somber tone to their moments of reflection.
Limited in formal authority to physical planning, community planners choose among and sometimes mix these
four modes of handling the social problems of their
neighborhoods—denial, referral, transformation, and translation. But none of the four adaptations allow the planner to
escape the basic dilemma: he cannot respond to the urgent social concerns of his community's residents without going outside the physical planning role prescribed for him by his employers.

City Versus Community:
The Priorities Dilemma

In the community planning programs we observed, the planner is charged with the dual responsibility to further community interests within the larger framework of furthering city-wide development. Unfortunately, the interests of the city and the planner's area seldom coincide completely, and they may be diametrically opposed. Most community planners find themselves beset with proposals that are beneficial from one perspective but disastrous from the other. In a typical comment, one told us, "We've found that whenever there's something that would help the city as a whole, it's a problem for the community." Each planning decision contains a priorities dilemma. For example, when a hospital in a community planner's area proposes to expand, should the planner place higher priority on the city's urgent need for improved medical facilities and favor the expansion? Or should he concern himself with saving the community's housing that lies in the path of the proposed expansion, and oppose the hospital's growth? If the housing in his area upgrades in value, should he make plans to reinforce the trend, or try to introduce lower value housing to ease the housing shortage for low-income residents in other parts of the city? If other areas have greater need of city resources than does the area he is assigned to, should he adjust his plans to take this into account, or disregard it and push for maximum city investment in his own area?

It is in these situations of conflict between city interests and area interests that the contradictions inherent in present community planning programs are cast into sharpest focus. The planner's training has usually been scaled to the functions and needs of cities rather than smaller or larger units. He works for a governmental body that deals fundamentally in systems administered and funded for the city, not the city's

constituent communities or the metropolitan region of which
the city is a part. For these reasons, he is inclined to be sensitive to city-wide needs. But his specific assignment, by whose
success he both judges himself and is judged by his department, links his responsibility more immediately to a smaller
scale unit. Moreover, he is expected to work closely with citizens whose primary concerns involve their immediate area
rather than the city. Thus he must be sensitive to community
needs. Beyond vague statements to the effect that planners
should consider the needs of both the city and their communities, the community planning programs offer no guidance to
planners torn between the two on a specific issue. The planners are on their own.

For many, choosing a course of action in these conflict situations is agonizing. Not only can they see both sides of the
issue in question, but they are also painfully aware that recon-
ciling the conflicting interests requires either resources that
are not available or powers the planners do not have. "I run
into conflicts of interest all the time," one told us, adding:

> The trouble is, even if I see a way to resolve them, I
> usually can't put it into effect. Take the open enrollment
> policy of the schools here, for instance. I'm really torn
> over this. I sympathize with the people in the central city
> who send their kids to the outer parts of the city, but I
> also see they are crowding these outer schools in my
> planning area. The inner city schools are now one-third
> empty. I wouldn't want to see kids forced back into
> them; they ought to be closed down completely. But the
> crowding out here is no good either. What we should do
> is to make educational parks, each serving a pie-shaped
> section of the city. This would require remodeling the
> whole school system, of course, which I can't do.

A similar story involved a large park, vitally needed by the
city's population as a whole but desperately resisted by the
community it would displace:

The master plan has this land in my area set aside for the park. The people here don't want the park; they'd like to see the slum go but they want it replaced with rehab housing or new housing. But what about the rest of the city that wants the park? We must have balanced land use; that means we have to have the park somewhere in a built-up area. It's got to affect *some* neighborhood. I personally think the proposed park isn't in the right location. [Where would you put it?] There's no simple answer. Maybe we should leave it to a regional planning body to provide a park in some undeveloped outlying area, but it would be out of our hands then; and besides, who would provide the transportation to get people out to it? There are so many obstacles to settling this conflict. We've been thinking of joint use of park and school land as a solution, but this is just in the discussion stage. We can't really push it without stepping on the toes of the board of education and the department of parks and recreation.

In some cases the planners can see possibilities for tradeoffs, some special benefits the residents could get in return for accepting the unwanted city facility. However, since such tradeoffs depend on the cooperation of private developers or other city agencies, the planner has no clout to bring about this kind of solution. "I remember going to meetings in the West End," said a planner. "We did all kinds of things to sell the idea of zoning changes to bring in industry. The city needs more industry. But when it came to tradeoffs, we couldn't promise any. So it didn't sell." With a touch of cynicism, another said:

There's a lot of conflict between institutional growth and community residents here. The conflict is bitter because of the low level of institutional responsibility. Many of the institutions haven't awakened to the fact that they can't just expand like this without doing something for the people around them. Look at the university. It has no relations with most of the surrounding area, even though it has displaced thousands of people and causes housing and parking problems. They do a little now with a community on one side of them, but it took a student sit-in to get that. They say they provide programs, but their activities are basically city-wide in nature. They don't do anything special for their own community. They don't think they're part of it.

Thus blocked from all mechanisms for resolving the priorities dilemma, some planners simply throw up their hands. Said one:

In my area, there's intense conflict over the 400 acres surrounding the stadium, whether it's going into parking or housing. The neighborhood's already cut in two by the freeway, and now the stadium wants parking on both sides of the freeway. The war is on until some kind of community plan can be made that fits the master plan. It's a real mess. I gave the problem to Joe [another planner].

Another planner in a low-income black neighborhood told us almost in panic:

I'm unable to keep up with my area. Whose interests do you look out for, the community's or the city's? I'm too young and idealistic to believe they are separate, and I don't know what to do when they conflict. The railroad in my area is supposed to be realigned. The city's master plan has it running right through the only park in the neighborhood. If the realignment goes through the people there threaten to blow up the tracks. What am I supposed to do about this?

The resolution of interest conflicts between city and community is not merely a technical problem. The planner's response is a professional decision involving basic assumptions about planning, power, and political organization, and the planner's self-identity as well.

The Role of Citizen Participation

As we saw in Chapter One, community planning was initially designed to encourage—or at least give the appearance of encouraging—greater citizen participation in planning. Most of the community planners we talked to are quick to endorse this goal on a high level of abstraction. Only in talking about specific cases does it become clear that they represent a wide range of attitudes on just how and with what authority citizens should involve themselves in planning their own communities.

In general, the planners' feelings about the proper degree of citizen participation depend on how they view *the relationship of planning to implementation*. Those who see the two stages as completely separate regard citizen participation basically as *public relations*. For those ambivalent or undecided about how closely planning and implementation should be linked, community input is a kind of *balancing act*. And for those who include implementation as a basic element of planning, citizen participation represents a *power boost* necessary to compensate for the weak position of planning in the United States.

Illusory Democracy:
Citizen Input as Public Relations

A number of community planners, sometimes without recognizing it themselves, reveal a total lack of sympathy with the concept of citizen participation. They are not necessarily insensitive to the problems of their communities, nor are they necessarily uncreative or opposed to innovations in planning. Rather, these planners define planning in a way that allows no room for input by amateurs. They see planning as a highly

technical professional effort isolated from all political considerations. Whether a completed plan ever reaches the implementation stage is a political issue, and thus irrelevant to the
technical task of good planning. Convinced that most citizens
lack both the interest to work on planning separately from
implementation and the training to deal competently with
planning concepts, these planners see no technical value in including community input in the preliminary planning stage.
The citizens' proper role is a political one, to lobby for the
plan once it is drawn up by the professional planner assigned
to their area. In the political realm of implementation,
democracy—that is, citizen participation—is appropriate;
in the professional realm of planning, it is not.

Although officially assigned responsibility for only one
community, planners taking this point of view are inclined to
give first consideration to the needs of the city in all their decisions. By their definition, planning means accepting the
city's administrative organization and budget level as given,
and designing a rational allocation of resources within these
limits. To push for extra benefits for their assigned areas at
the expense of other areas, they feel, would be unprofessional
conduct. The fact that community residents cannot be expected to share this concern for the rest of the city is further
reason to disregard their views in drawing up the community
plan. We were told:

> The planner has to have control, not the community.
> Even if it's a local problem. To solve it other things have
> to be taken into consideration. It may appear to be a local
> problem, but it never really is. The community only sees
> the local part of the problem, and doesn't ask, for in-
> stance, if the city has enough money to do what they
> want. The planner is trained to think in a broader
> perspective.

A planner deeply involved in community work said, "I'm
against citizens having excessive power in planning, basically.

It does more harm than good. It's a big slogan, citizen participation, but it's naive." "Communities are not responsible
enough to have veto power over plans," said another, adding,
"They should be given due process, of course. If they don't
like the way things turn out, they can use court injunctions."

Some resent the citizen participation they are forced to
allow by department policy or federal regulations. One planner, bitter over a conflict with his community involving
selection of a park site, said:

> I question the philosophy of citizen participation as it
> was set up here. They gave out too much power to the
> neighborhood. HUD said that all decisions must be made
> by the citizens. The Model Cities board has to approve
> all programs. When HUD tried to contract the power it
> just caused more conflict in the neighborhood. I believe
> the neighborhood has a proper place in planning. Profes-
> sionals should work with residents, getting together with
> them at certain points in planning to inform them, but
> the planners should do the basic work. But as it is now,
> the neighborhood's involved in the process of planning
> continuously. And when a professional says something,
> they will override him. [Has this happened to you?]
> Yes, it certainly has! That's how much power they've
> given out.

In a different city, a planner who had recently been hooted
down at a community meeting commented:

> It's not practical to get 100 percent community accep-
> tance of a plan! Some planners here think they shouldn't
> decide anything, just let the community decide every-
> thing from top to bottom. I think this is going too far
> with democracy. I don't know exactly how much influ-
> ence a community should exert, but one thing I do know:
> in my area, they've got too much influence. They want
> to lay down the law.

Complained a planner in yet another city:

It's not so much that they've been given the authority:
but they just take it. They shouldn't have taken so much
authority; they can't use it more positively than we can,
although that's what they think. They say: "You have
planned and it failed, you promised low income housing
for the people you dislocated and didn't follow through.
If you have made so many mistakes, why not give us a
chance?" Now, you know they're going to make more
mistakes than trained professionals would. They'll just be
worse off than before.

These planners do see some value in community involvement—as public relations work to give community
leaders the illusion of participation, coopt them, and thus
smooth the way for community acceptance of the planners'
final product. As one planner working in the inner city described this process,

The community should be kept aware of developments.
They shouldn't get involved in the technical work,
though. The planner might present several alternatives
that are within feasibility and let them choose between
them. But he should keep the neighborhood aware of
what he's doing so they will feel part of it. You can't just
give them something at the end and expect them to accept it.

Another planner, assigned to a similar area in a different city,
made clear his feeling that public relations considerations in
community involvement should never obscure the actual
power relationship between planner and residents:

What should be the community's role? Well, first they
should express their desires, and get the feeling of par-
ticipating. The planner, through expertise supplement,
should shape their desires into a workable program. Then
he should go back to the community and give them the
case for the problem's solution as he sees it. Then they
should accept it. If they don't accept it, it should still be

done. There has to be some control. The community certainly shouldn't have veto power.

Planners taking this position do not necessarily think of
themselves as "comprehensive planners" as opposed to "advocate planners." Although many of them are outspokenly hostile to advocacy planning, others are swept up in the aura of
democratic enthusiasm surrounding the community planning
effort. They are young and liberal, and they wish to identify
themselves as advocates because the term has become synony-
mous with social concern. However, unwilling to abandon
their professional concern for city-wide needs, they are
forced into mental gymnastics that stretch the concept of advocacy planning far beyond its original meaning. One planner told us:

> We should all be advocate planners. I am one. We advo-
> cate for the people of the city, not special interests.
> Advocacy planning is planning for everyone. That's how
> I work, as a planner for everyone in the city. I want to
> plan housing for all classes, not single people out on the
> basis of income and work for them. Something like trans-
> portation, you can't plan for just one group. If you work
> for just one group or area, that's not advocacy.

Somehow, but How?
Citizen Input as a Balancing Act

For the majority of planners seeking a mix of citizen participation and professional expertise in the formulation of community plans, the boundary between the creation of a plan
and its implementation is blurred. Rather than falling into
two distinct endeavors, one reserved for the nonpolitical professional community planner and the other for the community's nonexpert voting public, the two "stages" merge

into a messy process from which the citizen might be entirely excluded unless care is taken. After all, unless the community has prepared an alternative plan with the help of a private planner (an expensive and therefore unlikely possibility), the residents can only choose to support the community planner's ideas or go totally unrepresented by a planner. Seeing their plans as the only game in town, these community planners cannot comfort themselves with the thought that meaningful citizen participation will come into play in implementation decisions. By then, it is too late for the residents of the area to say anything but yes or no. Planners taking this position feel strongly that since the residents will have to live with the consequences of the plan if it becomes reality, their views should be included somewhere in the planning-implementation process. They see only one possible point of entry for these views: in the formulation of the plan itself.

Therefore, planners taking this position favor considerable community control, even veto power, over planning decisions in their area—as long as these decisions concern the local area only. When a proposal involves a regional facility, however, their enthusiasm for community determination of the plan quickly fades. In these cases, those affected by the plan's implementation are no longer limited to the community's residents but include the population of the city, the metropolitan area, perhaps even the nation. By allowing local communities to block planned regional facilities, planners would be failing to protect the interests of these larger populations for whom they also feel professionally responsible. Thus they strongly oppose "excessive" community participation in decisions involving city-wide or regional needs.

The remarks of these planners about their selective acceptance of community control over planning has a formulalike quality:

> I believe the people should have near total control in deciding what kind of facilities go in their neighborhood,

and the placing and priority of the facilities. They should definitely have veto power over the plan. Except, of course, with regard to large regional issues.

Some decisions can be given to the community, others not. Playgrounds, I'd leave that to the community. On locating highways, you can't give the last word to the community.

They should have considerable influence over factors that affect their own neighborhood, but less over city-wide things. They shouldn't be able to stop a freeway going from here to Florida.

Citizens should play the primary role in making up the plan for the neighborhood—all but the regional facilities. I believe in delegating the responsibility to the community, but they shouldn't have responsibility for regional-serving facilities like the university. The area around the university has to accommodate the required facility whether it wants to or not.

Certain things a neighborhood can make decisions about, and should play a major role. On local issues. But other large issues like open housing or expressways can't be decided locally, even if they work to the community's detriment.

Local people should have authority over things that affect them only. But things that go beyond the neighborhood, where the entire city is involved, should have a higher arena.

These neat formulations fail the planners, however, whenever specific proposals are resisted by the community. "I believe the community should frame plans and have veto power over those activities and projects that affect that community itself, but not for city-wide projects," a planner told us, then added, "only, I don't know who decides which is which." After trying to explain his position, another concluded, "Some things the people should have maximum control over, other things the city should have maximum control over, but it's hopeless to try and pinpoint it!" Some glossed over the dilemma with clichés: "The community has to respect certain regional needs like freeways, but then again, you shouldn't trample the people." "There's just got to be more communication and sincerity," we were told, and "when community leaders and planners disagree they should get together around a table and resolve their differences—but which one has the power, I don't know."

Without guidelines for determining which issues are local and which regional in impact, these planners decide the proper degree of community control on an ad hoc basis, balancing citizen demands and their own professional judgments about city needs as best they can. "This macro-micro problem is really something," said a planner deeply committed to the concept of citizen participation. "We got a proposal for public housing recently. My community didn't want it located here. I could see the inner city needed it, but I went with my district against my better judgment. But on housing for the elderly, which they also didn't want, I went for the needs of the city. I know that's inconsistent. It seemed the right thing at the time in both cases."

Planning in the Streets:
Citizen Input as Power Boost

For the planners most in favor of citizen participation, the professional task of planning is not only inextricably mixed with the political task of implementation, but it derives its *only* claim to validity from the political dimension. They feel that however elegant and creative their community plans may be, they will not be functioning as planners unless their work has some physical consequences. Without implementation, their product is not planning but rather an esoteric art form. One planner voiced the frustration common to those who see implementation as an integral part of the planning process:

> What I'm interested in is people, especially housing for poor people. At first I was very enthusiastic about planning, but now I see it doesn't relate to these problems. A lot of reports are done, they get stacked up in a storage room and covered with dust—what's it all for? Planning without action doesn't have any real significance for the people. How can you even call it planning, when you can't delve into the real problems and fulfill the real needs? The reports and plans are beautiful, but they *never get carried out*.

Since plans rarely reach implementation without active community support, these planners conclude that in the present institutional context, their greatest contribution as professional planners would be to mobilize the community politically. As a planner in an inner city area put it:

> All plans around here are meaningless without money, and there isn't any money. If you don't have money power, you've got to get people power. The purpose of the community planner is to organize the community, so that when the plan is completed the people can exert enough power to get the plan implemented. Planning without power is meaningless.

"Politicians will just laugh at you until you get community support," another told us. "If the planner is going to have any credibility with the politicians who control implementation, the people have to back him up." In the community of another planner, citizens were organizing to pressure the city government into using a large wooded area in their neighborhood for a new high school campus instead of selling it to a developer. The planning department's recommendations alone, this planner claimed, would never save the site for the school. "The only answer to meeting political objections to the kind of planning we want is to let the citizens play a very heavy role," he said. "They have to push it through or our plan means nothing." One planner, about to leave the department after a year of deep involvement in a poor black area, said bluntly: "The people have to control planning, because there's no teeth in regular planning. Real planning assumes socialism. In this capitalistic society, for planning to play any role at all the community has to be active."

Observing how badly city planning has served many of the communities they work with, these planners have developed a skeptical attitude toward the department's claim to professional neutrality. "Let's face it," said one, "the planning department was *set up* to help developers and real estate interests, not the people." Another explained, "I generally lean toward citizen groups when they're in conflict with the city. My premise is that most of their grievances are valid." Some come to the conclusion that the whole profession is biased against the needs of community residents. As one told us:

> If the community is informed and has its own plan, they should be given veto power. There's a lot that the profession doesn't know. Professional planners aren't always right. Most regular planners don't know their ass from a hole in the ground. On road improvements, I'd go with the community any day. On some recent road issues the planning department should have stood up and resigned en masse, but some here thought the road proposals were good planning.

Although convinced that planning requires a power boost from the citizens, these planners are acutely aware of the difficulties in generating community support. "Community pressure isn't the problem," said a planner seeking implementation for an elaborate area plan. "Our problem is, how do you build *more* of it. We're trying like crazy." Particularly when the residents are poor, their apathy and political ineffectiveness evoke a painful blend of sympathy and exasperation in the planners. One black planner said, "People in my area think of themselves as house niggers now, and they're so happy not to be field niggers anymore, they won't do anything!" "How do you get the poor to be active?" asked another planner, who had obviously tried everything he could think of to spark community interest in planning. "They're so strung out. How do you get them involved?"

Caught up in the struggle for implementation of particular projects, planners with this perspective often view the drawing up of formal community plans as a distraction from their "last ditch efforts" to give planning some relevance to actual city development. Explaining her total involvement in one specific project and her indifference to the overall community plan, a planner explained:

> This piece of land in my community is important and not only to the people here; if it goes, the same thing will happen in other areas. So we're organizing the community, trying to arouse them. We're acting like advocate planners. That's how important this thing is. I'll tell you, I'm becoming very disgusted with planning vis-à-vis politics. I don't like losing so many battles. By now I care more about politics than pure planning. If people only realized, that's what's important.

For these planners, the management of a project through the political system supersedes the formulation of comprehensive area plans; and in the political arena, citizen participation is the planner's only effective weapon.

The five basic problems reviewed here are inescapable. All community planners must find some way of coping with community distrust, decide what degree of responsibility to claim in presenting themselves to the community, set their priorities concerning social versus physical planning, develop a policy on the inevitable conflicts between area needs and city-wide needs, and determine the proper role of citizen participation in planning. In the next chapter, we shall see how the community planners' response to these problems is shaped and molded by the pressures they confront.

Notes

1. This is particularly true for the city's poorer residents, both black and white. The systematic neglect and marginal political influence of low-income residents in U.S. cities has been well documented in such major government-sponsored research efforts as the Kerner Report (*Report of the National Advisory Committee on Civil Disorders*, Washington, D.C.: Government Printing Office, 1968, Vols. I and II) and the Douglas Report (*Building the American City: Report of the National Commission on Urban Problems*, New York: Praeger, 1969). See also Joseph P. Fried, *Housing Crisis U.S.A.* (New York: Praeger, 1971); Harold M. Baron, "Black Powerlessness in Chicago," in *Majority & Minority*, Norman R. Yetman and C. Hoy Steele, Eds. (Boston: Allyn and Bacon, 1971); Charles Abrams, *The City Is the Frontier* (New York: Harper Colophon Books, 1965). Jewel Bellush and Murry Hausknecht, Eds., *Urban Renewal: People, Politics and Planning* (Garden City, N.Y.: Anchor Books, 1967); Fred Powledge, *Model City* (New York: Simon and Schuster, 1970); and Herbert J. Gans, *The Urban Villagers* (New York: The Free Press, 1962).

117

Five

The Community Planning
Pressure System

As the planning link between the city and the community, community planners find their activities the focal point of strong contradictory demands linked together in what might be called the *community planning pressure system*. On the one hand, neighborhood residents are demanding quick action in the community's interests on a variety of projects, some of which involve social services outside the planner's formal mandate. On the other hand, the planning department and the city government of which it is a part are expecting the community planners to produce relatively long-range area plans that stay within the physical planning sphere to which the planning department's mandate is limited, give the city's needs higher priority than any specific community's interests, and avoid any involvement in the political struggle for implementation of the plans. Squeezed by these opposing forces into dilemmas for which their professional training gives little guidance, community planners must construct

119

their own planning roles as best they can.

Many of the planners attracted to the community planning program are "antiestablishment" in personal style, liberal-to-radical in their politics, and extremely sensitive to the needs of underdog groups such as the poor, minorities, and community residents fighting industry and highways. In the confusion surrounding the limits and goals of the community planning program, these planners see opportunities to use the resources and contacts at their disposal to benefit the groups so often ignored or exploited in traditional city planning. Cynical about the "public interest" concerns espoused by most professional city planners, they embrace the idea of advocate planning with enthusiasm. In effect, they respond to pressures from their communities' residents rather than the planning department and city government. However, since the city government that employs them defines the goals of the community planning program more conservatively, their advocate role is usually covert. They become what might be called *administrative guerrillas*, working undercover for a specific client rather than the nebulous public interest they profess to serve as public city planners. Occasionally, as we shall see, community planners cease to mask their advocacy and openly challenge the planning department and other city government agencies, moving from administrative guerrilla warfare to *administrative insurgency*.

Of course, not all the community planners are willing or able to oppose the planning department that employs them, or reject the comprehensive planning approach they were trained to value. Despite the most intense community pressure, some strive to work in terms of the traditional priorities and methods of elite-encapsulated city planning. Others wish to act as administrative guerrillas on behalf of their communities but lack the personal characteristics and skills necessary for the role. These "misfit" community planners—a minority among those we interviewed—develop patterns of behavior we shall call *role resistance* and *role incapacity*. They usually show much more discomfort about their assignment to community planning programs than do the administrative guerrillas.

Even community planners who accept and successfully play the role of administrative guerrilla, however, are still plagued with difficult choices. In choosing to become underground community advocates, they have responded to the community planning pressure system and to some extent resolved the dilemmas of community planning. But as community advocates, are they to serve simply as *delivery agents*, working to gain whatever facilities and services the community demands? Or are they to serve as *change agents*, working to awaken the community's residents to unrecognized problems and sharpen their often unsophisticated perception of community needs?

In this chapter we analyze in detail the administrative guerrilla role forced upon community planners by the community planning pressure system. First we explore the strategies that planners seeking to become community advocates use to establish their legitimacy in the eyes of their "constituency," the residents of their community. We then focus on the administrative guerrilla in action, examining the undercover tactics commonly used in furthering the interests of the community residents. We shall see how administrative guerrillas painfully struggle to strike a balance between their functions as delivery agents and change agents. Finally, we look at how "misfit" community planners interact with their community residents in the alternative roles they play due to role resistance or role incapacity.

The Making of an Administrative Guerrilla

For planners who define themselves as community advocates, gaining community support is a prime necessity; without it, their advocacy becomes farcical. As noted earlier, however, community residents usually receive the planner assigned to them with clenched fists rather than open arms, or ignore him completely because they never heard of planning or they doubt the planner's ability to produce. They greet their would-be advocate with a combination of distrust, disinterest, and disbelief. Thus the planner's first task in gaining community support is to establish credibility as an advocate in the eyes of community residents. Unfortunately, having no direct control over the city's resources, he cannot prove his value and commitment to the community by producing actual facilities and services on demand. All he controls is information about the operation of city government and his own training in planning skills. He must somehow use these meager resources to convince the residents of two things: (1) he is on their side; and (2) he can be of service.

Proving Allegiance

The planner usually finds that the residents in his community view their relationship to city government in terms of warfare. To get what they want, or stop what they don't want, they expect to fight the city. Many of the planners seeking to establish themselves as community advocates share this conflict interpretation of city-community relations; others still view city needs and community interests as potentially reconcilable. But whatever their own views, the planners recognize that without control of city policy, they cannot hope to change the community's hostile orientation to city government. Would-be community advocates must work within the conflict model, somehow turning it to advantage in their effort to gain community support.

With battle lines so sharply drawn, the planner's association with the city planning department—the "city hall stigma" mentioned earlier—brands him as an enemy agent in the community. His loyalty is presumed to rest with his employer. Becoming a community advocate means changing sides, and as for all turncoats, his new loyalty is suspect and must be proven before he can be trusted. Thus before he can start planning with the community residents or acting as their advocate, the planner must solve a "political" problem for which he usually has little preparation. He must demonstrate effectively to the community that he is indeed a sincere turncoat. The trial and error methods used by the planners we talked to yielded two basic strategies for proving community allegiance, both involving the planner's only stock in trade: information. We shall call these strategies *community validation* and *agency betrayal*.

The *community validation* strategy consists of gaining the support of community insiders who can help sell the planner to the rest of the community as a trustworthy advocate. In some cases, this takes the form of classic cooptation in which the planner invites the participation of influential community leaders in a community planning organization. In return for the prestige and possible power of this position, the community leaders give public backing to the community planner's efforts, in effect vouching for his good will. However, the planner's community is usually too fragmented for this form of community validation to be very successful. As one planner complained:

> We have an image problem; we're continually having problems with communication. It's only through a long working relationship that I can get anything comparable to trust. I thought I had solved my communication problem with community organizations by setting up a five-person committee of community leaders which I normally deal with. But I find that when I have to talk at a public meeting to people who don't know me, I have the same image problem all over again!

Because they must gain the support of community factions of many different persuasions, planners may seek community validation through a more covert procedure: gaining the support of a community insider willing to act as a behind-the-scenes informer on community feelings. Much like a political campaigner, the planner then consults his informer before meeting different groups of suspicious community residents and tailors his presentation to deal with their concerns, thus gaining maximum community support. One planner described the Machiavellian aspects of this approach:

> If it hadn't been for my friend, this black community organizer, I couldn't have done anything. I accepted the distrust of the community and tried in my first meetings with them to set a good tone. This black community organizer helped me plan the meetings. He filled me in on the different groups' political hangups and background. For example, if they were Toms, I'd stress working together with the city. If they were tough, I'd challenge them not to cop out and tell them to treat me as their spy in city government, not necessarily to trust me. After a few months I got pretty good acceptance, not complete, but I could work with them.

Without a community insider to vouch for them publicly or coach them privately, many planners feel immobilized by community distrust. This is particularly true when the planner is of a race or ethnic group different from most of his community's residents. Until contact is made, they feel constrained to proceed with great caution, for fear of alienating potential validators. One told us:

> When I first got here I was reluctant to work with blacks, being white. I worked slowly. I used to sit around with people drinking wine, listening and not talking. I didn't want to say the wrong thing. I remember once I sat for three hours and didn't say one word.

While seeking community validation, some planners make attempts to advertise their commitment by altering their personal style, adopting the language peculiarities, dress, and mannerisms of their communities. They spend a great deal of time in casual interaction with residents, learning the community's mood and hoping to convey their good intentions to potential validators. Despite such efforts, after working over a year in their communities, some planners we met were still trying unsuccessfully to make contact. "They'll never accept me," mourned one planner working in a community of Oriental Americans. "I don't speak Chinese."

Community validation is only a first step in proving allegiance. However convincingly the planner conveys his concern for the community's interests, his commitment is suspect as long as it remains untested. Is he really interested in working for the community's interests, the residents ask, or are they being tricked? The planner is, after all, a city employee. What would he do if the chips were down? In an all-out conflict between city and community, would he put his job on the line? The community planner cannot settle into an advocacy planning role without first countering these doubts with a token of his commitment to the community.

To accomplish this, many of the planners we talked to use the strategy of *agency betrayal*. Given the warfare interpretation of city-community relations, they reason, loyalty to the community can be demonstrated indirectly by committing acts of disloyalty against the city planning department. One device commonly used for this purpose is verbal rejection. In their conversations with community residents, planners will ridicule and repudiate the department's policies and personnel, calling their fellow planners "hypocrites," "idiots," and "chickenshits." Although these insulting remarks often communicate the planners' true feelings, some planners who are basically in sympathy with the department also use verbal rejection to build community support. "I criticize the city government and the planning department every chance I get," one such planner told us, "because it gives the community confidence in me."

The most effective form of agency betrayal, however, is leaking information about the city's plans and operations to community groups. Revealing agency secrets has higher "treachery value" than verbal rejection, since the planner presumably undertakes a greater risk of losing his job. The betrayal is particularly useful for gaining community support if the planner is disciplined or rebuked for leaking the information. The injuries to his job security become "war wounds" suffered on behalf of his community, to be proudly displayed. Planners make sure the community is aware of the disfavor they are incurring with the agency's management. One planner described how he used the planning director's wrath to build rapport with his community:

> I often feed community groups inside information about the city. For instance, I didn't hesitate to tell people about the park [an unpopular proposal for use of the community's park land, which at the time was a closely guarded and politically sensitive agency secret]. It usually turns out well for me. Someone from a community group will tell the planning director what I said. He calls me down to the office, screams at me, threatens to fire me. Then I can go to the next community meeting and ask Mrs. Jones or Mr. Washington, "Why did you call my boss? I gave you that information in confidence. Now he wants to fire me!" This really helps me with the community.

Planners willing to have their disloyalty made public usually intend to leave the planning department soon for another job, or they place a low value on job security. The planner quoted above, for example, told us:

> My chances for promotion here are nil. The director wants to get rid of me; he just hasn't found time yet. I

don't care. I'm willing to make a low salary just to make a mark. The only way I can be successful in doing what I think is necessary is by being ruthless, petty, vindictive, and objectionable. I don't expect the planning agency to love me for that.

Many planners, however, take their position in the department less lightly. For them, the strategy of agency betrayal means walking a tightrope; they must disassociate themselves from the planning department enough to establish credibility as community advocates, without at the same time committing occupational suicide. Some who leak confidential information to community groups protect themselves by denying their transgression:

> We do come close to being advocates—as close as we can, up to getting into trouble. I'm embarrassed that community groups sometimes come down to protest because I supposedly told them to do so. Actually they come because of their own convictions, not because of what they thought I said. It could get sticky for me here if anybody really thought I was giving out information.

Others seek protection by getting "treachery value" out of disclosures that are not confidential and therefore do not jeopardize their jobs:

> Sure, I leak information. It can't help but increase the community's confidence in you. But I don't give out confidential information, just stuff that's helpful. I tell them for instance, about the reputation of a councilman, what he's up to and so on. That's not secret. But the community doesn't normally get any information at all, so you still get credit for letting them in on it.

But most planners using agency betrayal simply plunge ahead and hope for the best. As one told us, "I leak information, but I don't like to. It could get me in trouble. I worry a lot."

Proving Serviceability

Important as it is, gaining community trust does not in itself establish the planner as the community's advocate. From an advocate, community residents expect not only sympathy and loyalty, but effectiveness as well. However friendly his relations with the community, the planner finds himself put on the spot. If his advocacy is to be credible, he must demonstrate ability to deliver something the community residents want.

The residents' ideas about improving their area usually involve new physical facilities and improvements in city services—a school, a park, a rat control program, clinics, housing, better police protection, and so on. As we have noted, the community planner is at least two steps removed from direct control over these things. His recommendations on behalf of his area may founder within his own department if they conflict with the ideas of the planning agency's management. Recommendations that survive this trial may be ignored by the operating agencies and politicians who make the ultimate decisions in allocating city resources. Complaining bitterly about the department of education, a planner observed, "Our priorities are very different from those of the operating agencies. It's hard to convince them what's really needed. We're forced to make compromises. What finally gets built is usually our second or third priority."

The community planner's powerlessness reflects the weak position of the parent planning agency itself. Said a planner, voicing a common observation, "I can't put my finger on a single project that was generated, orchestrated, and brought to execution by the planning department. Nothing that actually sprang from this organization. There's very little tangibility to planning." Yet tangible results are exactly what community residents expect their advocate to produce. The community planner's problem is finding a way to deflect this pressure that will still satisfy the residents' doubts about his serviceability.

Many planners in this awkward situation rely on *delivery windfalls*, accepting credit for any new capital improvements in their area even if their influence in determining the location of the new facility was minimal. Planners commonly speak of "my recreation center" or "the schools I got for the community"—while complaining about their lack of influence. One planner told us about the support he gained in the community when the city decided to build a recreation center the residents wanted. "They brought their plan to us, and we approved it and said we'd hustle it for them," he said. "It'll be under construction next fall. The community thinks we got it for them. The real reason we got money fast was because they had a minor riot in my area a couple of years ago." Another planner was a hero in his community because a zoning change sought by an expansion-oriented university was blocked successfully. "The community knows I sided with them," he said. "I did a report condemning the university's proposed science center. . . . But it wasn't me or the community opposition that stopped the council from action. It was because the mayor hates the university, because the university treats him like a peon. You have to know these things to understand how I could 'deliver' so well."

The planner's exaggeration of his influence is not necessarily cynical. In the battle for his community's interests, the planner himself cannot always tell whether a victory is a result of his efforts, or more or less accidental. But because demonstrating serviceability is so important in generating community support, he is willing to accept delivery windfalls at they come. Planners try to stay flexible in their commitments to community demands so that they can take advantage of unexpected opportunities to appear influential and avoid revealing their actual lack of influence. One planner described the disastrous effects for his community support when he allowed himself to be pinned down to a specific demand, thus putting his influence to a direct test:

> The planning department is like an operating agency but has nothing to operate with—it's schizoid. Within the department, community planning is the most schizoid of all. It's the only section charged with delivering. We're on the line. When you become the community's man, you want to deliver. In my district they wanted a junior high school. I promised them I'd get it. I was trying to be an advocate, you see. But I hadn't done my leg work and the planning department vetoed it. This killed me with the community. I ran too fast. I undercut myself. I couldn't produce.

Some planners are able to garner community support through *symbolic delivery*. Rather than something tangible, they deliver a token of the city's interest and positive intentions for the community. As described by one planner working in a white working-class neighborhood:

> We try to show some sort of city concern. There's a lot of symbolism involved. There has to be; we are too understaffed, too undermoneyed, to affect much in the way of actual change. There are no federal programs in my area. It's not as bad as other areas of the city. One can believe that the work of the department might be significant, not by directly upgrading the community, but by making people *think* things are getting better. People have said to me, "If we could see some sign of faith in our area, people here would fix up their houses." A positive feeling helps to encourage a multiplier effect.

Another planner told us how the symbolic control involved in drawing up their own plans temporarily deflected the citizens' pressure for tangible delivery of facilities and services:

I'm trying to change the attitude toward the planning department, to restore confidence. [How do you do this?] Well, we plan little things like a playground where they want it. We let them design and plan it. This is exciting. We find out where they want it, and draw it up that way in the office. Then we hang the design in their Little City Hall office. People can look at it, say what they think, and make changes if they want. [Have they actually gotten the playground?] No, it's not started. The main thing is just to get them to participate. This kind of thing will work here—my area's ethnically homogeneous, Italian with no blacks, no rival groups.

Symbolic delivery, a stopgap measure, works only for those planners whose areas are not totally disillusioned about the city's intentions toward their community. Planners working in the inner city usually shun this strategy like the plague. Ghetto residents have little patience with "trick-bag" solutions to their desperate problems. For planners in such areas, symbolic delivery is the surest way to convey worthlessness as a community advocate.

Most of the community planners fall back on the strategy of *delivery conversion* to prove their serviceability. Unable to deliver what the community wants, they encourage the community to want what they can deliver. They try to interest the community residents in the value of the one resource they do control: information. Since the residents see city-community relations as warfare, the value of information is often explained to them in conflict terms. Information about the operations of the city's bureaucracy, the planners argue, is a major weapon presently being monopolized by the city. It matters little that much information important to the community is nominally public. For most community residents, it might as well be stamped top secret. For instance, notices of public hearings appearing in back pages of the newspapers are not public information if no one sees them or understands

how they affect the community. Citizen complaints are out of
the question if no one can figure out which of the hundreds
of city bureaucrats to complain to. The citizens can hardly
apply for services and programs they never heard of, or
mount opposition to planned policies they are unaware of.
Deadlines will always be missed if no one knows they exist.
Such recondite bits of information, which might be called
public secrets, are just as inaccessible to a community without
guidance as the city government's carefully guarded private
secrets. But suppose the community has an insider—like the
community planner—who not only understands all this red
tape but also has access to information about the city's activities in the community. Through him, the residents can lay
their hands on the weapon of information and attack unwanted city policies at their weakest points. Here is an example from a planner with a mixed community of blacks,
whites, residential neighborhoods, and small businesses:

> The community groups in my area benefit from having
> me there. For the first time people are learning to use the
> city. They're getting themselves on pertinent agendas.
> . . . I go out to community meetings quite a bit. After
> we decide to focus in on a particular project, I try to get
> it into the capital improvements budget. I show the com-
> munity how to follow up on the project, how to maintain
> pressure over the six years it might take to get it imple-
> mented. Also, I alert them about dangers to the commu-
> nity. For example, the planning department wants to
> reinstate the Monoxide Expressway on the comprehen-
> sive plan. It might never get built, but if it does, the com-
> munity would have to start opposing it at this point. By
> the time it's about to be built, it would be much harder
> to stop. People in the community normally don't realize
> this, or even know about the change on the plan. So I'm
> trying to alert the various groups where to testify.

Another planner working in an area on the fringes of the
ghetto explained:

I perform an education function, giving information to people in the community as to how the government operates—the different agencies such as planning, the managing director's office, housing, redevelopment, and the streets department. I end up giving a lot of information as to how decisions are made. They have already learned how councilmen perform. I tell them about the CIB [capital improvements budget] function; I tell them how it affects them. . . . I find myself moving into a new community and instead of planning, I tell them about CIB—how to go about affecting it. I tell them how to harass operating departments to get what they need. I show them how to put pressure on the city council.

Because of the existence of government secrets (both public and private), the planner's failure to deliver tangible facilities and services does not render him totally worthless to the community. He can still provide a vital service as a supplier of information, equipping the community residents to fight their own battles with the city. As their advocate, he can aid their struggle by delivering not victories but arms.

The Administrative Guerrilla in Action

To gather and dispense strategic information, the administrative guerrilla at some early point in his activities sets up a personal communications system that has little to do with the formal channels of communication specified in his job assignment. He must cultivate a network of informants within the city bureaucracy who will keep him abreast of any city policies that affect his community. This is necessary because other city agencies often jealously guard even the most harmless information about their operations, as we shall see in Chapter Nine. They are especially reluctant to reveal politically sensitive information concerning proposed public works, code enforcement policies, plans for school integration, trash collection schedules, and so forth. To accumulate such bureaucratic secrets, the planner needs an interagency underground of informal friendly contacts (sometimes explicitly referred to as "spies") in other departments. In addition, he needs a mechanism for disseminating information to the community quickly and covertly. For this purpose, he constructs a community underground of local organizations and individual residents, to which he can leak information without risking his own "cover."

The two parts of the information system, within the bureaucracy and out in the community, make up the administrative guerrilla's *double underground*. The double undergrounds we observed ranged from extremely rudimentary ones—based on occasional, almost accidental information exchanges among friends—to incredibly elaborate and self-conscious systems involving codes, preplanned daily reports, and secret rendezvous at night. In some form or another, however, the double underground seems to be an essential feature of the administrative guerrilla's work.

The planner may also use his knowledge and skills in various ways to bend the city's bureaucratic apparatus to his community's advantage. Within his own department, for instance, he may try to "soften up" the attitude of other staff members toward his community and thus gain the backing of the planning department as a whole for his area's needs. For example, when one planner found his agency was being asked to make recommendations on the amount of money to be spent on recreational resources that year, he set about lobbying for his area's interests within the department. "My area has a strong case," he said, "when we show how recreational resources have been allocated for the last ten years for various areas of the city. I'd like to know why my area, with 30 percent of the population, received only 5 percent of the resources over the last ten years." When questioned further, this planner confided that the figures he was using to argue his area's case were off the top of his head. "I'm not sure what the exact distribution is," he admitted, with a sheepish grin. "I requested the information from the comprehensive planning section, but they don't have it. It looks like I'll have to dig it out myself." In the meantime, since he knew the need for recreational facilities was urgent in his area, he added force to his argument by making up fictional statistics. Another planner undertook a covert campaign to create a receptive mood in the city administration for a community group he was interested in:

> NDP [the federally funded Neighborhood Development Program] is a success here; it works pretty well. A year ago, in April, I came across a neighborhood in my area that I felt was a good prospect for NDP. But it had to get its application approved, and no one in the city had ever heard of the Upbound Valley Neighborhood Association. They didn't have a chance as long as they were unknown. So my problem was, how do you get them known in city hall? What I did was to get them to write letters to the planning department director, and the head of redevelopment, and the housing department director. They didn't need the information they asked for in the letters—I could give them that. It was just a way to give them visibility, to make them seem important. Before too long I started to get feedback. The planning director asked me "What's going on in Upbound Valley?" By the time their application for NDP came in, everybody knew them. It worked so well that I'm doing the same thing again with a nearby group.

Creation of double undergrounds and softening up resistance to community demands within the city bureaucracy only set the scene for the administrative guerrillas' most important effort: managing the "battlefield encounters" between their communities and the city government. These planners view the precipitation and management of clashes between community groups and the city as the only way a planner can meaningfully affect his area's development. As planners, they are excluded from both the political arena in which policy decisions about city development are made and the operating agencies where policy decisions are carried out. Aside from a few weak review powers, their formal authority stops far short of implementation; furthermore, they lack the political clout to influence the decision-making system informally.

The same is not true of community residents. Their formal access to influence over city policies, though generally unused, is not inconsiderable. Moreover, they have the numbers to act as a significant political force. Their powerlessness does not, like that of the planner, represent a low power potential. Armed with information and mobilized for concerted political action, they could become formidable. Thus the planner seeks to circumvent the restrictions on his own power by developing and channeling the dormant power potential of the community residents. As one planner put it:

> Under the present structure, the present set of circumstances, the planner has to develop an underground role —feeding information to outside groups, talking to the community. He has to take on the role of the complete Machiavellian, overcoming restrictions on his actions by artifice or persuasion. He should lose his own personality, not look for personal credit—just find an effective way to get what's needed. The residents have power—they can bring political pressure and court cases—but they don't know how to use their power unless they're organized.

Another told us:

> We have a responsibility to influence the political machine in whatever way we can. Planners should develop an infrastructure of community groups, nonprofit organizations, and so forth, to feed information to. This would have to be secret and clandestine in the existing political structure with its rabid reactionaries. If it were known, it

would eliminate planning. . . . You have to work behind
the scenes.

Unable to wage battle for their areas' needs directly, most
community planners come to rely heavily on their "troops."
"Influence? Me? I've got none, and the same goes for the
planning department," remarked a planner in a typical comment. He added darkly, "But there are ways of developing
influence. There are ways. The community could do it, if
you float the right word and they're organized to listen to
you."

The administrative guerrillas we talked to vary widely in
how openly and deliberately they engage in mobilizing the
community to pressure the operating agencies, the mayor,
and the city council. The most cautious approach is using
community pressure to increase the planner's informal influence over policy decisions. For example, some planners cultivate the councilmen in their areas by engineering what might
be called *gratitude traps*. In this tactic, the planner uses his influence with community residents to create a political
problem for the councilman—for instance, a flood of letters
from residents who would not have articulated or pressed
their demands and questions without the community planner's guidance. Then the planner offers to assist the councilman in solving the problem. The councilman, grateful for the
rescue, will be more inclined to trust and consult the planner
in the future. If the planner handles the situation especially
well, he may even be able to generate a sense of obligation on
the part of the councilman and collect a reciprocal favor
later. "I've developed good relations with three councilmen
in my district," explained one planner using this tactic. "Let's
say a group wants a tot lot. I tell them to see their councilman. Then I happen by, agree to design the tot lot for him,
and he looks good to the community. I 'help' the councilmen,
and they appreciate it." Another planner told us:

One new councilman recently got a number of letters
from community groups demanding answers to specific
questions about the needs of the area. The area planner
there put them up to it. The councilman didn't know
what to do. After getting the letters he ran to the planning department and the area planners said they'd help
him answer the questions. The councilman had no idea
that area planners were behind the whole thing to start
with.

Since the community is usually already seething with sponta-
neous demands and grievances, the planner wishing to set a
gratitude trap need only steer protesting citizens toward the
proper target to create the desired pressure.

Another common tactic is the *democratic blitz*, which involves locating whatever legitimate channels exist for citizen
participation and flooding them with community residents.
The formal procedures of city government provide a number
of opportunities for citizens to influence specific city policies
and decisions—public hearings, special elections and refer-
enda, representation through councilmen, grievance procedures, and so on. Historically, these formal points of citizen
entry into the workings of city government have gone un-
utilized. The typical unmobilized community is too apathetic,
ignorant, disorganized, and intimidated to make use of them.
Few community residents even know they exist; they are
public secrets. Under the guidance of a planner, however, the
residents can activate these latent democratic opportunities
and use them for their area's advantage. The formal procedures are usually structured in such a way that citizens can
block an existing policy decision much more easily than they
can get a new one launched. For this reason, the democratic
blitz is usually resorted to in cases where the community is
threatened by some unwanted development such as a highway, hospital or university expansion, or public housing. The
administrative guerrilla, unable to protect the area himself,

shows the residents where to go and how to act to best protect themselves. As one planner told us:

> Back when urban renewal was first razing communities, planners couldn't do anything about it. Planners are politically impotent. They were as effective as they could be, but they didn't have the cards to play. Raising hell about it publicly wouldn't have had much impact; it wouldn't have been a creative thing to do. But now it's different. Now we can build support in the community through area planning, and get destructive programs stopped. Area planners are sending a lot of people to public hearings!

Another planner described with glee how he rallied his community to defeat his archenemy, the department of public works (DPW):

> The highway department of the DPW has been planning the North-South Parkway to go through my district. They have little regard for how their proposed road would affect the neighborhood; their prime objective is to move autos. They tried to pull a fast one in my district. First they proposed an 80-foot right of way and the neighborhood agreed. Then the DPW said there was no agreement, and they took 100 feet. I couldn't block this myself, but I could let everyone know what was going on. The information I gave the community is available to the public, but the public is not adept at getting this information for themselves. They need someone to explain, for example, the condemnation ordinance for roads. What I did was to point out the newspaper article that tells where you can protest the condemnation ordinance —in city hall, room such and such, at such and such a time. I saw that the whole neighborhood found out. That put a thorn in the side of the DPW!

The planner can also use community pressure to get at the operating agencies by way of the city council:

We have problems with the BZA [board of zoning appeals]. They're not responsive enough to the community. They have a definite commercial and developer bias. Understandable, I suppose—the BZA is made up of political appointees, lawyers and realtors, mainly white. They like to keep us at arm's length. But it doesn't work; we're still within stabbing range. The power relation is in their favor, of course. They can ignore us. We're just advisory. But we're not as helpless as it seems. When they try to put in something unpopular like gas stations, drive-in restaurants, a car wash, dance halls—anything we think shouldn't be there—we rely on the community. The solution is to use community pressure to get the council to slap an ordinance on them. You see, the BZA can ignore the community, especially when it's black. But the councilman *must* respond to community pressure. Because of the tradition of councilmanic courtesy, where the council automatically approves anything a councilman raises about his own district, any ordinance the councilman proposes is sure to go through on something like this. So community pressure can operate through the council to get us an ordinance affecting the BZA. And we help this process along a little. Myself, I rely on a guerrilla type operation. I research out the problem, get the data, and then call in an outside group. I rely especially on the Women's League of Voters and strong community groups. We structure the problem so a layman can understand it, and then let the community fight for it.

Another planner we talked to was awaiting the outcome of a carefully staged clash between the community and a number of city agencies, the culmination of months of preparation. Again, the battlefield was the city council:

We've been trying desperately to get a beautiful piece of undeveloped land in my district used as the site for the regional high school. It's the only way we can save it from the developer who presently owns it. His plans for it are horrible—a sea of asphalt. The board of education wants the school located elsewhere. Their site isn't as good as this one. We've tried everything to push this through. We've organized the community. We've given out behind-the-scenes information to arouse them against the developer. The community is forcing the city council to hold hearings. There's a subcommittee meeting tonight, in fact. I'd be delighted if a large number of community residents turn out and raise hell.

One planner who was manipulating citizen participation from behind the lines was also instructing his community in how to convert their informal veto power over a roadway into affirmative power to get a recreation center:

I'm always trying to scheme for more leverage. It's not enough to just stop at helping the community formulate their needs and problems—you have to find ways of implementing the programs they want. For example, the planning department wants to reinstate the Wideswath Expressway on the comprehensive plan for freeways. It cuts right through two of my communities. I'm trying to alert the various groups where to testify against it and show them how to gain from it. They're going to insist on a deal: in exchange for the community's tacit support, they'll demand a review of the recreation priorities for their area. They want an upgrading of the recreation facilities and programs. The community has come to see this highway as round one in a game. They'll use it now to their advantage for upgrading the neighborhood. Later, they'll ask to have the highway taken off the comprehensive plan, or changed, or rerouted.

A higher risk tactic used by some administrative guerrillas in staging city-community conflict is the *symbolic holocaust*. In this tactic, the planner arranges an incident that reminds city officials of the community residents' potential for violent uprising if they are ignored too long or pushed too far. The planner's problem is creating a "safe" threat, one that will convey a convincing sense of urgency without getting out of hand and precipitating violence. One method commonly used is "threat transmission." Unpopular city proposals often provoke anonymous rumblings in the community about bombing and arson to prevent the plan from going through. The planner can make sure such threats do not die unheard on the street by helpfully warning the operating agency involved of the risk it is running by disregarding community outrage. In this way, the planner uses the threat to pressure the city government without instigating violence.

In some situations, especially in communities that have been the scene of past riots, simply gathering a crowd of concerned citizens may be a credible but safe threat. If the crowd is poor and black, they may be perceived by government officials as a threatening mob even when they intend no violence. Thus planners are able to produce safe threats by organizing demonstrations, marches on city hall, and community delegations to the appropriate agencies and officials. One planner working in an inner city area told us:

> Agency heads panic in front of crowds in this city, if they think the people are pissed. I've used this consciously. Once I brought about fifty blacks downtown to city hall. I told the people to come down and beat on the city council and the mayor so the mayor would give them what they wanted. They went down not to hurt anyone, but just to keep from going crazy themselves. You should have seen it. City officials were hiding in their offices, afraid to come out.

Another planner, himself black and militant, explained that he frequently used the community to "intimidate" operating agencies. "The board of education's afraid of the students in my area," he said. "I can always threaten them with the community youth. They can't put their finger on it, but they know I do it. The mayor knows too, but he cringes at the thought of a school riot and lets me alone."

Where racial tensions are very high, the administrative guerrilla can create a safe threat by setting up a small number of particularly terrifying community residents as a "token mob." For example, one city we visited had recently held a school charette (a public meeting of the community and government officials) to discuss school policies in the inner city. The community planner for the area concerned made sure the meeting was "properly" attended:

> I used the Black Panthers. They were waiting outside in the hall, clanking their chains. This kept things in the proper perspective!

In very rare instances, the administrative guerrilla seeks to mobilize city-wide political pressure against the city in the form of a *public crusade*. This tactic, which has the drama and poignancy of a suicide mission, is undertaken only in the last extremity, when the physical survival of the planner's community is at stake. The city may be planning some development that will completely displace the residents. Or some planned major city expenditure may show such blatant disregard for the community residents' needs that the planner fears an explosion of violence. Rather than see the destruction of his community through clearance or riot, the planner may surface into public visibility as a full-fledged *administrative insurgent*. He throws aside considerations of job security and the "disguise" of professional demeanor and publicly leads the community's attack against the city government—sometimes against his own department.

This happened in one city we visited where the government was undertaking an exposition that would cost millions of dollars and fill the city's central park with fairground facilities. The plan had the support of the mayor, the city council, and most of the operating agencies including the planning department's management—but not the community planners. Many of the planning staff, particularly those whose areas adjoined the proposed fairground, had been waging for months an unsuccessful, semicovert battle against the plan. They wanted the fairground relocated somewhere away from densely populated areas, or at least planned in such a way as to incorporate housing, schools, and recreational facilities desperately needed by the surrounding communities as permanent benefits once the exposition was over. Their covert opposition to the city's proposal was rapidly gaining public visibility. At the time we spoke to them, six planners had just moved into open insurgency; they had issued a signed open letter to the press detailing some little-known aspects of the exposition proposal and condemning the chosen site. They were no longer secretly leaking information to a community underground. Instead, they were openly exposing the city's public and private secrets and calling for a popular uprising to block the unwanted development through massive political protest.

Although the cases where this occurs are spectacular, we found in general that few community planners are willing to act as public crusaders. Most feel that their communities are not sufficiently endangered to require such potential martyrdom. But many, frustrated by the thankless, inch-by-inch progress of their administrative guerrilla efforts, long to plunge into open muckraking. Even those administrative guerrillas most concerned with preserving their cover sometimes admit to having Walter Mitty daydreams in which they blackmail and embarrass the city into serving their community's needs, and then go off to Washington in a blaze of insurgent glory to demand federal funds. For instance, one planner excitedly confided his fantasies:

> You ask what we could do? Wow! I'll tell you what we could do! We could embarrass the shit out of the city.

We could do a hard-hitting evaluation of health care and publish it. This city has one of the country's highest urban TB rates and nothing's done about it; the head of the health department spends most of his time flying off to professional meetings. We could make that public. The same for other operating agencies. We could work out a good revision of the subdivision ordinance and publish it, showing the hanky-panky in the old one. We could use part of our budget to hire a good urban economist and do a hard-hitting exposé of city financing. We could examine the committees that set up the rules for financing. There are bankers on those committees; the system's lousy with conflicts of interest. This should be made public. Naturally, we'd blackmail them first. These documents should be given to officials first so they could respond. On the side, you see, we'd be giving the same information to community groups secretly. And then we might still publish it! . . . The city may seem more sensitive to the community's needs than before, but they wouldn't be if no one kicked them in the ass. The city pulls tricks on the folks. Like tenant leasing of public housing—that's a trick bag. Now that 40 percent of the public housing projects are losing money, the city gets the idea to transfer ownership to the folks. The planning department isn't helping the folks fight this kind of thing. We just tell people things informally. We should take a public stand. Then as the next step, we should go to Washington and lobby.

When it came to actually launching a public crusade, however, this planner demurred, explaining that the example of some of the more experienced administrative guerrillas in the department convinced him that public opposition might be "dysfunctional" compared to clandestine strategies for pressuring the city. "The gadfly approach seems irresponsible over the long haul," he said. "I'm uncomfortable about it. I'm not sure I know why I feel the position is untenable. It's probably a liberal hangup."

Delivery Agent or Change Agent?

The planner's choice of strategy is complicated by an ambiguity within the advocate role itself. To work for his area's interests as an administrative guerrilla, he must first arrive at a definition of those interests. Who defines them? Is the planner to accept the residents' own interpretation of what they need for community improvement, working as their *delivery agent?* Or is he to impose a professional definition of community needs by acting as a *change agent,* uncovering and bringing to the residents' attention community needs and problems they otherwise misunderstand or fail to perceive?

The tension between these two approaches to advocacy weighs heavily on many of the administrative guerrillas we talked to. In serving their areas, they want to show responsiveness to the views of community residents; but they also want to use their planning skills in attacking community problems. The two goals often seem contradictory. For example, acting purely as a delivery agent may mean offering up as a sacrifice the claim to any special planning expertise, as in the case of this administrative guerrilla:

> I've made it clear to the people in my community that I will advocate for whatever use they want for a site. I've found that some of my initial opinions were wrong— the people came up with a much better rationale for the use *they* wanted. Unless you go in with this attitude, better stay out of area planning. What I mean is, suppose there is a site for housing and the people want a recreation center which I don't think is needed because the site is better for housing. I'd advocate for the recreation center. If the people don't want housing, I'm not going to push it down their throats. In fact, if they don't want it, I'd try to stop it for them—even if I thought it would be better to have it. I'm a dedicated believer in organizing people and decentralizing power.

On the other hand, functioning as a change agent may mean overriding the will of the community. One planner devoted to the idea of citizen participation in planning mourned:

> People in communities don't know what they can have. They don't know what they are refusing. They don't understand the results of their decisions. You can't just leave them on their own.

Another planner, one of the more radical administrative guerrillas we met, told us with evident pain of the conclusion his deep involvement in an inner city area had led him to:

> The planner has a responsibility he can't abdicate. Especially in the poor areas, he's going to sometimes differ from the community in how he sees their needs. When that happens, he has to go with his professional judgment if he's really going to help them. There's a dangerous tendency in district planning—you can easily become a lapdog to stupid people.

Torn between community sympathy and professional insight, most administrative guerrillas shift uncomfortably back and forth between the two approaches to advocacy, sometimes acting as delivery agents against their professional judgment and sometimes as change agents against their democratic inclinations.

Some planners strive to dodge these difficult choices by "educating" the community into agreement with the planner's perception of the area's needs. The first step in this effort is to gain acceptance as a teacher. One planner working in a tough ghetto neighborhood told us of his latest moment of truth as a semiaccepted community teacher of planning:

> I was at this meeting and a major difference came up between me and the people there over a particular site loca-

tion. They didn't want to hear my arguments until I
made an analogy to a doctor. I said that a man with a
crushed hand wouldn't insist on deciding which finger
had to go if the doctor disagreed. If he didn't go along
with the doctor, his hand would rot off and he'd die. I
made the story gory enough so it caught their imagination. Fortunately, they bought it.

Specific techniques of educating the community include
anything the planners can think of, from formal lectures to
community games with visual aids. One planner, whose zest-
ful advocacy efforts bordered on administrative insurgency,
described the varied methods he used to increase the planning
sophistication of his community residents:

> I have meetings to explain the principles of planning. Not
> only that, I get them experts from all over the city—
> the more prestigious the better! . . . I get them to dis-
> cuss a hell of a lot of things. I use Polaroid and moving
> cameras to get people to "see" their neighborhood.
> They're so used to things the way they are, they don't
> notice anything wrong normally. For instance, the
> backyards and vacant lots here are all junked up with
> old tires and stuff. People have just written them off;
> they don't see it as usable space. But going around taking
> pictures makes it visible. They're amazed at what the pic-
> tures show, and start thinking about what can be done.
> I'm trying to develop a sense of consciousness of prob-
> lems they suffer from but aren't aware of.

Community education efforts of this sort seem more for the
benefit of the planner than the community; they allow the
planner to strike a shaky balance between being an advocate
and being an expert.

Role Alternatives

Not all community planners adopt the administrative guerrilla role, of course. One alternative pattern of behavior, *role resistance*, occurs among planners who refuse on principle to depart from the department's traditional planning approach even in the face of extreme community pressure to do so. These planners are unwilling to accept the arena-council, expansionist implications of the community planning program as legitimate or useful. Although formally assigned to work in an experiment in decentralized planning, they remain uncompromisingly dedicated to the ideal of centralized, comprehensive, long-range planning limited to the physical aspects of development and totally divorced from implementation. They reject involvement with citizen participation, political activism, and social planning as unprofessional and unlikely to yield rational land use. The short-range projects demanded by community residents are of little interest to them; they feel alienated from the project level of planning that the community planner is so often drawn into. "I get so frustrated dealing on the micro level!," exclaimed one. "I wish I could go back to working on problems on a comprehensive level."

Role resisters seek to reinterpret the community planning program as an extension of elite-council comprehensive planning, in which the purpose of drawing up area plans is to elaborate the city's master plan rather than determine the needs of each area as an independent unit. One planner explained his definition of community planning this way:

> We got involved in community planning to provide a better guide for the citizens. They know they have problems in their areas, but the Master Plan's not detailed enough for them to follow in solving their problems. We could see they needed a more detailed plan for each area.

> It's better for us to make up area plans than for them to
> hire a consultant, because we can make the community
> and its consultant aware of things they usually don't see.
> They usually are concerned with just their own little
> community. Actually, you have to take the whole city
> into account to make up a good area plan.

Another remarked, "I'd like to see community planning provide a set of district plans for the entire city, so community
groups and other departments would have a better guide for
their programs. We ought to get away from these short-
range things."

Community pressure for immediate action frustrates the
role resisters. Like the following planner, most of them feel
implementation is not their responsibility—especially when
the desired project is, in their view, misdirected:

> The first year I was here, I was involved in neighbor-
> hood planning. I tried to keep planning on a land use
> level, but invariably the community wanted, say, a new
> park—not because it would be good land use, but be-
> cause their kids needed a place to play. And so we found
> ourselves doing short-range implementation studies.
> That's not our bailiwick! We're supposed to be con-
> cerned with long-range land use planning. Maybe some
> economic and social planning too, but in any case, it
> should be long range.

Leaking information to community groups is out of the
question for these community planners; for them, the only
proper direction for information to flow is up. "I couldn't act
as a community advocate," ran a typical response. "My ultimate responsibility is to the city. My job is to provide information about the community to the city, not the other way
around." Similarly, citizen participation is viewed as a problem more often than a goal. For the role resister, political mobilization of the community interferes with planning. One
told us:

> There have been some structures going up in my area that people don't like, but we can't do anything about it. We can't stop industry! It's part of the planning department's policy to spread out industry. It's a shame people are organizing against it.

Another said, with obvious annoyance:

> Citizens' groups have backed the city planning department and operating agencies into corners. They start saying, "You've got to do something!" They don't recognize any city-wide responsibilities. They don't recognize the shortages of staff we have to work with. They tend to just damn the administration, and never present the case they're arguing in such a way as to help the administrator.

Caught up accidentally in a decentralized planning program, most role resisters care little whether their community residents trust them or participate in working out the area plan. The community tactics they develop revolve around avoiding community pressure rather than responding to it. They minimize contact with citizens whenever possible and make no pretense of delegating any planning responsibility or soliciting the participation of community residents. Often they shield themselves psychologically from community demands by constructing rationalizing myths about the needs, problems, and capacities of their area's residents. For example, one planner told us:

> I don't live in the area. I can't see all the problems. It's up to them to tell me if they really need something badly. For some of the problems they're talking about, they are going to have to implement the solutions themselves. Like a small vestpocket park. If they really need that, they would implement and maintain it themselves. Then it would be a new ball game!

Another planner, sublimely insensitive to the community's terror of massive relocation through urban renewal, assured us:

> This matter of displacement has been overplayed. All of us move fairly frequently. We're forced to, for one reason or another. It doesn't disturb us that much. It's not that bad to be displaced.

Not all of the role resisters are actively hostile to their community's residents, but they are profoundly unsympathetic with the resident's demand for entry into the planning process. As one described his feelings, "You war with yourself. Fundamentally, I'm an aristocrat. I'd like to believe in equality, but I'm too pessimistic about human nature." Without exception, the role resisters feel uncomfortable working in the community planning program. They frequently talk of transferring out of community planning into some other section of the planning department where they can do "real" planning.

A second alternative pattern of behavior is *role incapacity*. Some community planners who try to play the role of administrative guerrilla are unable to carry it off successfully. Despite their sympathy for both the plight of community residents and the decentralized approach to planning, they fail to establish the essential rapport with community leaders.

Often role incapacity arises from the planner's personal style. The administrative guerrilla role requires skills most planners received no training in and never imagined they would need. The planner has to be able to think on his feet. He has to present his arguments to skeptical, often hostile community leaders with enough eloquence to persuade them and enough forcefulness to inspire their confidence. In winning community acceptance, he is forced to function not only as a planner, but also as an actor, a politician, a salesman, a con man, perhaps even a charismatic leader. As one successful administrative guerrilla observed, "In this job it's not enough to know planning. You have to know how to bullshit, how to put off a couple of hundred people clutching for your throat." Moreover, to overcome the stigma of the "city hall image," the administrative guerrilla has to be prepared for and hardened to the community hostility and distrust he usually confronts. One planner, describing the verbal abuse he absorbed at every community meeting, said good-naturedly:

> It's only during the meeting that I'm squeezed. Before and after, I'm treated well. The community leaders just attack me during the meeting so that people will be aroused enough to come the next time. If I were a leader of a black group, with all the traditional hostility to redevelopment and urban renewal which has meant black removal, I'd do the same thing. I don't take it personally at all. My relations with the leaders of these black community groups are good.

Planners who become effective as administrative guerrillas develop these skills mainly through trial and error, sometimes aided by the counsel and example of more experienced community planners. Most report an initial painful period of confusion and mistakes before they learn to deal with community residents with some degree of control. Predictably, however, not all planners can develop the necessary presentation of self. Some planners are too shy, too thin-skinned, or too clumsy in managing interpersonal relations. They shrink from the community contact situations so critical to gaining the acceptance and support of their communities. They bungle chances to establish rapport with community leaders. They interpret community antagonism as a personal insult. However attracted they may be to the administrative guerrilla role, their personal styles render them incapable of it.

The position is an uncomfortable one. Planners experiencing role incapacity tend to adopt an apologetic, self-deprecating tone when describing their work. For example, one planner we met, whose personality was particularly retiring and gentle, had been assigned for over a year to the Model Cities area—clearly the most tense, hostile, and problematic of the city's districts. Dealing with the community residents had become agony for him; they shouted at him at meetings, overrode his suggestions, refused to listen to his arguments. In desperation, he had cut his community contacts down to the bare minimum. He told us:

> Although my ideas have changed from strictly middle class, I'm not oriented to this kind of planning. Maybe I'm not fully equipped to handle it. I was just thrown into it. I'm not trained for this. I do believe it's a good idea. But it's not for me.

Another planner, in the process of resigning from the planning department when we talked to him, also blamed himself for incapacity to win community trust:

> Initially I liked advocate planning—the Davidoff stuff. But I'm no community organizer! Beside that, the program's set up with such a loose structure that you lose people who aren't self starters—like me. I need guidance. It got to seem that there was nothing I could do or stop. I got completely frustrated and bored. I started going less and less into the community. I became a 10 to 3 planner. I heckled at department meetings. It's best for everybody that I'm getting out of this job.

Other community planners, especially those functioning successfully as administrative guerrillas, may add to the discomfort of those with "deficient" personal styles by urging them to change or by pitying them. The head of one community planning section, himself an active administrative guerrilla, remarked about one of the community planning staff members:

Cheddar's not involved enough in planning for his district. I had to tell him about a meeting of one of his own
community's groups last week. He felt they didn't want
him, so he didn't want to go. I said he should go no matter how they feel about him. You can't be that sensitive.
District planning is supposed to introduce a new attitude
toward planning, but you have to talk to people to do
this.

The colleagues of a planner who was leaving the department
for reasons of role incapacity made his departure all the more
embarrassing with their sympathy: "Poor Oswald. He was
just overwhelmed by his job. He didn't know what to do
with it. It was all out of his frame of reference."

Role incapacity can also arise from premature delivery failures in which a planner new to the community makes promises he cannot honor. As we have seen, most would-be administrative guerrillas try desperately to avoid direct tests of their
serviceability until they have built a buffer in the form of
"delivery windfalls," "delivery conversion," and general
community rapport. During the period when community
faith in their abilities and allegiance is too low to carry them
through a delivery failure, they try to evade commitment to
specific projects requested by the community. A few community planners, however, get tempted or forced by community
pressures into demonstrating their value as advocates by engaging in an all-or-nothing attempt to produce some particular urgently desired facility or service improvement. This
"sudden death" approach is a gamble. Success establishes the
planner's credibility as a community advocate more solidly
and quickly than any other method; failure often brings
about instant role incapacity, no matter how dazzling the
planner's interpersonal skills may be. The planner who starts
out with a major delivery failure usually finds his credibility
as an effective community advocate damaged beyond repair.
To function as an administrative guerrilla after this happens,
he must change communities. One planner, a victim of pre-

mature delivery failure who then became a highly active administrative guerrilla in a new community, told us:

> My district has two subareas, one white and one black. I started out working in the white area at first, but I had to leave it because right away I lost a school. The director didn't back me up, for political reasons. I was left holding the bag. That's why most district planners leave their districts: because they lose battles. After that I devoted most of my time to the black area. I didn't want to screw up again so I was more careful. I researched things out, learned the politics of it, before I acted.

Unwilling to conform to the expectations of the city's bureaucracy but unable to respond successfully to the expectations of community residents, the role-incapable planner becomes a target for both sides in the community-city "war." In the following account we find a role-incapable planner caught in a crossfire between the city and his district's residents, helplessly watching the destruction of his relationship with all involved:

> I've had problems from the start with the Ratsville district. The residents submitted a proposal for neighborhood redevelopment, but there was no dialog between them and me in drawing up their proposal. They didn't want my help. They just gave me their proposal, with no chance of modifications. Since they were so firm, I didn't see any reason for discussion, and I sent their proposal on as it was. So in a way, what happened afterward is my mistake. It turned into a mess. The plan included demolition of some old buildings. The building department didn't like the Ratsville group doing demolition; they wanted to see that it was done under their control. They split up the area for demolition and said that the Ratsville residents could do a third of it. But only if they followed all the city regulations: licensing, bonding, and insurance. The Ratsville group didn't know they had to have all this. I tried to tell them, but they thought I was against

them because I wouldn't get them money in advance, before they worked out programming for the demolition effort; so they weren't listening to me. I told them money in advance would be illegal. I guess they thought I was lying. I've been trying to get insurance for these people so they could do the demolition, but it takes a long time because it's high risk. The planning director promised me he'd find a way to take care of the insurance, so I told the Ratsville group I could get it for them. Then the planning director found out the premium would cost $12,000, and now he says he can't pay it after all. The community thinks I sold them out again, even though I'm still out on a limb in the department negotiating for them.

Last month the Ratsville people decided on their own to get started. They rounded up a lot of students and community people to begin demolition. But the buildings assigned for them to tear down weren't condemned yet because their organization hadn't fulfilled the bonding, licensing, and insurance requirements. No work could legally be done. I was there. I had to tell them they would be arrested for destroying private property. They had all these people out with crowbars and sledge hammers—they weren't about to go home without tearing something down. So they moved into Area II—the building department's area—and started in on a building that had a condemned placard on it, even though technically they were forbidden to tear it down. There was nothing I could do. I must admit, they did a good job! The building commissioner was furious, and I was on the spot for a while, but it blew over. No one sued us. Thank God no one was hurt. In the community, I took the blame for all of this. For his own political reasons the neighborhood leader has tried to discredit me and the planning commission at every opportunity.

I still want to do neighborhood planning, planning with the residents. But I feel I've been taken advantage of and used as an instrument of local politics. I don't want to say I'm cynical or skeptical of neighborhood planning, but I know now that it isn't easy. It's not a case of a planner and residents in a friendly, cooperative relationship.

Next time, I'm not going to let the neighborhood submit a
proposal to me on a take-it-or-leave-it basis. It will be
negotiated. The only problem is they say if I don't
accept their plans without changes, they'll join with the
university students and march on city hall. I didn't take
it seriously at the time the threat was made, but now
I don't know.

For this would-be administrative guerrilla, there is really no
way to put the pieces back together again. To overcome role
incapacity this extreme, he would have to start out again in a
new city.

The striking feature of the two major role alternatives is
their rarity. All of the 70 community planners we talked to
had started work with their roles almost entirely unspecified;
they received little guidance from colleagues as they went
along. Yet at the time of the interviews, only nine (13 percent) could be called role resisters, and only seven (10 percent) suffered currently from role incapacity. The remaining
54 (77 percent) were acting as administrative guerrillas or insurgents. It is no accident that so many developed similar
ways of defining and carrying out their mission as community planners. The pressure system clamped down around
them presses them relentlessly in this direction. As community planners, they are expected to work closely with the
residents of their areas. The residents will cooperate only if
the planner can demonstrate total allegiance and serviceability to the community. The only way the planner can do
this with his skimpy resources is by revealing inside information about city government and helping the community
residents use this information to pressure the city government. However, since the bureaucracy the planner works for
also expects exclusive loyalty, as well as nondisruptive behavior, this means of gaining community cooperation must be
kept undercover. Thus simply by struggling to survive in the
pressure system, the community planner drifts into betray-

ing his agency's secrets and clandestinely mobilizing the community for political action. Before he knows it, he is deep in administrative guerrilla activity.

In a sense, all the different modes of behavior we have described represent alternative ways of resolving the contradictions in the community planning pressure system. The administrative insurgent, a rare and usually short-lived figure, disregards the bureaucracy's pressure toward elite encapsulation in favor of the community's pressure toward arena expansionism. The administrative guerrilla, as the most common adaptation, combines pressures from the bureaucracy and the community in a precarious and shifting balance. The role resisters, a minority among community planners, disregard the community's pressures and conform to the traditional type of planning sanctioned by the bureaucracy. Role incapacity, unlike the other alternatives, does not represent a response to the pressure system but rather a failure to respond, in which the planner is totally blocked and his efforts disorganized. These different ways of handling contradictory pressures are summarized in the accompanying table.

Clearly, the most common product of the community

Responses to the Community Planning Pressure System

	Administrative Insurgents	Administrative Guerrillas	Role Resisters	Role Incapables
Bureaucratic pressure (elite-encapsulation)	−	±	+	−
Community pressure (arena-expansionism)	+	±	−	−

+ indicates acceptance, − indicates rejection.
± indicates partial acceptance and partial rejection.

planning pressure system—the administrative guerrilla—engages in planning activities likely to prove disruptive in an elite-council, encapsulated planning department. On the basis of the theoretical observations discussed in Chapter Two, we would expect to find the community planning innovation being quickly suppressed by its parent bureau. To see why this does not happen, we now focus on some unusual organizational features of the planning departments that sponsor community planning experiments.

THREE

THE PLANNER
AND HIS DEPARTMENT

Six

The Significance of
Organizational Chaos

To understand how the community planning experiment fits into the operations of its parent bureaucracy, one must realize that in most cities the planning department is not a bureaucracy in the Weberian sense. Often it is almost antibureaucratic, militantly resistant to "rational" authority hierarchies and procedural routines. Within such agencies, the contradictions and frictions between the elite-encapsulation assumptions of traditional planning and the arena-expansionist implications of the community planning program take strange turns. In this chapter we outline the chaotic organizational structure typically found in city planning departments and show how it simultaneously frustrates and protects community planning as a bureaucratic innovation.

Counter-Irrationality

One of the most striking characteristics of city planning departments is the Kafkaesque quality of their internal organization. At first glance, the planning department seems almost a parody of bureaucracy. Hiring practices have little relation to personnel needs. Salary scales are often inverted, with new staff members earning more than those with long tenure. The different sections within the department work along in sublime uncoordination, sometimes unknowingly duplicating each other's efforts, sometimes even producing incompatible plans for the same piece of land. Few staff members work consistently on one assignment until its completion; instead, everyone jumps around madly from project to project, often abandoning in midstream assignments never to be finished. Reports are written, sent up to higher levels, and never heard of again. Data are compiled and never referred to. Since planning work is not related to implementation, staff members sometimes find themselves laboring over plans that have already been vetoed by the mayor or city council. Lines of authority are so vague and overlapping that responsibility often cannot be successfully delegated within the department. The planning director, as the only certain authority, becomes overwhelmed by the burden of ruling on department functions at every level, and proposals are sometimes held up indefinitely waiting for his signature. Despite constant complaints that nobody is ever informed of anything, staff meetings are avoided by the staff whenever possible. With some variation among individual departments, the general picture is one of numbers of people furiously engaged in irrational and uncoordinated activity. But there is method in this apparent madness.

To some extent, the internal organizational chaos of the planning department represents a defensive response to the insecurity of its mandate. As we have mentioned, the concept of rational centralized city planning fits awkwardly into the fundamentally irrational value system of a "liberal" society. Granted, the political and economic framework of the American city diverges significantly from the completely laissez-fare institutional system of the ideal liberal model. However, the physical shape of the city is still determined primarily by private developers who follow the logic of individual profits rather than rational land development, and the administrative policies of city government are usually based on considerations of politics rather than planning. The city's decision-making process is fragmented, pluralistic, and inhospitable to pleas for rational land use and service delivery systems from a relatively powerless and easily ignored advisory body like the city planning department. Moreover, the planning department's budget, work assignments, and influence in city government are not stable and dependable but change erratically with the political climate. Under these circumstances, rational internal administration becomes both difficult and self-defeating. Like logical Alice adapting to the illogic of Wonderland, the administrators of the planning department find they must work in terms of their surroundings, however bizarre, to make any impact at all on city development. In the effort to survive and function in an irrational social environment, they turn to what might be called *counter-irrationality*.

Some of the apparent breakdowns of "good" administration endemic in planning departments take on a new significance when viewed as counter-irrationality. For instance, consider the common practice of pulling staff members off their regular work assignments to work on crash projects of various kinds. With a limited staff, this method is the only way the planning director can respond to specific requests from the mayor and councilmen, who come to the planning department asking for everything from aerial photographs of the central business district to an estimate of off-street parking needs ten years in the future. The planning director knows that ignoring these requests would insure his department's ineffectuality, since the ultimate fate of planning recommendations lies in the hands of these politicians. He is therefore forced to use his staff to serve their needs, even if it means bypassing the department's section chiefs and making a shambles of the rational scheduling and continuity of the staff's regular work. One planner described the results of this practice:

> The planning director uses the staff here as a great funnel of information to him. He makes all the decisions, with very little delegation of authority. He has a whim of iron. When he wants to start something, or know something, he just pulls people off whatever they're doing to work on his pet project. He refuses to allocate staff according to priorities. It sounds absurd to even phrase it that way. Around here, there *are* no organizational priorities!

The idea of counter-irrationality also helps explain the poor match between the department's personnel and its current programs. This situation grows out of the instability of the department's budget. The director cannot count on getting budget lines on demand, or having the resources for projects that would match the skills of the planners he hires. Neither can he tell in advance which programs are likely to attract the continued support of the city government, or which will bring in future state or federal grants with any dependability. Therefore he resorts to "staff banking" and "program stockpiling." He hires as many planners as he can wring out of the city budget, even if the activities they are hired for are not yet under way. Similarly, he starts new programs without waiting until personnel with the requisite special skills can be added to the staff. He follows planning fads, trying to get as many programs as possible started in hopes that one will capture the imagination and backing of the politicians who govern his department's resources. The more he proliferates staff and programs, the more favorably the department will be positioned for maximum opportunism. The resulting program overextension and jumble of staff members unsuited to their work assignments become necessary evils, a counter-irrationality made unavoidable by the irrationality with which the department's resources are determined.

These practices wreak havoc in the department's internal structure. In city after city, the planners we talked to described their departments' "lousy administration" with a tone of almost desperate levity, marvelling that such a "strange animal" could hold together at all. Many of them observed wryly that the planning department could use some planning itself. The following complaint is typical:

> Would you believe that we created the area planning program without increasing the staff? The only personnel adjustment at the time was to shift one comprehensive planner to area planning, even though he was totally unprepared for that kind of work. That's the way things go here. The director likes to hire only designers. Say the comprehensive planning section is overworked and a position comes up. The director won't wait to let you find a good comprehensive planner. He'll fill the position with a designer. He subverts both the rest of the department's management and the programs group. They'll say, we don't *need* a designer. It doesn't matter. Without consulting them, he'll go out and hire three designers.

In another city, a planner described his department this way:

> What you have here is an ineffectual staff groping for direction. The problem is the way in which district planning and current planning staffs are used. Either their time is misused, or the resources they need are lacking. They need to lop off some activities around here. Some of the projects that are initiated shouldn't have ever been

started. They're just pipe dreams that can't be carried out. And we don't have enough staff to cover them all. But everybody here thinks their own things are most important. Right now this department is like European monarchy in its early stages. There's a king, I'm a duke, we have lots of barons. Except nobody knows who is whose vassal. The knights undercut the barons, the king bypasses the dukes, and so forth. The system encourages everyone to ride roughshod over other people's projects.

Rational lines of authority are also weakened by the director's counter-irrational adaptation to the salary schedules he must work within. The department's pay policies are sometimes out of his control, fixed by the city's civil service system or some other part of the city's bureaucracy. His funds for salaries are limited. The salaries he can offer are, to put it mildly, noncompetitive with the salaries his staff could be earning as private planning consultants or architects. As one planner told us scornfully, "Their top salary here is just about a proper starting salary." As a result of these limitations, the department's pay policies often yield inverted salary scales that reward junior more highly than senior staff members. In setting salary levels, the planning department concentrates its limited resources in relatively high starting salaries to compete successfully with other public and private planning organizations for talented planners seeking new jobs. Correspondingly less is left over for pay increases for the staff already employed. As starting salaries are forced up from year to year by competitive pressure, the salaries of previously hired staff fall behind. Thus planners commonly join the staff at starting salaries higher than those of planners who have been with the department for several years. The only way the longer tenured city planners can win significant salary increases, over and above the yearly civil service increments, is by going on the market themselves and taking advantage of the higher starting salary bid of some other department. They are further encouraged to move by the promotion structure of the planning department, which might be described as a very flat pyramid with few positions of real authority at the top. To move up the ranks, planners usually must also move out of the department and enter another at a higher level.

Planning directors, acutely aware of the irrationality of their department's advancement opportunities, respond with counter-irrationality. They try to combat dissatisfaction by offering their staff nonmonetary rewards such as autonomy and status recognition within the department. "I'm concerned about staff morale," one director told us. "Our staff is so different from other city employees. They're professionals. They're young. And they know they could earn more and move up faster by leaving the department. They must feel they are listened to; otherwise they'll leave." New titles and "promotions" without a major change of duties or salary are handed out with little regard for the effects on internal organization. In two departments we visited, whole new administrative subsections had been created out of thin air for the sole purpose of mollifying senior staff members who felt they deserved to be chiefs of their own section.

The resulting internal structure defies description in a diagrammatic table of organization and leaves many staff members confused. Most of the planners in the department pay little attention to the formal chains of command even if they understand them. It is generally acknowledged that administrative titles are symbolic rewards rather than functional positions in a rational bureacracy.

Two other common features of the department complicate its internal structure. First, the planning staff may not be concentrated in one physical location. Frequently, different sections of the planning department occupy offices on two or even three different floors of an office building. In one city we visited, some sections were located in a building three blocks away from the main planning department offices. This physical fragmentation hardly aids in coordinating the different sections. Second, the staff is always in flux. As one director remarked ruefully, "Turnover is a big problem. Right now I'm spending 60 percent of my time on recruiting." Many of the planners we talked to, particularly those in community planning, conceive of their work in the planning department as a short stint to be followed by private practice as a planner or architect, or a career in teaching, writing, or art. One planner told us, "Most of us can't conceive of being here ten years from now." Many expressed the intention to move after a specified period—two years being a popular time span—to avoid getting "stale." In some respects city planning departments find themselves functioning as postgraduate training institutions. "Lots of students want to come here as a training ground, to get experience," a director told us. "It's usually their first job. Their professors advise them to come here. I remember being advised this way by my own professors. It helps our recruitment; but it also accentuates our turnover problem." High staff turnover on the order of 15 to 20 percent a year means not only continual vacancies that need filling but also new staff members constantly breaking into unfamiliar work and outgoing staff members withdrawing their efforts as they prepare to leave. With the department personnel perpetually coming and going and scattered in different locations, rational administration recedes even further from the realm of possibility.

Innovations in Counter-Irrational Bureaucracies

The chaotic organization produced by counter-irrationality creates a unique and paradoxical setting for bureaucratic innovations such as community planning. Parallels do exist between the development of community planning and the typical life cycle of bureaucratic innovations described in Chapter Two; but they are distorted and transformed, as if viewed through a kaleidoscope. Organizational chaos in the parent bureaucracy, even while it creates unusual problems for an experimental program, seems to function also to shield the new program from attack and provide unexpected opportunities for strengthening and expanding the new approach. From its very initiation, the community planning program begins to depart from the model suggested by Downs and other theorists of bureaucratic innovation, as it simultaneously suffers and benefits from its confused context.

Instead of being established with fanfare and the full support of the parent bureaucracy like the typical bureaucratic innovation, community planning starts out casually, as just one more poorly defined experimental program with pitifully inadequate resources and staff members haphazardly thrown together because they were handy. The new program's formal goals are so vague that the community planners we talked to found questions about their mandate amusing. As one planner put it, "District planning is like a piece of mud thrown against a wall: all over the place in no particular pattern." Another planner told us that in his agency's community planning program, "There is no definition of what area planning is. Area planning is nothing. It's anything. There's only one thing you can say for sure: we do give each area of the city a name!"

The vagueness and low-keyed nature of the new program's mandate deprive community planning of the special access to the parent bureaucracy's resources commonly enjoyed by bureaucratic innovations, often leaving the community planning staff crippled for lack of support services. Assigned to cover singlehandedly areas which are often as large and complex as a small city, community planners constantly point out the need for more resources if area planning is to work. "We have just one secretary for the whole community planning program," lamented one overburdened planner, who confessed that he sometimes didn't answer his phone when it rang because he had too much work to do already. Community planners usually do their own drafting, complaining that they have to wait too long to get assistance from the draftsmen hired by the department and that in any case, "no one here is capable of drafting our stuff but us." One planner remarked nastily, "The draftsmen they expect us to use are so dumb they draw lines for streets right through buildings." Often community planners even type their own reports and keep their own files, grumbling about being "the highest paid secretaries in town." Their pleas for more back-up staff and equipment fall on deaf ears. "If we gave each community planner a back-up staff, we'd have to increase the total staff here by eightfold," explained one planning director. Another director, in an unconscious echo of Ebenezer Scrooge, scoffed:

> What, give a staff to each district planner? We're not to the point of needing that! When I see them here on holidays, *then* I'll believe the problem is critical.

On the other hand, the vagueness of the community planning program's mandate affords the community planner considerable freedom. His position is not one of specific duties but rather a *position of opportunity*. His job can be whatever he wants to make it, as long as he exercises minimal caution. Planners relish this freedom:

> I have a remarkably free hand. I can do everything or nothing. I can wait till someone tells me to do something, or I can just start something on my own. It's a fantastic opportunity, providing you don't rock anyone else's boat.

A planner in a different city explained:

There are two types of people in this agency. Those who are technical types, concerned with knowing what their job is and doing it right and following channels of communication and so forth. And then the others, like in area planning, who realize how loosely structured the department is and see that they can run around and make contacts and get into the really hot projects.

In some departments, the community planner can escape close supervision by his superiors almost entirely by leaving the office:

We're supposed to work from 9 to 5 here, but it's not enforced for community planners. It can't be, because the work takes us out of the office. I come and go as I please. You've got a perfect excuse: "I'm going out to the field" [that is, the planner's community]. I end up putting in more than my seven hours a day, but for all they know, I go home and sleep. The section chief likes us to check first before leaving, but often he's not in the office himself! It's a free and open situation. I feel like I can do anything appropriate. There aren't any policies; the community planners are let to do what they want to.

By judicious maneuvering of his position of opportunity, the planner can increase his actual authority in the department even though his formal position remains unchanged. One planner told us:

We have very incompetent and insecure leadership here. They don't know enough about my job to supervise me, so they leave me alone. He who spends a little more time on some project than anyone else, becomes the instant expert and others will defer to him. That's the way it is generally here. Like for instance, there were problems about a street in my district. I was the expert on that street. Whatever I said about that street carried a lot of weight at meetings. Planners tend to be impressed by the appearance of knowledge, even though we all know we use the most ridiculous ratios and ball park figures.

"Many of us in community planning are freewheeling men," observed another planner. "It's such a helter skelter thing, it's the only way."

For the occupants of these positions of opportunity, every element of confusion of the planning department's internal structure becomes a paradox. For instance, many community planners complain that their work is blocked and frustrated by the absence of rational lines of authority and clear spheres of responsibility in the department. The following comments are representative:

> The organization here is extremely bad right now. There's no chain of command. All the staff have to speak directly to the planning director. He handles a tremendous volume of information. It's difficult to see him when I need to, or get his signature on a letter. It doesn't work out.

> The director here is involved in the details of all activities. He hasn't delegated responsibility to anyone. Of course it's difficult to get his approval on every little thing; he doesn't have the time. You have to go to him, but often he's not accessible. No matter what it is, I have to work out the details with him before I can make a move. There's no one else I can go to. All of us in community planning have this problem.

> This planning department does not have good administration. We have an administrative consultant, but he doesn't do anything but limit the number of Xerox copies we can make. We work together poorly. I don't even know exactly who I'm responsible to. The section chief of area planning says to me, "You work for such and such an area planner, but I can come in and override him, and thus you work for me." The planning director, of course, can override the section chief and often pulls people off what they're doing to do something else for him. I feel like I have several different full-time jobs. I'd like to do one thing or the other. I develop a great deal of personal anxiety trying to figure this place out.

On the other hand, the same planners prize the de facto autonomy that often results from the department's organizational chaos. Some seem puzzled over whether they want more rational administration or not:

> This section is poorly set up, all right, and some of the projects carried out here are worthless—but you know, some are great.

> I don't have enough communication with the section chief of area planning. There would be some benefits if we had more conferences. Well, more benefits for him than for me. I guess I'm equivocating because I don't want him to butt into what I'm doing!

In a similarly paradoxical fashion, the community planning program is simultaneously weakened and strengthened by its parent agency's counter-irrational efforts to curry favor with the city's politicians. Unlike the bureaucratic innovations described by Downs, community planning enjoys no special insulation from the general organizational concerns of its parent bureaucracy. The staff of the planning department is too small and its position in city government too marginal to exempt the community planners; they are expected to carry their weight in helping the department survive. Therefore, as the planning department seeks to demonstrate its utility by responding instantly to political officials' requests for specific information or projects, the community planners cannot avoid being swept up in the constant shuffling of work assignments this entails.

On the one hand, this intrusion of unrelated projects hampers the community planner by overloading him and interrupting his regular work. This problem is often voiced as a major complaint:

> My big problem is that at times I'm told that important projects have to go out of the office quick. I'll be thrown

off schedule to get on to it. This can really mess you up, especially when you're already carrying twice as much work as you can handle.

Around here we go from crisis to crisis all the time. We're always being caught off guard. Somebody'll say, "Oh my God, we've got to look at that!" and we'll all be asked to do a quick study. This happens all the time. Someone in the highway department just asked the director to do a project; we just heard about it today. I'll probably get pulled off what I'm doing, which isn't my regular work anyhow because I'm just finishing up another job for the director. I had to drop the back alley study I was doing for my area a while ago when I got roped into working on a project for Earth Week, making a display. Before I could go back to it I was put on George's economic survey. Now I'm working on a booklet for the director. Next week, who knows?

Community planners we talked to were particularly bitter about these interruptions when they saw little value or follow through in the "crash projects" for which their work continuity was being sacrificed:

Around here we respond to crisis demands; we're always putting out brushfires. I've been trying to get into general studies of my area, but I get interrupted by a variety of other studies, like that damn vacant land study the director asked me to do. I spent three days running around on that thing. Later I asked what came out of it, and the director said vaguely that a sketch was being drawn up and it was supposed to be sent to the head of residential development. I never heard anything more about what happened to that plan. That's what's getting disgusting: the lack of feedback here.

The problem of area planning is the way we work day-in, day-out. The procedural aspects of our work make it a multitude of crises without a stage or audience to make the end product a meaningful one with any connection to implementation. For example, I did a study for the director, a crash effort to do something he was interested in. I had to interrupt my work to do it, but by the time I finished it he had lost interest. Nobody cared about it, it didn't fit in anywhere. I presented it to the staff—big deal. Or another example: I helped draw up development standards, but what good is this with no follow-up with developers to see what their plans are and whether they conform to our standards?

Some planners incensed at the amount of time spent on projects with no apparent function, scoffed at the idea that the department was accomplishing any useful purpose. "Most of our activity around here is mental masturbation," remarked one. Another suggested, "The only people who benefit from the work done here are the staff, because we get paid for doing this silly stuff." One planner, after describing his scrambled work schedule, said:

> This department spends 40 to 50 percent of its time servicing itself. It's ridiculous. We spend more time talking about doing things than actually doing them. We do projects for the benefit of each other. Take these six guys working full time on Earth Week, for instance. Their time isn't best spent this way. It doesn't help pollution, just helps the department. At least in that project you can see some indirect benefit. Some of the people here, I don't know what they're supposed to be doing!

Thus the pressure to prove the planning department's political value by being responsive to "crisis" projects fragments the community planners' work.

On the other hand, however, this same pressure helps the community planning program by providing a built-in rationale for continuing and even expanding community planning efforts. The counter-irrational method of work assignment, which places highest priority on those projects that can be presented as favors to the powerful, gives the community planning program special leverage. Community planning is the one section of the planning department that can pose as an answer to civil unrest and citizen pressure—urgent concerns for the city's governing officials. Community planning is thus valuable to the planning department as a token of relevance. This interpretation leads some community planners to assume an almost cocky attitude about their program's invulnerability to administrative curbs:

> The director told us to do "reconnaissance reports" of our areas. He said it was to get us familiar with our areas and other departments. Bullshit. They need the reconnaissance reports not for our benefit, but to show that the planning department is doing something about the urban crisis. What else can they show the mayor—a bullshit land study? They need us to show that the department is with it.

As we shall see in later chapters, however, the community planning program enjoys the security of indispensibility only up to a point.

Even staff turnover presents a paradox for the survival of the new community planning experiment. As we have noted, turnover rates are high for the department as a whole; but in the community planning program they reach astronomical proportions. Judging from our interviews, we estimate the average tenure of the community planners to be between two and three years. In several of the cities we visited, approximately one-third of the community planners were preparing to leave the department within the year and another third had been employed by the city for less than a year. "District planning has a huge turnover," we were told. "Everyone is used to coming and going all the time."

Why is staff turnover so much higher in the community planning section? Part of the explanation is that factors producing high turnover among city planners in general seem to operate with greater intensity within the new program. For example, as we have seen, the pay and promotion mechanisms of city employment motivate many planners to leave because they tend to work to the economic disadvantage of planners who stay in a planning department rather than moving. In the community planning section, both the pay and the promotion disadvantages of staying put are at their most extreme. Planning departments, anxious to attract top-notch staff for the experimental program, bid unusually high starting salaries for new community planners from prestigious schools. Community planners already on the staff, like planners in other sections, do not receive commensurate salary raises. The resulting salary discrepancies between the existing community planning staff and new community planners just joining the program may be as high as $3000 to 4000 a year, a gap that makes it painfully obvious to the longer tenured community planners that leaving the department is in their economic interests. Similarly, the promotion opportunities are more restricted in the new program than in other sections because of the relative youth of the community planners. As one told us, "I'm 28 and looking to rise in city planning, but my section chief is only 32. I won't be replacing him anytime soon! To advance, I'd be forced to look for another job, where I could come in on a higher level." Moreover, again because of their relative youth, community planners are not tied as strongly to the city as their colleagues in other sections of the planning department. They are less likely to own homes in the city, or to have children in school, or to wish to settle down. Thus they are more inclined to respond to blocked advancement opportunities by moving. One community planner explained his situation:

> My chances of promotion are slim because I'm at the top of my ladder. This would be a reason for me to leave. Civil service allows no way for me to go higher. The only way I can get major pay increases now is to move.

> And I've got no special reason to stay in this city. I'm
> unencumbered. I could leave tomorrow.

Also, as we have mentioned, a large number of planners
enter the city planning department with no intention of
building a career in city planning. They aspire to enter private planning firms, perceived as a higher prestige and higher
paying level of professional activity, and undertake a stint in
the city's planning department out of curiosity or to gain
experience—"to get it on their record and then leave."
These planners with high turnover potential tend to gravitate
toward community planning because it offers opportunities
to gain the kind of experience—small-scale projects and
contact with community residents—that they perceive as
relevant to their career goals. For example, a community
planner working on a major redevelopment project for his
area told us that he hoped to attract attention with his innovative plan for the project and perhaps win a professional
prize, because "this will help me later when I set up my own
planning firm." He confided:

> We lose a lot of people because it's not attractive enough
> for talent to be here, where it's needed. The rewards and
> the low image of civil service work against talent staying.
> It's not just the money. The work isn't glamorous. After
> about two years you lose animation. The planning opera-
> tion gets stifled. You feel you're not being challenged.
> Routine gets to you. There's no innovation.

Most important, the pressure system that community planners work within exposes them to contradictions and dilemmas from which the rest of the planning staff is relatively insulated. Community planners often feel driven out of the
planning department by sheer frustration. "The reason we
have a high turnover in area planning is because we can't get

things done," one community planner told us wearily. "I'd tell you to go talk to the planner for the Model Cities area about the incredible lack of cooperation and obstacles he faced, but he isn't here—he quit last week!" We shall explore this reason for the community planners' short tenure in detail in Chapter Eleven.

For the survival of community planning as a bureaucratic innovation, this unusually high turnover situation offers an ironic mix of disadvantages and benefits. On the one hand, high turnover strikes at the heart of the new program: it destroys the hard-won working relationship of planner and community. Decentralization of planning requires community cooperation, and the administrative guerrilla role adopted by most community planners requires not only cooperation but community trust. As we have seen, winning community trust is no easy, cut-and-dried accomplishment for an employee of the city. Since community residents feel the structural aspects of city politics are stacked against them, the planner gains their trust only by disassociating himself from the bureaucracy he works for and proving himself trustworthy and useful as an individual. His relationship with his community's residents follows the course of a stormy love affair, full of tests and sudden doubts, crises and reconciliations, before he is finally accepted. Unfortunately, building trust in this highly personal way is a slow, time-consuming process. Where turnover rates are high, planners may leave before they build up enough trust to work successfully with their area's residents. "You have to be in a community a long time to be effective," we were told, "but this doesn't happen. Guys leave just as they're getting started."

Planners who stay long enough to win acceptance as community advocates usually find that the community's faith in them is nontransferable. Some outgoing planners make efforts to smooth the way for their successors by introducing them to the community at meetings. Others, like jealous lovers, throw obstacles in the way of their successors as they depart. One outgoing administrative guerrilla told us, for instance:

> Wunderkind's supposed to replace me—that's stupid. They don't need him. I'm going to talk to my people, and have them send a letter to the planning director to say screw it, they don't want a new community planner. I'll give information to the community on who to call in the city, if they'll buy it, and then they can take care of themselves.

But whether the new planner's advance notices in the community are glowing or damning, he must ultimately pass through the long testing period and win community trust on his own. Thus with high turnover, community planners— and the community planning program itself—are always "starting all over from base one." The program continually starts all over again administratively as well. Since community planners generally rank low in seniority, the new program has trouble developing the clout to draw more heavily on the department's scarce resources. New entrants into community planning may complain about the department's deficiencies, but they feel reluctant to urge reorganization or challenge the department's management until they have settled into the job for a year or two—at which point they often leave.

Paradoxically, however, high turnover protects the community planning program from some of the internal processes thought to inevitably stifle bureaucratic innovation. Routinization of tasks that demand flexibility and creativity, proliferation of red tape, goal displacement, cooptation, and empire-building among the innovative program's personnel —these creeping forms of breakdown are blunted or blocked by the constant input of fresh, enthusiastic, often idealistic young planners. Knowing that their stay may not be permanent, many community planners throw themselves into their work with the dedication of missionaries, VISTA workers, or Peace Corps volunteers. They see their relatively low salaries as voluntary sacrifices in the interests of public service—as one planner put it, "the price I pay in order to make a mark." Some involve themselves so totally in community interaction that they jeopardize their health or their family relationships. Such fervor can usually be sustained only for a short time, a matter of a few years, before the planner leaves. But although this high-commitment work style may drain and exhaust the individual planner (a problem we shall explore further in Chapter Eleven), the community planning program itself benefits enormously. Not only does the new program avoid rigidity; it also enjoys an unanticipated expansion of its resources through effort volunteered beyond the call of duty. Money could not buy this mobilization of talent and energy. However, as in VISTA and the Peace Corps, the high-commitment work style goes hand in hand with the disadvantageous consequences of high turnover rates.

Thus simultaneously sheltered and smothered by the organizational chaos of their counter-irrational parent bureaucracy, the community planners thread a tortuous path through the paradoxes surrounding their positions of opportunity. We next begin to examine the intricate moves and countermoves of the community planners and their colleagues as they clash within the loose structure of the planning department.

Seven

Polarization in the Planning Department: Old Versus New Planning

Frictions between community planners and their colleagues do not surface immediately. As we have seen, the community planning program initially represents merely one among many vaguely defined programs, obscured in hazy rhetoric about "working with the people" and "providing a link between government and community." The disruptive implications of decentralization usually are not foreseen. At this stage the planning department's management and most of the planning staff are neutral or mildly favorable to the new innovation. Its goals are viewed as congruent with the department's overall efforts. Its activities seem innocuous, primarily public relations, no threat to the department's organizational interests.

But as the new program begins to operate, community planners are squeezed by the pressure system into a type of planning activity antithetical to the traditional pursuits of the department. They begin to act as community advocates, as

185

administrative guerrillas. They become politically active. As this happens, a gulf begins to open between them and the rest of the department's planners. In some cities we visited, the community planners and their colleagues eye each other with conscious resentment and contempt. In others, mutual antagonism is muted and softened by the general organizational confusion of the department or the newness of community planning. But in all of these planning departments, there are signs of a major cleavage developing between planners dedicated to traditional elite-encapsulated city planning and the community planners who take an arena-expansionist approach. Even where the struggle between proponents of the two contradictory planning approaches is being carried on with some decorum, each side questions the other's basic methods, professional competence, moral commitments, and very justification for existence. Translated from the plane of ideas into an organizational structure with scarce resources and insecure status, the clash of perspectives turns planners against each other, sometimes bitterly.

The diffuse sense of mutual distrust and dislike between community planners and many of their colleagues, present in all the departments we visited, seems to arise from three sources of irritation:

1. The perceived differences in personal style, background, and work attitudes commonly found between community planners and planners in other sections of the planning department.
2. Differences in the definition of planning, with community planners tending to differ with most other staff members over the proper degree of political activity planners should engage in, the legitimate scope of planning, the proper degree of citizen participation, and the most useful time frame for plans.

3. Problems of coordinating community planning with the other activities of the planning department.

These friction points are, of course, interrelated. In combination, they can polarize a planning department, driving normally reasonable planners into open threats and name-calling, personal vendettas, shouting matches at staff meetings, deliberate sabotage of one section by another, and conspiracies to change the department's internal power structure.

Personality Frictions

Frictions between community planners and other staff members need not be crystallized into disagreements on specific planning issues to polarize the department. Frequently community planners and their colleagues rub each other the wrong way simply because of differences in personal style, background, or work attitudes. They are, we were repeatedly told, on "different wavelengths."

For one thing, community planners as a group are much younger than their colleagues. In the departments we visited, the average age of community planners was 27, that of the rest of the staff 34. An age cleavage this sharp between nominal peers would probably prove abrasive in any organization, but in the planning department, such a gap involves far more than the usual clash of cautious, experienced elders vying with impatient, idealistic youths. Because of the rapidly changing nature of the profession of planning, different generations of planners may not even speak the same technical language. Their training may in some cases be contradictory. Most of the older staff members entered the profession when planning schools were fewer in number and, compared to present graduate programs, limited in terms of curriculum. Some lack any formal training in planning, owing their positions to the looseness of past employment standards and the protection of the civil service system. Most were trained primarily in the technical skills of architecture and land use planning and had no contact with social science as part of their academic preparation. Younger planners, educated more recently, come from a very different academic tradition. In the last decade, many planning departments have departed from their previous exclusive emphasis on architecture, introducing sociology, systems analysis, "problem solving," and urban design in a quest for greater relevancy. Although it is still possible to follow a traditional course of study in planning, most younger planners have been at least exposed to this broader kind of training. In some cases they have dismissed the earlier tools and techniques of planning almost entirely as outdated and inappropriate for coping with current urban problems. Many planners we talked to spoke of the "old" and the "new" planning. "New" planning evades precise definition, but there is a pervasive sense that young planners are somehow different—as one community planner put it, "you know, part of The Movement."

The correspondence between age and planning style is by no means perfect; occasionally young planners profess "old" planning ideas and some older staff members are "new" planners. Moreover, young men and women with "new" planning ideas are sprinkled throughout the department. However, because the younger, more radical planners are attracted to the community planning experiment and tend to concentrate in that section of the department, the community planning program generally comes to be considered the major stronghold of "new" planning. One community planner, trying to summarize the differences in style between his section and the "projects" section, explained:

> The people down there [in the projects section of the planning department] aren't educated planners. Some are

ex-draftsmen. They all come from this city, they went to public school here and maybe night school at the local university. The people up here [in the community planning section] are educated—you might say supereducated—and intellectual. In the projects section, they're interested in government today, not in revolution. They're more realistic about government today. Here in community planning, guys are very learned but not knowledgeable about government today. We'd like to change it, not fit into it. The projects people think we are longhairs, we think they are squares.

Each faction casts a jaundiced eye on the planning style of the other. From the younger planners' perspective, for instance, many of their older colleagues are living fossils, parochial in their outlook and hopelessly unprepared to grapple with the needs of the city. One community planner exclaimed impatiently:

I definitely feel we should do advocacy planning. That's what the district planning program's trying to do. But first you have to get rid of the deadwood. Then the newer generation can get on with real planning! The problem is, we still have people in the department who never went to planning schools; they worked their way up from being draftsmen. They don't understand what it means to work with the people.

Another, deep in the midst of an ambitious project in his city's worst slum area, remarked in disgust:

Most of the people in this planning department don't even keep up with the social dynamic. They don't read anything, not even newspapers—nothing. It's fantastic. And it makes their theories baroque at best. I bring in news articles and circulate them here, but nothing gets through to them. Except for district planning, the planners here are zombies. They close their eyes to the world. You know what I'd do with most of them? Put them on a barge and sink it!

To "old" planners, on the other hand, the younger staff members seem irresponsible and unprofessional, lacking in deep commitment to the city, deficient in useful skills despite their prestigious educational backgrounds. One "old" planner remarked:

> My division has more responsibility than the area planners do. They're not under as much pressure as we are. Many of them seem to regard what they're doing as an extension of their studies in school. They have high turnover. In my division it's different. I guess it's the different backgrounds. They're mainly out-of-towners, working here just because they came here for the university. But us—we're native born, and we really care about the city. Not like them, here today and gone tomorrow. And you know, when those area planners really need to get something done, they have to come see us. Even the freelancers, the radical ones, have to check with us because we're old timers and know the city better.

Another aggrieved "old" planner complained:

> To a great extent the area planners feel superior to the projects division because we deal with the council on a day to day basis. Hell, projects is the best division here! A lot of the area planners seem to act as if they were above the tools of the decision-making process. They look down on us because of our contacts with politicians. They aren't realistic. They talk about time as if they were the president of the United States. And they won't give up any time for discussion with us. They may be bright, but they sure are egotistical.

As these remarks suggest, the tension between "new" planners and "old" planners goes beyond their specific disagreements. By their mere juxtaposition, they threaten the legitimacy of each other's claim to professional status. Since there is no consensus within the profession as to what constitutes planning, the two factions feel entirely justified in measuring each other—and finding each other wanting—by different standards of planning competence. "Professionalism" becomes a weapon of personal attack, meaning whatever the planner wants it to mean. Those who agree with his formulation of planning are "professional in the true sense," and those who don't are "professional" only in the sense of occupying a job category called city planner. Both sides use this verbal weapon freely, usually prefacing it with something like "a lot of planners seem to have a distorted idea of what planning is all about," or "planning isn't a body of skills, it's mainly an approach; and I'd say only half of the 'professional' staff here has it, even though they all *think* they do."

As a result of such barbs, the interaction between "old" and "new" planners is heavy with status tensions, hurt feelings, and one-upmanship. Planners become so familiar with the hostility that they can even empathize with their detractors. For example, after describing his colleagues in other sections of the planning department as "mainly clerks and administrators," a community planner went on to give the other side of the picture:

> I know they think we're on the wrong track, just like we think they are. The people upstairs say we in community planning aren't doing any real planning, just messing around. There's a definite feeling that we're pretentious and snobbish. We don't participate enough with the rest of the planning department. They feel what we're doing isn't the right way to handle the problem.

Some view the status tensions wistfully. Said one "old" planner:

> I'd like to see the two factions here combined. I do my best not to alienate them [the "new" planners in the community planning section]. I'd like to attend their informal meetings on ecology and social problems, but I

just don't have time. I guess they think I'm not interested. I am, though. If they'd just try to come halfway
—they're not interested at all in what I'm doing.

Others greet the status contest with glee—this "new" planner, for example:

There's a district planner here who's doing fantastic
things with his community. Most of the older staff hates
him. He's black, so he can get back at them by using
their hangups about color against them. Also, he knows
what he's talking about. And if his approach is right, that
makes them irrelevant as planners. They know this, and
resent him. All "professionals" do horrid things to their
own minds to prove they're relevant. He rather enjoys
their discomfort. He knows he's right.

A particular sore point in the stylistic differences between
community planners and their colleagues is adherence to
minor formal procedures and regulations such as signing out
when leaving the office, filling out forms, sending routine
memos, and drawing only the allotted amount of supplies at a
time. In most of the departments we visited, community planning was under fire for its staff's lighthearted disregard of
such rules. The vehemence of the feelings expressed over this
issue indicates that the bureaucratic rules have acquired a
symbolic significance in the status struggle between "old" and
"new" planners. Nobody really cares whether the time sheets
are precisely accurate, whether a planner exceeds his Xerox
allowance, or whether he takes a dozen Magic Markers instead of the specified two. But to some of the "old" planners,
adherence to such details indicates an implied acceptance of
established city planning, a willingness to work as part of the
team, a token of cooperation. Failure to abide by the rules is
construed as a rejection of the planning department itself. To
the "new" planners, on the other hand, these procedural regulations are not only annoying and unnecessary rituals, but

symptoms of the malaise they feel haunts the department's planning efforts. They are symbolic of the "civil service mentality" that stands in the way of "truly professional" city planning.

Community planners in particular feel almost duty-bound to disregard minor bureaucratic rules. Out on the "front lines" of the battle to save the city, they find it infuriating that anyone should distract them with this "bureaucratic crap . . . Mickey Mouse stuff." "We shouldn't have to concern ourselves with red tape," fumed one outraged community planner. "These things ought not to be an issue. We are planning with the community! We shouldn't have to worry about picayune things." Most noncomplying community planners feel entirely justified, even noble, about their antibureaucratic behavior. In one city, the head of the community planning section explained:

> I find it difficult to impose regulations that I don't believe in myself. You put this kind of regulation on professional people and you'll just demoralize them. It's bad for morale. Area planners have more autonomy than other planners; it has to be that way. My position is that a job has to be done and as professionals, they can work as they see fit. I'm not interested in the technical details of how they work, like their time in or out of the office. But in the planning department's administration, they're very upset with us. The administrative manager says we're inefficient and troublesome because we don't follow all these trivial rules. You should have been here during the Great Xerox Conflict, when they were trying to tell us we could only make so many copies per week! We've got work to do; we can't worry about such things.

In general, then, community planners tend to be cosmopolitan, "new" planning oriented by their training, and inclined to follow work styles patterned on the independent professional. Many of their older colleagues in other sections of the department, on the other hand, tend to be local and "old" planning oriented, and they work in the style of the civil service bureaucrat. Each faction feels threatened symbolically by the other. Each can legitimate its own claim to professionality only by denying the claim of the other faction. Casual insulting remarks behind other planners' backs are common, with community planners referring to their "old" planning colleagues as "that clown," the "bureaucrat-rat," "the pig," "inhuman opportunists," and so on. "I retch at the sight of the department director," said one community planner, adding quickly, "but that keeps me strong." Community planners reap their share of insults in return, being called "the social workers," "the hippies," "naive bleeding hearts," "do-gooders," and "raving fanatics." "Those area planners!" an associate director complained. "They ask questions that are impossible to answer."

The general sense of strain generated by these personality frictions lends a hidden irrational element to all specific conflicts and disagreements within the department. One community planner we talked to had become so fascinated by the turmoil within the department that he was taking time away from his planning activities to study it. He told us:

> I'm writing a paper on personality, on how it fucks up the work here. We say at AIP [American Institute of Planners] meetings that planners are receptive to new ideas because of their training. That's not true. Anything the area planners say, the other planners here take it as personal attack. I'm the same way when they criticize what I'm doing in my area. If they had a good suggestion I'd never even hear it, because I hate them too much to listen to anything they say about my area. These interpersonal jealousies are a son of a bitch to work around. You know who suffers? The people, and the whole field of planning.

Professional Conflicts

With this background of mutual irritation, the "new" planners in the community planning section usually find themselves at loggerheads with other staff members over the many specific issues that are mushrooming into theoretical controversies within the profession. Does planning stop at the edge of the drawing board, or should planners involve themselves in lobbying for their plans' implementation? Should the planning department's efforts encompass only the physical aspects of the city's development, or social services as well? Should planners work politically to increase their control over private developers? Who can best determine a community's interests—the planner or the residents? Does it make any sense to draw up long-range master master plans that are never followed, and call this "planning"? Conversely, is it "planning" when a staff member gets caught up exclusively in short-range projects? Conflicts between community planners and their colleagues often boil down to contradictory definitions of proper professional behavior.

The sharpest clash revolves around the question of *political involvement*. When it comes to the implementation of plans, planners have sealed themselves off from direct influence with a wall of professional restraints. Traditional professional ethics direct the planner to a straight and narrow path of strict political neutrality. However deeply planners may feel about the fate of the city, tradition holds, they should express their public service concern through the production of technically excellent plans. The question of implementation should be left up to the workings of democratic politics—a decision-making system which, however flawed, represents an awesome and almost sacred principle that must be respected. Any direct involvement of planners in the political sphere, either

to block ill-advised policies or to lobby for their own proposals, represents unprofessional, irresponsible behavior. At best,
it threatens the planner's objectivity; at worst, it smacks of
corruption. "Old" planners tend to feel that any breakdown
of political aloofness threatens the very foundation of professional planning. Summing up an attitude we found in all the
cities we visited, a community planner told us:

> Many planners here don't think we should be in politics.
> They see the function of the planning department as ba-
> sically serving whoever is in power. When they speak of
> politics, they mean it in the worst sense; they put a nega-
> tive connotation on it as something beneath them. Their
> attitude is, "We are technicians, professionals—and
> professionals do not lobby."

From the perspective of the "new" planners, on the other
hand, this tradition of political aloofness has become an obstacle preventing the profession from having any practical impact. They regard it as professional irresponsibility (as well as
self-deception) to labor over rational plans for urban development and then stand quietly aside to watch the city move in
the opposite direction because of what some cynically call
"the crooks" and "the hacks," with their "trick-bag approach" to serving the needs of city residents. Abstention
from politics might be responsible professional behavior in a
perfectly democratic rational system, they argue, but in the
context of the imperfect political systems that actually exist in
cities in the United States—financially overburdened, rid-
dled with special interests and patronage, frequently incompetent or ignorant or outright corrupt—political aloofness
among city planners amounts to dereliction of duty. Simply
because they understand the complex implications and ramifi-
cations of policy decisions better than most, planners have a
professional obligation to break out of the stultifying division
of labor that locks them out of politics, and start concerning

themselves with the implementation of their plans. Otherwise, their work will be meaningless. Here is a common view, voiced by a community planner whose area could easily have absorbed the whole city budget:

> The heart of the matter is getting federal funds. We can plan schools and so forth on paper, but the city just can't afford the construction. This leads to hopelessness. Most of the younger planners here say: shove comprehensive planning. It can't possibly be effective. The next step, what we really need to do, is lobbying for more funds and power.

For "new" planners working in the community planning section, of course, this point of view constantly receives reinforcement in the form of pressure from community residents, to whom planning without implementation makes no sense at all. A typical reaction when asked if the community planners get involved in politics is, "Oh my God, yes. We wouldn't get anything done if we didn't." Most of the community planners we talked to are intensely concerned with the political fate of their area plans, and many are working actively for implementation. Because of the planning department's official adherence to political neutrality, their political activism is usually indirect and clandestine, taking the form of administrative guerrilla activity. However, while pursuing this underground role, some also proselytize within the department for a new definition of professional responsibility and seek to move the planning department and their professional organizations into a more active political role. At the time of our interviews, change-oriented community planners reported that in their estimation, faith in the strict separation of planning and politics seems to be eroding slightly in national professional organizations such as the American Institute of Planners. They take the emergence of national groups such as Planners for Equal Opportunity as a sign of a trend toward legitimization of political involvement. In the city planning departments themselves, however, tradition continues to reign supreme. A community planner told us:

> I suggested here in the department that we all donate $500 to create a political lobby. I said we could be the first to do so; it might set a national precedent. They laughed.

The question of *citizen participation* creates another professional gulf across which "new" planners and their colleagues glare at each other uneasily. Most "old" planners consider the concepts of citizen participation and advocacy planning of questionable legitimacy—probably a passing fad, and certainly never meant to involve any real concession of the professional planner's final authority over what goes into the plan. Some of their comments have about them a tone of nostalgia for the good old days when nobody felt it necessary to ask city residents what they wanted:

> Things were far better before the citizens got involved. The willingness of citizens to get involved far outweighs the capacity of the city administration to respond. Look at the Model Cities area. The citizens there got a voice and now they want more than the city ever expected.

Even when contact with the community is accepted in the abstract, "old" planners interpret it in a highly restricted sense, more as pacification than participation. We were told, for instance:

> The planner has to become a good salesman. When the council has accepted a zoning change and people don't like it, it's up to you as a planner to convince them that it's for their best interests.

In one planning department, an assistant director tried to explain just how far he wanted advocacy planning to go—far enough to involve his department with community residents, but stopping short at the first sign of trouble for city hall:

> Our area planners shouldn't oppose the city government. Hell, they work for it. They should serve the city. I do expect them to fight for their area; in fact, they don't do it enough. But they should do it in a way that lets them still serve the city. I'd like to see my area planners fighting for playgrounds for their areas when the Capital Improvements Program comes up, things like that. Things the city can afford. Little things. If they try for more, they'll get the city and the planning department in trouble.

Since rigid opposition to citizen participation is an unpopular view, the majority of "old" planners paid some lip service to the concept. But like this planner, they were wary:

> [What should the department be doing that it isn't doing now?] Well, of course, we should get more directly in touch with individual citizens' views, as distinct from dealing only with other agencies and economic interest groups as in the past. But you know, I don't know how to reconcile comprehensive planning with more citizen involvement. No matter what plans you prepare for the ghetto, you're going to get a negative response.

"New" planners, on the other hand—particularly those in community planning—favor increased citizen participation. Despite some reservations about the machinery for including residents' views, they commonly regard the current experimentation with this approach as a salutary democratic reform, long overdue in a profession whose primary (although unacknowledged) client groups have historically been the city's large institutions, industries, and commercial interests. One community planner, convinced that all planning done without involvement of city residents is tainted with an unconscious pro-business bias, suggested:

The city planning department should scrap the general plan. Just throw it away. We should develop new city-wide goals involving citizen participation, then work from this for an updated—and, at long last, balanced —master plan.

A "protector of the underdog" image crops up often in the comments of community planners; for example:

I'm an advocate for the impoverished, for those who have always lacked power. I'm already classed by the city managing director's office as a troublemaker. This is true of the area planning section in general. I like to see planners doing this. We do get somewhat isolated from the Establishment in the process. This is a danger for area planners.

These community planners tend to view themselves as the vanguard of a new, democratic style of planning. Still, like this planner, most acknowledge that in their department the traditional view holds sway:

Some planners are changing, but most of them here still have an attitude of "I know better than you, so let me take care of you." They see it as a matter of high (them) and low (the people). I hear it every day. They say, "What do these people know?"

"A lot of planners here are really screwed up," another community planner told us regretfully. "They have this attitude that big business is paying our freight and has to be kept in the city, so we should plan for whatever big business wants —even if it goes against good planning principles and hurts the people living in the city."

Another professional issue dividing the "new" planners in community planning from their colleagues is the proper *time frame* for planning. "Old" planners, steeped in the tradition of long-range master plans, favor plans stretching over a ten to twenty-year period or longer. Foreseeing long-range effects of present policies is not just one of many possible kinds of planning. It has a mystique about it. It represents the very *raison d'être* of planning, the essence of the profession's distinctive contribution. Since long-range planning has traditionally been defined as the only real planning, time frame preference is also tied up with "old" planners' ideas about professional competence. The more experienced and highly trained a planner is, they tend to feel, the further into the future he should be able to direct his attention. The intense concern for current problems and immediate results displayed by younger planners signals immaturity—not necessarily incompetence, but an underdeveloped grasp of what the planning profession is all about. For example, an assistant director explained reassuringly:

> Some young planners do get disillusioned when they start working in city planning, because nothing seems to come out of their efforts. I tell them, don't give up. Eventually something will be accomplished. I felt that way myself ten years ago, after my first three years in planning; but eventually some things broke through. With experience, you learn that there are different levels of planning accomplishment in terms of time. For an architectural project, it takes about three years. In city planning, it takes fifteen years. It's like space exploration.

The community planners we talked to express considerable frustration with both the traditional emphasis on long-range planning and the paternalism of their older colleagues who expect them to adopt this approach automatically as they gain experience. Most of them regard the effort to plan more than a few years ahead as patently absurd. What good is it, they ask. With uncontrolled developers and a city government that shows less commitment to rational public service than to political expediency, long-range plans are doomed to increase steadily in irrelevancy from the moment the ink is dry. A planner who gears his efforts to the glacial pace of traditional long-term planning ends up planning for no one but himself and the few others sharing his dream world, with no relation to ongoing city development. From the viewpoint of "new" planning, the "old" planner resembles nothing so much as the ineffectual antihero of a wistful Beatles' song:

> He's a real nowhere man,
> Sitting in his nowhere land,
> Making all his nowhere plans
> For nobody.

"New" planners know this is not for them. Many favor a redefinition of planning that deemphasizes long-term plans and instead concentrates on explaining the complicated present interrelations of the existing urban system. Such plans would be constantly changing, kept current and tied to specific problems. Their time frame would necessarily be short. As one community planner, an outspoken critic of long-range planning, explained the position:

> A long-range plan can end up being a series of maps and drawings that doesn't do anything, kind of like an Alice in Wonderland plan. Most of the plans I've seen around here are like this, bad. My idea of a good plan is one that offers specific recommendations and solutions for a particular problem of a city, like housing or transportation. It should be a clearly spelled out program for the next five or ten years. Certainly never more than ten years, and it should be continually updated.

Other planners were more direct:

> No plan that's written down is worth a damn. If it isn't in a looseleaf binder, throw it away!

The time frame conflict among planners partially explains the enthusiasm of so many younger staff members for community planning. The community planning program offers "new" planners a legitimate way to circumvent their department's long-range orientation and deal with current city problems. This motivation showed up especially clearly in one department just starting its community planning program. One young planner working there explained with some embarrassment that after producing a master plan, his department had degenerated into a data gathering service. Apparently oblivious to the city's acute current problems, his colleagues devoted themselves to amassing endless quantities of general information and working up special reports for political officials. He looked to the community planning program as a means of professional redemption for his department:

> This department has been doing little in the way of planning, but it's not going to work this way when this new district planning program gets underway. Many of us here are hoping to see more planning get done, planning that really leads to something. Not data gathering.

Another young community planner working in the same department explained his enthusiasm for the new program in much the same way:

> I've gotten sick of writing reports! I like dealing with current problems. That's the real reason I wanted to work here: these guys in district planning deal with current problems. The way I see it, we know what the story is. We don't need any more projections and analyses. Now it's time to deal with the problems.

This feeling that in the community planning program the department would finally achieve some relevance to urban problems was echoed by young planners in city after city. Some "new" planners in the experimental program, guarding their turf, militantly resist the slightest intrusion of traditional long-range planning methods. For instance, one community planner we spoke to—more extreme than most, but not by any means unique in his views—resented bitterly being asked to write a "reconnaissance report" of his area:

> We are wasting time on these stupid reconnaissance reports. It's a disguised form of comprehensive planning all over again. As long as you can't really push the hard issues and run with them, fuck comprehensive planning.

More often, community planners say they would prefer to strike some kind of balance in the time frame of their plans. However, their department's continued preoccupation with planning for the distant future proves so alienating, and the demands from their community residents so irresistible, that the majority of community planners find themselves drifting inexorably into total immersion in current project planning. Like this planner, some are not entirely comfortable with what they end up doing:

> One problem I see in district planning is that the planners might get involved in current projects to such an extent that they don't do the in-depth studies of their districts needed to really understand the overall problems. I'm working on a general study of my area; even though I'll have to work overtime to finish it, I intend getting it out. I'm also very interested in working on current projects and getting more into this all the time, but it could present a problem for doing long-range things that are also important. I want to do both if I can.

But even at its worst, they feel, community planning is at least a step in the right direction for the planning profession, an attempt to wrestle with immediate and urgent urban problems. To the "new" planners, anything is better than a "no-where plan."

With these divisions over the proper methods, the proper participants, and the proper time element in professional city planning, it is hardly surprising to find another deep cleavage between "new" and "old" planners concerning what kind of urban problems constitute the proper *target* of planning. Consistent with their training, older planners tend to express their concern for urban problems in physical terms. When they set out to analyze the city's needs, they look at its land use patterns rather than its service systems. The improvements and solutions that occur to them involve structures, not programs. Pressing and deplorable as the city's social decay may be, they feel, the professional planner's job is first and foremost to tackle physical blight. The resistance of so many younger planners to this physical emphasis dismays and puzzles them. If the young planners care so much about the city, why do they reject the tools of their own profession in the effort to improve urban life? For example, a baffled "old" planner remarked:

> The young planners here seem so unhappy with the degree of site study their work requires. At a meeting just the other day, a planner stood up and said, "I don't want to do a site plan!" To me, that's hard to understand. It's a matter of different generations of planners. The older, physical-oriented planners are out to renew the city; they want concrete results. It's hard to put your finger on what the younger, goal-oriented planners want. As far as I can see, they don't do anything.

"Old" planners are especially skeptical about the direction that community planning seems to be taking. As they see it, the staff members working in this experimental program do not function as planners at all. They have become informal social workers, community organizers, counselors, ombudsmen—all on a nonprofessional basis. Their activities erode the department's professional integrity. Some "old" planners resentfully castigate the community planners for their maverick behavior:

> This department should be generating more new ideas in a more comprehensive way. There should be less nit-picking, less housekeeping. It's the younger planners who are responsible for it, you know. They spend all their time trying to get streets cleared of garbage and the traffic lights fixed, rather than trying to solve the basic problems of the physical environment. That's why we don't have more creative programs in this department. And that's especially true of the area planners. They want to use every vacant patch of land in their area for recreation, regardless of whether it's good planning.

To more sympathetic "old" planners, the community planners are unfortunate victims trapped by community pressure into sacrificing their proper professional role:

> One of the problems with this department is that there's too little work going on that would project future trends. It's a function of time and too many current problems. The area planners, for instance, deal with community groups directly and can't help being crisis-oriented. They end up doing community organization or social work rather than planning physical facilities for the neighborhood. There's got to be some other way of doing all this preliminary organizing. Maybe some way to fund private advocacy planners. We desperately need a way to handle all the hassling so that the area planners on our staff can be free to get back to planning.

But whether the emotional tone is peevish or pitying, "old" planners agree that the community planners have definitely strayed from the professional fold.

Community planners, on the other hand, usually come into

the department convinced that physical urban blight is only a symptom of a deeper, more serious social malignancy. Because they feel it obscures the real problems, they have an almost visceral negative reaction to spending their time pulling and tugging at the city's physical environment. The quality of life matters more than its physical setting, they argue. What good is a physically well-planned city if it seethes with racial hatred, if street violence drives its inhabitants to cower indoors, if its youth commit slow suicide with drugs, and its impoverished slum dwellers are driven to burn it down out of sheer desperation? True, traditional planning has not encompassed social problems, and the techniques available for dealing with such problems are crude and less developed than the refined tools of physical planning. Planners are unprepared by their training for social planning. But in the view of the "new" planners, the challenge cannot responsibly be avoided on these grounds. The mission of planning is to keep the city viable, no matter where this may lead the profession. To ignore the city's social crisis is cowardice and, in the most profound sense, unprofessional.

"New" planners working in community planning programs express these sentiments with a special intensity, born of their frequent and intimate exposure to the human suffering caused by the social problems of their areas. Their patience with their traditionalist co-workers wears thin. They feel, in the words of one community planner in a city where relations between "old" and "new" planners were particularly strained, that "most of what was technically impressive in planning, the physical part, is just outdated and irrelevant." Some adopt the epithets of their older colleagues proudly, as badges of courage and progressive thinking. "I started out as a straight physical planner, but I mainly do community organization work now; planners can't do one without the other," remarked one particularly active administrative guerrilla defiantly. Another community planner explained, "My role isn't

traditional planning. I'm more of a predevelopment coordina-
tor. I look at it as the most constructive thing a professional
planner can do in this situation." Many community planners
favored "balancing" the perspective of the department by
bringing in specialists from professions relevant to social
problems—sociologists, lawyers, economists, criminologists,
and so forth. Some spoke excitedly of the need for "new"
planners themselves to develop more refined methods for
handling social problems:

> In the last ten years, planning schools have gotten more
> sociological, which is a step forward. But lots of the very
> young planners coming out of these schools get very
> vague in discussion, circular in their arguments. It might
> be good in graduate school, but it's bad here. We need to
> go the next step, to practical applications of sociological
> analysis. We talk, but we don't know the specifics of finan-
> cing mechanisms, politics, the economics of housing, and
> the workings of the real interfaces of capital in public and
> private investment. Maybe nobody knows. But we have to
> learn the nuts and bolts of social planning if we're going
> to be effective.

Much to the frustration of community planners, tradition
again has the last word within the planning department. Un-
daunted but thoroughly disgusted, one community planner
recounted his futile efforts to stimulate department interest in
nonphysical problems:

> The management has assigned us the task of making these
> meaningless reports on our areas. Their reaction to our
> complaints is just to let us complain until we get tired. I
> constantly try to explain why the study is wrong, ill con-
> ceived, and useless. I show the director articles from pro-
> fessional journals, theoretical articles. What we're doing
> needs some serious thinking, I tell him. We need to really
> hash it out and try to find out what we are really trying
> to do. We should take three or four days, whatever it

takes, and look at alternatives. To me it sounds like a reasonable suggestion. But somehow the director never gets
into the substance of what I'm saying. He's the big boss.
He just brushes suggestions aside.

At the root of the professional disagreements we have discussed lies a gut-level division over whether the city remains
a viable social entity. Most "old" planners feel the city is in
trouble—even in crisis—but salvageable through traditional planning methods. Total urban collapse is an overstated
abstraction, "scare-talk" unworthy of a trained professional.
"New" planners, on the other hand, are haunted—even in
their sleep, some told us—by an apocalyptic vision of a
whole social order crumbling around them, a way of life in
the process of being irretrievably lost. They regard planning
as a last best hope as time runs out for American cities, but
only if planners can break out of the straitjacket of caution and passivity which their professional traditions have
wrapped around them. They regard the need for redefining
planning as self-evident; the festering city itself gives daily
testimony to the bankruptcy of "old" planning. What is
called for, they believe, is an aggressive, try-anything approach, and they view their colleagues' stubborn adherence
to an apparently dead-end style of planning almost with hor-
ror. One community planner, fighting a losing battle to maintain communication with planners in other sections of his department, said in despair:

> Nothing could be more severe than the in-house
> problems we have here. There's a tradition among plan-
> ners, and especially in our management, of long-range ra-
> tional planning. Even when it's obviously impossible, the
> commitment to do this kind of planning persists. The
> older planners here know there's an urban crisis, but they
> have no sense of urgency. Or maybe I should say, they
> have a middle-class technician's sense of urgency. They
> don't think the community planners should get so emo-

tionally involved. Planning should be respectable, not a place for hot shots. They live dual lives, as citizens and planners, split right down the middle. For us in community planning, our work and our lives are the same thing.

In another city, a community planner soberly spoke of how his colleagues who clung to traditional definitions of professional planning were driven into betrayal of their humanistic principles:

> Planners who don't fight the system get trapped into impossible moral dilemmas. As long as they accept the low level of federal commitment to the cities and try to plan rationally within that framework, they're forced to act inhumanely. It's like having one life raft for a hundred drowning people. For instance, I mentioned at a staff meeting that the Model Cities area will go under unless massive renewal action is taken now. The section chief of area planning said, "I haven't told any of you about this before, but there's one line of thought which holds that under conditions of limited resources it may be necessary to let some areas go under." This will provide cheap land for clearance, he implied. In other words, if you let an area go for four or five years, the area will clear itself. If it's hell on the people who live there, that's tough. Now, this guy isn't a monster. He's a sensitive person, in fact. He's taking this ruthless line not because he wants to, but because he has the responsibility to divide up limited resources. Unless he rebels against the system, he has no alternative but to screw the areas that need the most help; it would take too much to save them. This is an attitude forced upon planners as a result of the untenable position they are put in by limited resources and unlimited needs. That's why some of us feel we have to go outside the system.

Coordination Problems

The rift between the community planners and the rest of the planning staff yawns all the wider because of the community planning section's isolation within the department. The new program usually operates as a self-contained entity, with minimal administrative interaction with other sections. Often community planners are isolated in a physical sense as well, located on a separate floor or even in a different office building from their colleagues. Their work is considered, by both themselves and the rest of the planning staff, as only tenuously related to the department's other activities. They may not even see much of their colleagues. Describing a typical situation, a community planner told us:

> I don't really work with any other sections. We tend to get split off to our own districts. I just don't have that much contact with other planners.

Many staff members both in and out of community planning express concern over the lack of coordination between community planning and other sections. This feature of the planning department is, in fact, the single most commonly cited bit of evidence for the "lousy administration" most planners seem to feel they work under. However, their remarks about coordination carry a curious but unmistakable undertone of ambivalence. To understand why they have mixed feelings, we must turn back to the counter-irrational organizational characteristics of planning departments.

As we have seen, counter-irrational bureaucracies turn many accepted principles of rational bureaucratic organization inside out, transforming them from self-evident advantages to actual threats against the bureaucracy's survival. So it is with coordination in the planning department. Because of its weak formal mandate, the planning department is not in a position to offer its professional staff competitive salaries or a sense of power. An increased emphasis on professional autonomy, granting promotions within the department, and an appeal to idealism—in effect, the creation of the "positions of opportunity" discussed earlier—represents practically the only reward at the management's disposal. Rational coordination between sections would undercut the capacity to dole out this reward, devaluing the only coin with which the department can buy talent. Thus the efficiency benefits of imposing coordination must always be weighed against the job-satisfaction benefits of perpetuating chaos. For the management in the planning departments we visited, chaos clearly wins the day.

Since the deliberate choice of organizational chaos over coordination is felt to be somewhat embarrassing, it shows up in the planners' remarks in disguise—a hasty second thought embedded in a nest of complaints about fragmentation and compartmentalization. For example, in the words of an assistant director:

> This is not a tightly structured department. Coordination is one of our main problems. There are lots of disadvantages to our setup here. Duplication for one thing, and people disregardful of things going on in other parts of the planning department. There's the physical problem of being spread out over three floors. District planning is completely isolated. And also, personality problems. Comprehensive planning and district planning are not meshed well, to say the least. The district planners haven't made use of comprehensive planning and comprehensive planners haven't reached out to provide a framework district planning can use. But then, there are certain advantages of loose structure, you know. It encourages individual initiative and creativity. Bright young planners get lots of responsibility right away. This keeps them happy, and some do impressive work. Look at the district planners, ones like Dave, Joe, and Ron.

The district planners named by the assistant director confirmed his interpretation. One told us:

> There are definitely problems created by compartmentalization. District planning doesn't have much in the

way of resources—staff, research, drafting—and we can't get the backup we need from other sections of the department. It doesn't make much sense to have these seven little sections all operating independently. But it sometimes is a great advantage to be on your own as a sort of one-man planning department in your area. I like district planning the way it is. It's the main reason why I stay in this dismal city.

Where community planners do favor sacrificing autonomy for better integration among sections of the department, they clearly have somebody else's autonomy in mind:

We should coordinate comprehensive planning better with the current planning level. It's not happening now. It's a drag now. The hangup is that the comprehensive planners have their own power interests. They want to get credit independent of area planning. They're supposed to be working for a goal, but it's all one-upmanship. We need to cut down on internal competition and put more emphasis on reaching our objectives of a more livable city. Comprehensive planning should be made to realize that it's no good just to collect data for their own sake. They should tie their efforts in with the needs of our section. If their data aren't helpful to us, what's their reason for collecting it?

Since coordination is something of an administrative sacred cow, formal attempts to knit the different sections of the department together occur frequently despite the general preference for chaos. Staff meetings proliferate endlessly; intricate procedures for sending intradepartmental memos are established; some departments hold staff retreats and hire communications consultants to discover where the department is going wrong. Not surprisingly, these formal mechanisms for coordination fail, usually miserably. No one openly questions the desirability of increasing coordination; no one openly suggests a preference for the benefits of anarchy. But in an unacknowledged conspiracy, planners quietly subvert all formal mechanisms for integrating the department.

The "staff meeting cycle" is a good example. Envisioned as an opportunity for mutual exchange of information among different sections and between staff and management, staff meetings tend to turn instead into subtle sparring matches in which the goal is to guard one's secrets while seeming cooperative. Revealing information means risking autonomy. The less said about one's work the better, and what does get said must be carefully phrased and justified. One planner explained the atmosphere in her department's meetings:

> I expected there would be more of a team effort here, but there isn't, and there's such a lack of communication that I see no possibility of change. Even having discussions with the director and others is progress. But our meetings turn out to be merely instructional. Every time we've had meetings, they're not constructive. When questions are raised in all good faith, they're treated defensively as an attack, and people share only the information that makes them look good. It's a ridiculous way for professional people to act.

Since little actual information is being exchanged, staff meetings tend to degenerate into boring rituals which planners avoid if possible. This had happened in several cities we visited, where community planners assured us that staff meetings were "worthless," "a waste of time." In the view of one:

> The management in this department makes no attempt to draw out the ideas of the staff. Our formal meetings are a lot of bullshit. It's the director's psychiatric couch. He uses the meetings to feed his ego. It's a pretty sick scene.

Another told us:

> A lot of people who should be at staff meetings just don't come. And we're not being given all the information we

should have; it's being withheld, consciously or uncon-
sciously.

In two cities, staff meetings had been temporarily suspended
as hopelessly unproductive. However, they seemed unlikely
to die away completely, for as soon as they were discarded as
useless, pressure to reintroduce them in a different form
would begin to mount. "We don't have enough staff meetings, just occasional administrative announcements," said a
planner who had joined the department during a low point in
the staff meeting cycle. "All the planners here are discussing
the problem to see if we can get some worthwhile meetings
going." To distinguish a new wave of meetings from its "useless" predecessors, departments usually invent some special
designation—for example, "offbeat" meetings as opposed to
"onbeat" ones. In this way, elaborate systems of different
types of meetings are built up, consuming considerable staff
time without much actual coordination resulting from any of
them. As one community planner complained, "Sure, we
have staff meetings, all the time. That's why we don't get
much done around here."

A similar fate befalls the paper channels of information between community planning and other sections. Several departments have tried to establish a formal mechanism to keep
community planners abreast of any department action concerning their areas of the city, usually by sending memos to
the appropriate community planner. In return the community planners are supposed to feed their first-hand knowledge
of their areas into the work of their colleagues in other sections, also through memos or reports. These written exchanges become immediate casualties in the struggle to
preserve section autonomy. Planners in all sections tend to
feel the information should flow one way only: toward them.
Receiving information becomes far more popular than giving
it. Why help a rival section? Why take the time? One com-

munity planner, exemplifying the righteous indignation that
commonly accompanies breakdowns in the memo system,
muttered:

> There ought to be a more effective interplay between
> comprehensive planning and area planning. Anything
> that comes in about Fleaville—that's my area—I should
> get a memo. As of now, I get memos on only about three-
> fourths of what's going on there. The one-fourth I don't get
> infuriates me. The department administration ought to
> crack down on this! Things need to be tied together better
> here. As the Fleaville area planner, I should be kept aware
> of anything systematic that's happening there.

At the same time, this planner denied that other staff members could legitimately make information demands on the
community planning section. Community planners were too
busy working with the residents in their areas, and besides, in
his view "comprehensive planning should be an instrument
for community planning," not the other way around.

As they work along independently, the community planning section and other sections of the department frequently
get in each other's way. Sometimes, for instance, they unwit-
tingly work against each other, discovering their contradictions only when they unexpectedly collide head-on after
weeks or months of independent work. Here is a case of this
cross-purpose planning, described by an aggrieved community planner whose section found out the hard way about the
department's other activities. Intimating deliberate sabotage
of his section, he told us:

> People here think we are illegitimate, and won't send us
> the information we need or cooperate with us in any
> way. The people upstairs have been making plans for our
> areas on the basis of whim without consulting us. For in-
> stance, take the area I'm working in. They never told us
> about the placement of schools they were working out

upstairs. Now it turns out they planned one right in the middle of what we intended as a pedestrian corridor. It messes up everything! We made all our plans with the community assuming the school would be over by the side of the park and the residents are counting on it. We've made such a big deal about community participation, about not putting any tricks over on them. Now this happens! We should have had the information in time to resolve differences in our plan and the plan from upstairs, but now it's too late. The planning department has made its public commitment to put the school in the wrong place. We lost before we knew it was a problem. One of the area planners blew up at a staff meeting a couple of weeks ago, shouted and demanded that people send more information down to the area planning section. But I don't see much change.

Similar imbroglios occur when the community planners fail to pass information back to the rest of the department. One staff member from the comprehensive planning section recounted with some bitterness the embarrassing situation dumped in his lap by a noncommunicating community planner:

> The lack of communication between different divisions of city planning is the big problem; it's like a caste system, everybody avoiding contact. To give you an example: recently a controversy came up over a parking lot. A bakery had gone to the BZA [Board of Zoning Appeals] to get a waiver to build the lot. But the community found out about it, probably from the district planner there, and fought it at the hearing. They won. So then the bakery came before the planning commission to get the zoning changed. Nobody in the planning department told me about it even though I'm working on that part of the master plan and should be informed of any zoning actions. I heard about it accidentally, from someone I know in the community. I asked around the department and was told about a community meeting that night. I thought I'd go to see what it was about. When I got

there, it turned out that the district planner had sent
them a letter about master plan zoning. I had never seen
it; he didn't mention anything about it when he told me
about the meeting. But when they found out I was from
the planning department, they asked me what it meant.
They expected me to know all about it, and when I
didn't they thought I was playing games with them. I
couldn't explain that each section in the planning department thinks it's an entity in itself and feels its business
isn't anybody else's business. To that community group,
city hall is just one big monster devoted to doing them
in. They kept yelling at me, "What do you mean, you
don't understand it? You just mailed it to us!" I had to
read the letter and try to interpret it on the spot in front
of all those people. I looked like an idiot, and so did the
city planning department.

Most of the contradictions arising from cross-purpose planning are small, a matter of stepped-on toes, inconvenience,
and injured pride rather than irreconcilable conflicts. Sometimes, however, different sections develop a large time investment and emotional commitment to diametrically opposed
plans. When this happens, the department starts to pull apart
in opposite directions. In one city, for example, we found the
community planning and comprehensive planning sections
unswervingly committed to different renewal plans for the
same blighted residential area. As one of the community planners summed up the conflict:

The area is presently designated for industrial use in the
master plan. Our section wants what the people living
there want: to make it residential. But the industrial plan,
backed by the comprehensive planning section, is also
part of the department's thinking on this area.

In this particular case, the planning department was under
unusual pressure to present a united front because a public-
spirited development corporation wanted to build low-cost

housing in the area and demanded a plan before they would start. Since the development corporation's intentions were public knowledge and housing was desperately needed, the planning department's management feared that any delay in producing a plan would cost them dearly in bad publicity. But recommending one section's plan meant alienating—possibly losing—the staff of the other section. The course of action finally chosen was to leave the contradictions in the two plans unresolved but papered over with a bizarre compromise to give the illusion of unity. The area remained slated for industrial development in the "long-term plan" but was marked out for residential development in the "short-term plan." In effect, the planning department proposed building homes now to be torn down later. Although many planners in both the conflicting sections jeered at this recommendation, they accepted and worked in terms of it. However absurd, the maneuver postponed a dangerously divisive policy choice and thus placated the department staff.

We have seen how personality frictions, disagreements on professional issues, and the strains of coordinating two radically different planning approaches divide the planning department into opposing factions of "old" and "new" planners. What does the planning department do about the growing rift in its ranks? How does management deal with the "new" planning activities of their wayward community planners, potentially so dangerous for the department's organizational survival? In the next chapter we analyze some of the controls commonly applied to community planners, as well as the evasions commonly used by those acting as administrative guerrillas to counter departmental controls.

Eight

Department Controls
and Guerrilla Evasions

Like the legendary dragon's egg, community planning programs are usually hatched with little understanding of how hard to handle they may become. The original motives of the planning department's managers in setting up the new program—to seem "with it" professionally, to impress the city's political leaders, or to improve the department's public relations—reflect a comfortable assumption that the program is theirs to shape and manipulate in the best interests of the department. Confident that their planning staff will act largely as directed, they do not usually even entertain the notion that the new section might develop an identity of its own and swing into self-initiated action toward goals of its own choosing. Thus it comes as something of a shock when "new" planners, with their strong commitment to a radically different definition of professional conduct and objectives, begin to concentrate in the community planning program and develop it in unanticipated directions.

Aggressive community planners, correctly perceiving that the department's loose structure lends itself well to innovation but poorly to supervision, begin to take advantage of their positions of opportunity to test "new" planning ideas without the knowledge or prior approval of their superiors. In the case of full-fledged administrative guerrillas, they may even take pains to conceal their actions from those in the department who are committed to traditional "old" planning. With a growing sense of unease, the department managers watch control of community planning slipping from their grasp. Their apprehensions are hardly lessened by the triumphantly possessive tone with which some community planners speak of their section. The following remarks, coming from planners in different cities, represent a common sense of having outfoxed the Establishment by turning the community planning section into something management never expected:

> Originally, the director wanted us to do project planning here. You know, work out cute prospectives to impress people with. More or less eyewash. He didn't want real community planning from us. But the way we run things, he's getting a lot more than he wanted! Our unit has grown—well, not exactly into a monster—but definitely into an animal.

> The director here is a tremendous opportunist. He wanted to jump on the community planning bandwagon by creating this section so he could look progressive. He even said that community planning is the wave of the future. But actually he's opposed to community planning. It's foreign to his thinking and what he has written in his book. He doesn't want us doing community organizing, and he's unsympathetic to planning that isn't strictly physical. But we do community planning anyway, in spite of the pig.

Signs that a sizable proportion of community planners are not going to function as cooperative "members of the team" (a phrase frequently used by department management to indicate staff docility) are everywhere. Community planners, not content with "their share" of department resources, constantly badger their superiors for more staff in their section, more secretarial and drafting help, additional office space and equipment, funds for social science consultants, and so forth. They object to being assigned projects they consider irrelevant to their community work. They agitate for increased power within the department on matters of policy and staffing. They get themselves involved in controversial social planning activities far beyond the department's usual scope of action. From management's point of view, they "lose perspective" by drifting from community contact into community advocacy. Most threatening for management, they seek to push the department into a more politically active role, and they sometimes take political stands that embarrass the department. What looked at its inception like a harmless new planning gimmick is transformed by the unexpected vigor of its staff into a formidable challenge to the department's time-honored traditions of encapsulated and elite-council planning.

In curbing the disruptive actions of community planning staff members, management faces a dilemma: how to exert pressure without driving this volatile staff out of the department. As we have seen, community planners as a group are young, highly trained, and extremely conscious of their capacity for job mobility. Many speak of the Masters in City Planning (MCP) as a "ticket" enabling them to relocate easily. In fact, they usually enter the department with the expectation of fairly short tenure there. Those (the majority) whose career interests lie in the private sector see their city planning work as a temporary public service stint to gain experience and satisfy their idealistic impulses, not as the first step of a career in the city bureaucracy. Even those who hope to make a career of public city planning anticipate a se-

ries of moves to different planning departments before settling down permanently. Under these circumstances, the
managers of the city department they happen to be working
in at the moment have only the most tenuous hold on them.
The usual control devices of salary and promotion are only
marginally effective. The only reward of real significance is
the very freedom of action that management wishes to curb.
And if the planner finds this freedom of action effectively
hampered by the department's controls, chances are he will
leave for a less restricted position elsewhere. Unfortunately,
the better the planner's talent and training, the more easily
he can find alternative positions in other departments. Thus
department administrators who crack down hard on their
community planners face the dismaying prospect of driving
out the most capable and imaginative staff members and
watching their new experimental program gradually fill up
with planners that nobody else wants. They may, in effect,
end up trading insubordination for incompetence.

Some administrators speaking of control problems seem immobilized by this dilemma. For example, in the words of an
associate director:

> Certain staff members do what they want to do rather
> than what I think needs to be done. I guess it's a popular
> attitude nowadays to take a liberal attitude toward disci-
> pline. I really don't know how to handle it. I'm torn be-
> tween letting them do what they want to do and direct-
> ing them to do what should be done.

Other administrators, like this community planning section
chief, hopefully cling to the belief that the community planners will grow out of their stubbornness:

> I have a problem with my staff here in community plan-
> ning. We have a young staff, a staff that sometimes per-
> haps reacts to specifics. They're not thinking of the

larger perspective. It's just because they're new. There are two ways to go when you leave school; play it close and do what you're told, or rebel until you've made the point that you're not a student any more. We just got some who chose the second way. It'll pass.

And some express a sense of helplessness as their creation takes what they consider a wayward path:

Some of the staff here, especially the community planners, are taking public stands against the department. It's insubordination! I don't like it. It's childish. It seems to be part of the new movement. In this recent case [an open letter to the newspaper opposing a department recommendation] I couldn't stop them. I tried everything. And this kind of thing is increasing. I didn't act that way as a young planner. I guess it's a product of our age.

Attempts at control are by no means absent. However, with community planners touchy about their autonomy and the planning department management unsure of its ground, they tend to take unexpected forms. Often they appear as what might be called *control by training*, imposed on new community planning staff members when they are hired. The administration tries to head off trouble by correcting the new community planners' "misunderstanding" of what city planning properly involves. The new staff member is encouraged to reject the idea that his "new" planning orientation represents a valid alternative definition of professional city planning, and to reinterpret it as naivete and inexperience. For example, one administrator told us:

Area planners, being new, can lead people on and make them think they are going to get something. This results in trouble when it doesn't materialize. Our planners must be trained not to commit themselves or the city to projects that are not likely to be achieved. We've had a problem with this, so now we—that is, the section chief

and I—warn new area planners not to make rash promises. They should tell people they might not get what
they want, and that if they do get it, it's likely to take a
long, long time.

We found many community planners who recall being re-
galed with this kind of veiled threat masquerading as training.
Reporting a common experience, a recently hired community
planner said:

> When I came in, the director told me that I would be
> doing very mundane things, not changing the world, and
> that it wouldn't be helpful for me to proffer my revolu-
> tionary philosophy here. He advised me not to rock the
> boat.

Another community planner described control by training in
her department this way:

> When a district planner first comes here, he is expected
> to put in an apprenticeship. He's expected to go to meet-
> ings with a more seasoned planner so he won't be able to
> embarrass the department or commit it to anything.
> They don't let you have much contact with the public on
> your own at first.

Control by training represents an attempt to socialize the
new planner into nondisruptive conformity to the department's traditions. Our impression is that this type of control
accomplishes little except to heighten the cynicism of "new"
planners. "The first thing I learned here," a particularly radical community planner remarked, "is that they want no challenge. They want sheep here." Asked if there were any informal rules in her department, a community planner snapped,
"Yeah—don't air your opinion if you disagree!" Another
planner remarked with a smile, "One thing you notice about
those in high positions around here, who tell you how to go

about planning: they definitely aren't young dynamic people who are trying to change the place." We found some planners who were currently undergoing the control by training process to be anticipating conflict with their superiors almost eagerly; as one new community planner told us, after describing the cautionary advice rained down on him by his department's administrators, "I'm sure I'm going to be in conflict with these people pretty soon. It hasn't happened yet only because I just got here." The outward conformity sometimes produced by on-the-job training in "old" planning often seems no more than a cover beneath which "new" planners can go their own way unhampered. "I'd like to discuss changes with the director more, but there's no use making a battle over it," we were told by an administrative guerrilla. "It'll change over time anyway, and meanwhile I'll do what I can do on my own."

The department also attempts to impose what might be called *operational controls* in the form of sanctions applied directly to violators of "old" planning norms. Here the emphasis is on coercion rather than socialization. This is a particularly difficult form of control for the department management to apply. As we have seen, because of the way the department is organized, direct supervision over community planners becomes almost impossible once they start working in their assigned districts. Thus many activities that would earn department disapproval can be concealed, allowing the planner to escape the department's operational controls. This, in essence, is the appeal of the administrative guerrilla tactics favored by so many community planners. However, community planners do carry on some department-based activities that are more easily monitored, such as the innumerable rush projects they are pulled off their regular work to do. A planner who resists being distracted from his community work by such demands can hardly escape the scrutiny of the department. A planner in this position told us, "I've refused to do projects that I felt were insignificant. I was—well, not exactly reprimanded for it—but they kept sending me memos as if I had no right to refuse. I'm still getting them."

More serious department pressure falls on administrative guerrillas whose cover begins to slip. The more active community planners sometimes find their clandestine community organizing, leaking of information, and political involvement becoming so extensive and well known to community residents that department attention is inevitably attracted. When this happens, they are called on the carpet. Some planners report being "screamed at," "bawled out," and put on the "shit list." One told us, "I face a lot of blow-ups here. There's a feeling on the part of the executive staff here that I shouldn't get so involved with community groups. I've been accused of being an advocate planner." He added, "I've been thinking of leaving because of this."

In cases of outright administrative insurgency, where the community planner's "disloyalty" to the department and its planning traditions goes on public display, the embarrassed administrators pull out all the stops on operational controls. In the instance of administrative insurgency mentioned earlier, involving several community planners' public criticism of a department recommendation, the associate director listed his futile attempts to rein in the dissident group:

> I let them know that what they were doing wasn't the proper recourse for disagreement within the department. I told them that it will affect my judgment as to the amount of responsibility I give them in the future. I even told them right out that I won't invite them to important meetings if they can't keep their mouths shut. They just went on as before with their insubordination. They ignored me.

In a different city, an administrative insurgent told us, "I'm expected to check and double-check everything I do, because

I'm considered deviant and not trusted." Another recounted the operational controls she saw at work in her department this way:

> Some of us here are known as agitators. The director is frightened at the things we might say. He's not sure of what we are going to do next. It's a real thing here. He has been known to cancel names off lists for meetings because they are agitator types, and he fears they might get the department in trouble. I'm known as a ringleader, so I get a lot of flak. Like for instance, I met the personnel director in the hall the other day. He said, "Better watch out!" He mentioned I was hurting my chances for raises and advancement. He made it like a joke, you know.

Another administrative insurgent told us, "The director wants to get rid of me because he thinks of me as a troublemaker. No sweat, they need me more than I need them."

The most striking feature of these operational controls is their almost total ineffectiveness. For most administrative guerrillas they constitute only a minor annoyance; administrative insurgents view them almost as a necessary proof that they are accomplishing something. Whereas they represent the mainstay form of control in many other bureaucracies, coercive operational controls prove relatively useless for dealing with a highly mobile staff in a counter-irrational bureaucracy like the planning department.

The third kind of control that departments impose on their deviant community planning staff—and by far the most effective—is *control by inertia*. This consists of simple refusal to alter traditional department policy. As individuals, community planners find they can evade or even defy the department's attempts to limit their actions as administrative guerrillas or insurgents. As individuals, they are relatively free to operate in terms of "new" planning—opening the planning process into an arena council involving community

residents, expanding their planning activities into social services traditionally under the authority of other city departments, acting as advocate planners, taking political stands,
and lobbying for their plans. But when it comes to transforming the planning department itself into an instrument for
"new" planning, a step often cited by community planners as
absolutely necessary if the city is to be saved, the department
administration has the upper hand. Cleaving to its traditional
path of encapsulated elite-council planning, the department
refuses to be pushed into a new role. Warnings, reprimands,
salary cuts, and threats of being fired only spur the dissident
"new" planners on; but the blank wall of department inertia
stops them cold.

Control by inertia operates particularly effectively on the
issue of the department's political involvement. As we have
seen, planning departments traditionally adopt a passive, responsive relationship to the city's politicians. This is a
counter-irrational adaptation to the fact that city policies are
determined irrationally on the basis of politics rather than
planning. Department administrators feel that faithfully serving the needs of politicians is the only way to gain enough informal influence to compensate for the department's lack of
formal power to shape city policies rationally. By counter-
irrational logic, independently taking firm political stands as a
department means lessening the department's effectiveness as
a rational influence in city government.

"New" planners, unpersuaded by this argument, ridicule
the department's "low political profile" as cowardice, abdica-
tion of professional responsibility, and insensitivity to the urgency of the urban crisis. They interpret the department's
claims to aloofness from city politics as self-deception; the department is already politically involved in an innocuous sup-
porting role, they argue, and should not shrink from political
involvement in a more meaningful initiating role. By "new"
planning logic, independently taking firm political stands as a

department represents the best hope of increasing the department's effectiveness as a rational influence in city government. The remarks of many community planners reflect a desire to "stiffen the political backbone" of the department. They speak of their planning directors who are unwilling to speak out publicly on controversial issues as "timid," "beaten men," "cynical," "irresponsible," "opportunistic." The general feeling, voiced here by a disgruntled community planner in a department severely polarized between "new" and "old" planning staff, runs:

> The supervisors here reject innovative ideas not because they are poor, but because they might not be accepted by the heads of other city agencies or the mayor. All the programs we have are evaluated not in terms of their good for the city but for the good of the mayor's political future. We are serving the mayor's needs, not the needs of the city. We should function not as a staff serving the mayor, but as a consultant coming up with recommendations. What's lacking here is leadership. Very seldom do we take a position as a department. In fact, most of the time we don't have one! We should be much more forceful. But it seems impossible to implement this view in the bureaucratic context here.

Community planners also argue that a new social planning dimension should be added to the department's activities; as they see it, "most of the issues we should be concerned with are nonphysical in nature." Social planning, they point out, implies adding new kinds of expertise to the department staff, thus departing from the established policy of hiring only planners and architects. Such sentiments formed a leitmotiv for community planners' complaints about their departments in every city we visited; a common phrase was, "We need to get things going!"

However, no levers present themselves for prying the department out of its traditional passive, encapsulated role. We encountered many community planners who had tried without success to interest their superiors in publicly backing "new" planning ideas generated by their section, as in this case:

> This is a big bureaucracy with no room for the individual. You are given assignments to complete, or else left on your own. But they don't expect us to initiate new projects for the department. They ignore any independent work. Projects don't get initiated by the planning department as a team. And as a result, what I think would be effective for my district is being ignored by the rest of the department.

In another city we were told:

> I wanted to see us get involved in ecological problems. Not as a pollution control agency, but working out the political difficulties of environmental planning and design. This department has no ecological control. No one in the city has. No one is responsible, not the department of health, no one. I wrote up some stuff on this issue. What I wanted was for the director to make a press statement on the lack of ecological considerations in planning, so we could pave the way to move into this area of need. The director refused to even look at my statement.

"New" planners face similar unyielding barriers in channeling department resources into their personal projects:

> I was working on a report aimed at defining needed changes in the quality of service delivery systems, a social planning issue. I lost a battle with the administration about getting more staff working on it. I needed a core staff to do this full-time work with the community and the agency. Without the manpower to do the job, I just ran out of gas. One person couldn't carry it out.

Others, trying to institute more democratic hiring procedures within the department so they could bring in staff congenial to "new" planning, find their suggestions falling on deaf ears:

My difficulty here is relating to the management of this agency. No one with area planning background or sympathies sits at the level of the three top administrators. What I'd like now is more say-so in who they hire. We area planners should have some role in the evaluation of candidates. They [management] talk to the area planning section chief, not to us. There's no sign anybody is planning to ask us anything.

An outspoken administrative insurgent in community planning told us ruefully of his attempt to democratize the selection of a new director:

Six staff people here asked me why we couldn't have more influence in selecting the new director. I didn't see why not either, so I raised hell about it with the management. They acted like they didn't even hear me, which intimidated all the rest of the staff. Four of the six who raised the question in the first place came up to me later and said I shouldn't have made so much trouble.

In three of the departments visited, some staff members, most of them from the community planning section, had organized "revolts" within the department aimed at changing its internal organizational structure or public stance in directions more compatible with "new" planning. But, they reported, the effort is much like pushing a string, and it is dangerous for the individuals involved. One radical "new" planner in a community planning section recounted her experience:

Several months ago there was a meeting of the entire district planning section staff at my apartment, at night. Several of us set it up; we felt some changes should be made in the department and asked people to come and discuss it. Most came. We talked about problems and made a list of proposals. The recommendations included a restudy of the planning department to improve internal communication, and getting the department more in-

volved in standing behind its proposals politically, and
also getting the department to initiate things more ag-
gressively. There were some differences of opinion, but
the overall consensus was that we needed change. Four of
us from district planning drew up the formal proposal
and gave it to the director. He promptly pooh-poohed it
and said that's what we are doing already, and nothing
ever came of it except that some of us have been known
since then as agitators.

For her unsuccessful efforts to alter the department's internal
organization and public role, this planner was being pressured
out. She left the department under a cloud while we were
there, one of the few firings we ran across. In another department where a reorganization drive was brewing, with secret
memoranda being circulated and talk of conspiracy in the air,
one of the community planners involved explained his apprehensions:

> Tension here is increasing. It could all let go. There's in-
> ternal dissention over how far you go to influence politi-
> cians, and over how much activism is called for. If this
> reorganization move breaks open our deeper conflicts,
> I'm convinced the more conservative chickenshits would
> win out. They have control of the department, the posi-
> tions of strength. And most of the activists here are inex-
> perienced. Half would lose their heads in a fight.

When administrative insurgency is directed at pushing the
department into a new role, the department's inertia proves
to be the ultimate control. Throwing their weight against
such an immovable object, the insurgents simply batter themselves to death.

How, then, do community planners counter these
constraints—control by training, operational controls, control by inertia? Again, we found many of them resorting to
undercover administrative guerrilla tactics. For instance,

some community planners cultivate allies among the young planners working in other sections of the department or, occasionally, in the lower rungs of management. These contacts can be utilized to advance the interests of "new" planning in general and the community planning section in particular. Allies pass along information that might otherwise not reach the community planner, sometimes informally expand the resources available to the community planning section, and lend moral support and numerical strength to attacks on department inertia. Sometimes the relationship between community planners and their departmental allies is sincere, a matter of mutual dedication to "new" planning. However, the community planners' alliances can also be quite Machiavellian. One community planner involved in a "revolt," for example, remarked:

> Our reorganization movement is aimed at getting the "front line work" groups, the ones that have community relevance, to operate together under one chief. We've got one of the younger administrators interested in heading up the new section. We decided we needed an administrator for legitimacy, and we chose him because he was the most aggressive and political one available. The depth of his planning skill is questionable, but when planning's in this much trouble, that's irrelevant.

In addition to this tactic, community planners can induce other sections to lend support and resources to the community planning section by using their contacts with community groups. For example, clandestinely arranging for community groups to barrage the comprehensive planning section with carefully planted questions about the master plan can force planners in that section to seek closer relations with the community planners, who can presumably help them deal with this unaccustomed source of pressure.

This technique had been used with considerable success in

one city we visited. Without the trauma of a struggle over formal reorganization, the community planning section had subtly begun to spread its influence into other sections and tap into their manpower. One planner in the comprehensive planning section of this department told us:

> My biggest problem here is all this community group work. I expect it to increase because more groups seem to be developing all the time. I don't know why they need to deal with me when we have community planners. It makes divisional responsibilities awfully hazy around here, because we have to work more closely with community planning. This last group that came to us all excited about the master plan was one that community planning was working with. They should have tipped us off, or gotten us involved earlier. In the future we need to work together with the community planners in order to know what to expect.

This comprehensive planner of course was unaware that community planners had suggested to the community groups in question that they go down and demand information about the master plan. Another planner in this department observed almost with desperation:

> The lines of the different divisions here seem to be getting blurred. We are all beginning to be drawn into community work.

While these senior staff members felt disturbed about the creeping expansion of the community planning section, the chaotic organization of the department in general obscured what was actually happening and blunted "old" planners' reactions. We heard remarks such as "there ought to be more of a division of labor," and "we need to further define the responsibilities of the different divisions around here," but no one seemed quite sure how to confine the aggressive new section. Just as the department's inertia acts against the expansionary interests of the community planning program on the formal level, it favors them on the informal level.

A last countermeasure used for evading department constraints may be called "resource pirating." Since the department provides such scanty resources in the way of staff and support services, community planners sometimes "borrow" resources from outside sources. The Model Cities organization usually presents a tempting target. Other city agencies, particularly urban renewal and housing, may also fall victim. Successful pirating seems to carry a certain prestige among administrative guerrillas, because of the special skill and finesse required. Community planners who use this technique are prone to brag:

> The planning department gives us space and pays our salaries, that's all. We hustle things from other agencies: Model Cities, housing, and so on. We get secretarial help and everything from outside. It's tricky, because other agencies have budgets too. You have to do it just right.

Other community planners spoke of having volunteer teams of students to help out during the summer. Still others, who had developed close relations with their community, had put together amateur staffs of unpaid community residents. One planner spoke mysteriously of having "scrounged up enough of a staff to man eight subareas in my community." His staff seemed to be made up of community residents paid by Model Cities, which had overlapping jurisdiction in part of his area. He told us somewhat apologetically that he had to conceal the origin of his informal staff because, as he put it, "some of the guys here who are working all alone in large areas near mine might hear about it and want to steal some of my staff." In resource pirating, it appears, even one's fellow community planners are fair game.

FOUR

THE PLANNER
AND CITY HALL

Nine

*Crossing the Lines:
Community Planners and
the Operating Agencies*

We have seen how the community planners, torn between community demands and departmental constraints, are driven into the underground role of administrative guerrilla. Let us now turn to a third element in the community planning pressure system, one which heightens the contradictions and tensions of the community planner's role and drives the new program's staff to ever more devious—and more perilous —actions. This third element is the city's operating agencies.

Confrontation between community planners and these operating agencies has an air of inevitability about it, like a Greek tragedy. Even without community planning, the planning department's ambiguous status in city government generates a high potential for strained relations. Most of the departments that commonly make up the city's bureaucracy are *line* agencies in the sense that they have been delegated administrative authority; these operating agencies implement the policy decisions of the chief executive and city council.

The planning department, on the other hand, is a *staff* agency. It implements nothing and can only offer recommendations. Yet the planning department, as part of its assignment to guide the city's operation and development, must informally and sometimes formally review the operations of the line agencies. Planners find themselves in the awkward position of evaluating and recommending policies over which they have no positive controls. Worse yet, their review efforts, usually regarded as unwelcome meddling by the operating agencies, are easily thwarted. Operating agencies can—and do—keep their activities secret, refuse to cooperate, and hire "safe" planning consultants of their own to work out plans for the city services they administer. The more closely related the operating agency's service to the planning department's current activities, the higher the potential for tension and "interference." Recognizing this, planning department administrators often speak of their "classic conflict with the department of public works," the "inevitable clash with housing, whose interests overlap with ours," and a "natural conflict with the urban renewal department."

As we have mentioned, the planning department has two choices in this uncomfortable situation: it can *encapsulate* itself, tacitly agreeing to a division of labor that avoids open conflict with operating agencies; or it can undertake *expansion* of its control over the operating agencies, in effect taking over some of their line responsibilities. In the interests of organizational survival, planning departments have traditionally chosen encapsulation, limiting their efforts so as not to invade other agencies' jurisdictions. For instance, to avoid conflict with urban renewal and housing, large sections of the city may be ruled out of bounds; as an administrator confided, "We have informal agreements with housing and community development [HCD]. We stay out of HCD neighborhoods."

Another encapsulation technique is used to avert dangerous power struggles with particularly strong operating agencies:

the planning department simply forgoes effective review of
the powerful agencies' operations. For example, since directors of the department of public works (DPW) or its equivalent customarily enjoy formidable political clout, planning
departments tend to tread cautiously in their review of the
DPW's proposals for building city facilities (usually called
the capital improvements program, or CIP). In some cities we
visited, the CIP escapes planning department review alto-
gether and may become, as one planner put it, "the crude and
irresponsible tool of hack politicians." In other cities where
the city charter or mayor requires CIP review by the planning department, political realities often reduce the review
to a rubber stamp. A planning department administrator described for us how this works in his city:

> Well, our conflict with the DPW is a little unequal. The
> public works director not only is one of the planning
> commissioners, he also sits on the board of estimates,
> which has a say over the budget of the planning depart-
> ment. By an unfortunate accident-on-purpose of timing,
> our review of his CIP coincides with his review of our
> budget! He usually gets whatever he wants.

As we have seen, the planning department has also traditionally encapsulated itself by steering clear of social planning, renouncing all decisions about programming as the un-
contested province of the operating agencies. Thus even
when planners make recommendations about the location of
schools, police stations, and city health facilities, they leave it
to the operating agencies to determine whether the schools
should remain open for community use in the evenings and
during the summer, whether law enforcement funds should
be spent on weapons or gang control programs, whether mobile medical units might reach more citizens than centralized
clinics. Many planners—even "old" planners whose training and definition of professionality emphasize physical land

use planning—chafe under these restrictions. "New" planners tend to favor alteration of the planning department's formal powers to increase its legitimate control over operating agencies. But given the planning department's present marginal status in city government, most staff members in the noncommunity planning sections of the department, however reluctantly, accept encapsulation as a necessary political expedient. We were told repeatedly, "The planning department has to work within the power structure, play ball, compromise."

Into this precariously balanced set of relationships between the encapsulated planning department and operating agencies, the community planners drop like invaders from another dimension. They are foredoomed to be disruptive, for unlike the rest of the planning staff, they find expansionism built into the very premises of their work. Planners in other sections of the department work in terms of *segmental responsibility*, each dealing episodically with limited aspects of the city's development. Because their contributions are made within the framework of a complicated division of labor, they can feel disassociated from the end product; if the city's problems remain unsolved, someone else is to blame. Even when sympathetic to expansionary "new" planning ideas, they can accept encapsulation as a necessary expedient without feeling personally threatened. But this psychological defense fails community planners, for they work in terms of *total responsibility* for their assigned areas. If urgent problems of any sort go unsolved in their areas, most of them feel a sense of failure; it matters little that some other city agency was supposed to be taking care of the problematic situation. Community planners define their task in terms of community needs, not feasibility or bureaucratic etiquette. The idea that they should ignore part of an interrelated system of needs to avoid offending touchy bureaucrats in the operating agencies strikes them as ridiculous and hypocritical. Accepting encapsulation, they feel, would be a cop-out.

Close contact with community residents, another unique feature of the community planning program, drives community planners even further into expansionism. Community residents are singularly unimpressed with the niceties of encapsulated planning. They expect "their" planner to help plan solutions for the problems that concern them most, regardless of agency jurisdiction. Summing up the common community attitude in a single doleful example, a community planner told us, "Everywhere I go, people ask me why their garbage isn't getting picked up!" Community residents also expect help with the implementation of plans that pertain to them, for to them, as another community planner explained:

> Planning and delivery are all part of the same thing. We have good relations with community groups in terms of planning, but when the work is taken over by the redevelopment authority for implementation and we're supposed to bow out, the community groups want us to hang in there—not abandon them.

In situations like this, community planners could fall back on encapsulation, explaining that they have nothing to do with the sanitation department's garbage collection schedules and that plans can be implemented only by an operating agency like redevelopment, housing, or Model Cities. But this explanation would lead them into what we have called the paradox of role restriction: by stressing their limitations, they would convince the community of their uselessness. Most community planners, taking the establishment of community rapport as the major challenge of their assignment, would far rather reject the encapsulated role itself. Thus they find themselves on a collision course with the operating agencies.

Friction between community planners and operating agencies is made all the more inevitable by the convoluted mechanisms through which state and federal urban development grants filter into the city bureaucracy. Since some state and most federal programs now require the filing of a plan reflecting some degree of citizen participation, it would seem reasonable to channel them all through the planning department and particularly through the community planning section of that department. However, this frail bit of logic is drowned out in the din of city agencies swarming around any new program, competing for control of it. For a city department, the capacity to bring in outside funds means more than mere access to additional money. Grants are understood by all to be the symbolic currency of respect and influence in city government, the very wellspring of agency power. One community planner put it succinctly:

> If the planner has his own federal money, he can more or less dictate what he wants. Even though the city council has a theoretical say, there's always the stick over their heads: if they don't approve the plan, they will lose out on the federal money. But when the planner doesn't have federal money, he must depend on other city departments. He's at their mercy. The worst is when the other departments have control of federal money themselves. Then they call the shots, and the planning department is nowhere.

In the cities we visited, we found major federal programs like the Neighborhood Development Program (NDP) and the Community Renewal Program (CRP), as well as smaller scale housing and park grants, all rolling around like juicy plums from department to department, located and transferred according to the dictates of local politics. Often they lodge someplace other than the planning department—in an existing operating agency, in a specially created ad hoc agency, or even split between the planning department and some other city agency. Since these programs require compliance with federal guidelines on planning and citizen participation, operating agencies that win control of them have to seek cooperation from community planners or create something resembling community planning with their own staff. In either case, community planners find themselves linked to the operating agencies in a shifting, overlapping, and conflict-filled network of duplicated effort and hazy authority. Describing the community planning tangle that has developed in his city, for example, a planning department administrator commented:

> We just had the housing department "borrow" some of our staff. I'm not happy about losing planners to them so they can expand. With the changing nature of planning in our department, toward district planning, it can only cause confrontation if other city departments start trying to do their own community planning. This is already happening with urban renewal. As that department [urban renewal] broadens itself out to include NDP, sending people into the community, it runs into our district planners who are already there. Other departments and us, we're all getting more involved in similar areas. The CRP is another area of overlap. It started out in this office, then the mayor formed a separate staff for it. He wanted to give high positions to some personal friends and also create a new department he could use to do a lot of odd jobs as well as the CRP. Now our district planners have to confront a new department doing basically the same thing they are.

In the fluid, multiple-agency systems set up to administer federal programs, authority and responsibility shift around like quicksilver. Many community planners themselves lose track of who controls what. This planner's confusion is typical:

> It's sometimes difficult for me to pin down the policy of the planning commission on various projects. This is one of my biggest problems. For instance, on this vestpocket

parks project I'm working on. It's a joint program of
HUD and the city, written up by the beautification department working with the cooperation of Model Cities.
Since I've been working with neighborhood groups in the
target area, I've gotten involved too. I don't know
whether I'm supposed to run the show or what. I'm the
community planner, but am I supposed to tell beautification what to do? Nobody can figure out who does what.
To make it worse, it seems to be left up to me to find
enough park sites by the deadline, but Model Cities won't
approve my sites unless all the adjoining residents accept
having a park next door to them. It'll be difficult for me
to do all the necessary contact work and even harder for
the beautification department to do it, because the residents distrust city people. But Model Cities won't help
because they say it's our job and why should they use
their resources to do it. The grant is for $300,000 and if we
don't submit contracts to HUD on time, we lose $21,000 a
month as a penalty. I don't know if the problem is duplicate
work or not enough work. I don't know how to play it. I
wonder if my contacts with the other groups involved
mean anything.

Another community planner told us almost in despair:

There's too much division. The department of parks,
public facilities, housing, building—they all do their
own planning. They are all involved in the same thing
we are involved in. I see duplication and competition and
things not getting done because of it. None of the right
hands know what the left hands are doing!

Obviously, this blurring of jurisdictional boundaries among
agencies administering community development grants further vitiates encapsulation as an option for community planners.

Thus the community planners—propelled by the special
nature of their responsibilities, their unusual exposure to community pressure, and the dynamics of community develop-

ment financing—are forced out of the planning department's traditional encapsulated framework. Even the more conservative of them end up engaging in an unprecedented amount of contact with the city's operating agencies as an unavoidable side-effect of community planning. Their work demands it; they have no choice.

The community planners' drift toward expansionism is not only *unavoidable* but also *irreversible*. Faith in the utility of encapsulated planning hangs by a fragile thread, sustained only by the conviction that its marginal influence on city development is better than nothing, or that an "invisible hand" somehow makes use of it in the grand scheme of things. Community planners, responsible for troubled communities in which encapsulated city planning clearly has little impact, can hardly escape questioning this faith. The scales, as it were, are ripped from their eyes whether they like it or not. And having once doubted that encapsulated planning accomplishes anything important, they can never again take it seriously.

The community planner's expansionism also tends to be *self-accelerating*. The more closely he examines the operating agencies' activities in his area, the more appalled he becomes at their mode of operation, and the more urgently he feels the need to put their functions under some kind of control. Almost with disbelief, community planners relate tale upon tale of how operating agencies bungle things and work against the interests of community residents. For instance:

> I know it sounds ridiculous for a coordinating agency, but it's only in the last few years that we've had much interaction with other city agencies. The more we see of them, the more we realize they don't do their work right. For example, the department of education doesn't have the faintest idea where it should put schools or what kind to put. . . . They're presently building an elementary school in a neighborhood where ten years from now

there won't be any schoolchildren. . . . They reinforce segregation, maybe without even knowing they're doing it.

Another planner said incredulously:

Our relations with the DPW [department of public works] are terrible. They decide things like straightening out a curved road requiring removal of 30 homes and a lot of 100-year-old trees as if arranging things neatly on a map were the most important consideration. They don't even inform us of what they're going to do, that's how far they are from planning. Right now the DPW wants to build an inner belt that would rip a stable black neighborhood in my area to shreds. They are actually planning to destroy a middle-class black neighborhood full of good houses! Good houses!

For community planners helplessly watching the consequences of such activities in their communities, expansionism comes to mean more than merely a desirable administrative reform. Their remarks about operating agencies take on an emotional undertone of righteous indignation; expansionism begins to sound like a holy crusade against the infidels. To understand this fury, we must recall that many community planners regard their work more as a vocation than a job. The attraction of the work is its presumed opportunity for creative public service; for many, it is simply an extension of previous interests in VISTA, the Peace Corps, even the priesthood. In almost identical words, community planners in every city we visited told us, "This kind of planning isn't just a job—it's my life." One spoke cheerfully of working till 5:00 A.M. out of sheer enthusiasm. Another, voicing the thoughts of many others, remarked, "Serving the community is a heavy thing—a profound, almost religious experience." To these ego-involved community planners, any operating agency that thwarts their fervent service orientation is a personal threat, a force of evil against which the planners must wage a just war.

So powerful is this sense of moral outrage that community planners usually must talk their way through several levels of invective and ad hominem attack before suggesting structural reasons for their inability to work cooperatively with the operating agencies. The first explanation takes place on what we might call the *jeering level*. This involves personal insults and name-calling focused on "the enemy's" incompetence and lack of imagination. The operating agencies' top management personnel are said to follow their present undesirable policies because they are "rednecks," or "pension types," or possessed of an "1890s mentality," or habituated to keeping "both hands up their ass." Their outlook is condemned as "complacent," "insufferably arrogant," "hidebound," "racist," and "dripping with middle-class bias." Personnel in the hated department of public works, as keepers of the streets that so many community planners blame for destroying communities, come in for special epithets such as "the gear heads" and "the road gang." "The head of the DPW is a typical engineer," we were told, "All he knows is how to pour concrete." One community planner describing the management of the department of education could hardly speak for laughing:

> No wonder I have problems with the department of education. All their middle management people are World War II types who went to second-rate land grant colleges. And the head of that department is a walking disaster. He's so lethargic, it's unbelievable. He's like a great tortoise. [Here the planner crosses his eyes and demonstrates with slow hand movements how a tortoise moves.] He's preposterous. His own staff laughs at him.

The second explanation for conflict, on the *fishy eye level*, involves attribution of the most ignoble motives imaginable to the operating agencies. For example, speaking of the department of education, a community planner suggested, "Whatever we recommend, they always say they can't do it, just to avoid extra work." We were told that the education department's personnel were unwilling to experiment with scattered classrooms because "they want something they can control, a building, so the kids can't escape their clutches." The parks department in one city was accused of vetoing additional parks because it didn't want to bother with the extra maintenance responsibilities even though it had the resources to provide them—in other words, because of sheer laziness. Some community planners hinted darkly at kickbacks, bribes, and other assorted corruption. One pointed out that in his city, the former head of the department of public works had retired to take over the presidency of a large sand and gravel company which had monopolized city contracts for years.

Although loath to abandon completely the comforts of "jeering" and the "fishy eye," most community planners eventually suggest that their differences with the operating agencies are rooted in the organization of city government, so that conflicts of interest would arise even if all concerned were mentally keen and morally pure. On this *structural level* of explanation, planners report four contradictions in basic approach that dig a yawning gulf between themselves and the operating agencies. These contradictions involve (1) multiple versus single-purpose objectives, (2) service versus unit-cost concern, (3) bureaucratic enfranchisement versus product delivery as the measure of success, and (4) "outside" versus "inside" reference groups. We shall examine each set of clashing assumptions in turn, to see why community planners are so firmly convinced that they and the operating agencies are pulling in different directions and must inevitably come into conflict.

Multiple Versus Single Purpose Objectives. Community planners generally consider operating agencies narrow in purpose. The housing department, organized around the single objective of increasing the supply of housing units, cares little about alternative land uses, the long-range viability of its housing, or the way housing fits into a community's perceived needs and priorities. The department of education's only interest is schools, not the social and physical relationship of schools to the rest of the community. The streets department concerns itself only with roadbuilding and speeding the traffic flow, not the social impact of one-way streets or the possibility of closing streets to make a mall or park.

Community planners, on the other hand, are dedicated to balancing multiple objectives, and therefore unwilling to concede automatic top priority to any single land use. Indeed, community planners usually favor combining land uses and opening facilities for multiple uses wherever possible—putting well-baby clinics in library basements, for instance, or opening schools in the evening and summers for community recreational and social use, or building day-care centers into apartment complexes. As one community planner summed up the difference in perspective:

> We have this big problem with the housing department. They have vested interests in putting up housing, so they push as hard as they can to use every vacant site for housing and only housing. But it's our function to push for the *best* use of the site for the community and the city, which might be recreation, or a school, or some combined use. With the streets department it's the same problem; same with recreation. Each has one goal, while we're trying to weigh the value of one kind of improvement against another.

Because of the incompatibility between the planners' multiobjective approaches and the predetermined priorities of the operating agencies, they often clash over the proper use of specific sites.

Service Versus Unit Cost Concern. Community planners perceive a fundamental contradiction between their goals and those of operating agencies. Operating agencies, they feel, tend to measure success *quantitatively* in terms of how much they can produce at the least cost in the least amount of time. Community planners, on the other hand, measure success *qualitatively* in terms of how well community needs and desires have been satisfied. Unfortunately the two concerns often dictate different policies, since the type of city facility or program with the lowest unit cost rarely coincides with the type preferred by the community.

Planners, tailoring their recommendations to fit urgent community needs, tend to favor experimentation and decentralization in the provision of city services and facilities. They report meeting constant opposition from conservative, "rigid" operating agencies on the grounds that such policies would push up unit cost. One planner told us:

> The parks and recreation department uses standards that are simply out of date; they refuse to try new innovations. My area needs recreation facilities desperately. Kids are playing in the middle of traffic because there's nowhere else they can go. I recommended that the city buy a few vacant buildings and make a tot lot. Or they could close some alleys and make a strip park. Or they could close off a street for recreational use from 9 to 4 in the summertime. Anything would be better than the present situation! But parks was dead set against it, because it was a new innovation. They don't want anything smaller than three acres in size, they said, because little parks on scattered sites are more expensive to maintain.

Another planner, speaking of the department of education, mourned:

> Some of our communities are four or five schools behind. They'll never catch up at this rate. The immediate need

is so great that we ought to try some weird things, like converting existing buildings into temporary classrooms. But the education department people scream at this. They see their job as producing "real" schools that can be run "efficiently."

Summing up the problem, a planner observed:

> There's a basic difference in the point of view of planning versus the operating agencies. You can see it in our relations with housing, the department of streets and traffic, the department of recreation, and so on. They want to develop more of the same kind of facilities they've used to meet needs in the past, because they can predict how much these things will cost to build and maintain. They're not interested in things that are different. They don't want to see things in stages, or fit what they're doing now into an overall system that might end up serving community needs better in the future. They're more anxious to follow old rules than new ideas, and they consider us idealistic and extravagant.

Ironically, planners point out, the operating agencies' fascination with unit cost can end up producing inefficiency in the long run. In several cities, planners related how the housing department ultimately defeated its own ends by choosing the cheapest possible sites for acquisition in order to keep unit cost down:

> HCD [the department of housing and community development] picks up houses for rehab purposes that are only ten feet wide! There's no demand for such tiny houses. No matter how much money they put into that kind of housing, it'll still be a piece of crap.

> Sometimes the housing department rehabs one house on a block that's being abandoned. Their rehabbed house ends up surrounded by vacant derelict houses and people are scared to live there.

The housing director's office is for hurrying projects along. They are under such tremendous pressure to put as many units together as possible that they follow the path of least resistance. They look for the sites where they can build the most units for the least cost. In a renewal area, they won't undertake to do a complete job in order to insure that their work will have a lasting effect. For example, if there's industrial property in the area, the housing department will generally build around the factory, because the cost of incorporating the expensive industrial property would push their unit cost up. Because of the tremendous pressure to put up the maximum number of units, they'd rather not spend extra money to take out factories. But what they don't realize is that old factories are the most blighting influence in the area, and that leaving them may destroy the whole project in the long run. Blight is like a cancer; either you get it all, or forget it.

Moreover, some point out, the housing department's concern for unit cost leads to a misguided enthusiasm for cheap-to-produce types of housing (such as housing for the elderly) to the exclusion of more urgently needed but costlier types of housing (such as units for large families). From the planner's service-oriented perspective, operating agencies acting in the name of efficient resource allocation almost invariably gravitate toward the most deplorably insensitive policies possible. Conflict, the planners say, must inevitably result.

Bureaucratic Enfranchisement Versus Product Delivery. Another difference in goals is commonly offered to explain the continual disagreements arising over the issue of citizen participation. The operating agencies, planners say, are organized for product delivery. To them, considering and responding to input from the amateurs who happen to live in the target area represent a waste of time. As one planner put it:

> Urban development is an operating agency. They are ac-
> tion oriented and don't want anything to stand in their
> way. Therefore they just don't buy citizen participation.

Another planner reported that in his city a group of operating agency heads in charge of a federal "interim assistance"
program had refused to have anything to do with the largest,
most militant community organization in his area. "They told
us," he said sadly, "that getting involved with neighborhood
groups meant getting burned for nothing."

The community planners' perspective, as we have seen,
could hardly be more different. They are concerned with ac-
tivating community residents, linking them up with city hall,
giving them a voice in deciding policies that affect their
neighborhood—in effect, bureaucratic enfranchisement. They
hold that "you have to work with the community to
get anything accomplished" and "to know people's needs you
have to consult them," but their commitment to citizen participation runs even deeper than these comments suggest. In
the view of most community planners, citizen participation
represents not a means to an end but the end itself. Delivery
of a tangible product, though important, is secondary. In fact,
as discussed in Chapter Five, for many community planners
the prime significance of product delivery is its key role in
arousing community interest and confidence, and thus sus-
taining a high level of citizen participation.

This clash of priorities, planners feel, automatically pits
them against the operating agencies. Highly critical of various agencies' "highhanded" treatment of community residents, some planners point out the dysfunctionality of this
"arrogance" for the operating agencies themselves. For example:

> Redevelopment is rarely in tune with community groups.
> Usually there's a complete breakdown of communication.

For instance, in the redevelopment plan that's affecting
my area, community groups couldn't get their hands on
the redevelopment authority's application until two days
before the city council meeting. When they saw it, they
were appalled. It was full of glaring errors, like showing
more blocks needing relocation than there are blocks in
the area! We quickly made a list of errors needing revision and embarrassed the redevelopment authority at the
council meeting. They needn't have put themselves in
that position. If they'd involved the community in the
first place, there would have been no problem. My area
residents wanted to work with them, and it would have
been so much easier for them. But they claimed that this
is the way we've done it before, and that the community
group wasn't capable of helping them with anything.
They missed the boat.

We heard numerous instances of ill will resulting from priority differences in the citizen participation issue, sometimes involving not only the community planners but the entire planning department as well. The following is a classic case:

Where does planning end and implementation take over?
How much change can the department of urban development make in the original plan for reasons of implementation? That's where the battle shapes up. We
have an urban development director who feels that planning is subservient to implementation; that if he feels
plans are not feasible, they can be changed or disregarded. He says to himself, "Hell with planning, we'll
change it when we get to implementation!" This is disastrous for our community contact work. We deal with
community residents in making up the plan now. When
the carefully negotiated plan is changed in its final stages
without community participation, the residents get mad
at our department. They feel we made promises that
aren't getting carried out. But if our department director
objects to urban development about the plan changes,
he's called an "obstructionist," a "goody-goody." They
tell him, "You think too much of your community people

and not enough about the hard facts of the cost of development." He's the first to admit he's getting treated like
the proverbial horse's banana, but he's not willing to put
his job on the line to fight for our community-based plan.

"Outside" Versus "Inside" Reference Group.   As community planners see it, they and the operating agencies are both
deeply involved in local politics, but in profoundly different
and incompatible ways because they do not share the same
reference group. The heads of the larger operating agencies,
as line personnel administering major portions of city funds,
often occupy strong positions in the city's power structure.
As political appointees who in turn control large numbers of
jobs, they are usually intimately tied into the patronage system. Some have personal political ambitions. According to
planners, this membership in the city's power elite produces
in the operating agencies an abiding sense of loyalty to an
"inside" reference group: the incumbent city administration
and its primary supporters.

Planners, working in a staff agency with negligible political
clout, feel much greater responsibility to "outside" reference
groups. For planners in general, this reference group tends to
be the planning department itself if they are local in orientation, and a national or international body of professional
peers if they are cosmopolitan in orientation. For those working as community planners, the reference group is usually the
most "outside" of all: city residents with a history of almost
total exclusion from direct participation in the formation of
city policies. Because of this basic difference in reference
groups, the community planners say, they and the operating
agencies are natural adversaries.

As we have seen, the dynamics of community contact
work seem to require that community planners disassociate
themselves from city hall. Far from viewing members of the
city's power structure as a reference group, they work as ad-

ministrative guerrillas to alter or subvert city policies when those policies seem inimical to community residents' interests. To illustrate what they are "up against," a number of community planners told us how the activities of operating agencies were "distorted by politics." One, for instance, told us of how the site was selected for a large sports stadium being built in his area of the city:

> Choosing the stadium site was never seen as a planning issue. From the beginning, strong political forces were at work. As the district planner for the area where it was going to go, I should have been involved in picking the site; but I was never consulted. The director of urban development didn't care what planning said; all he wanted was to make a splash, to build it in a central, highly visible location so that he could proudly point to what he had accomplished. The site they ended up selecting was all wrong. It's located near a stable middle-class neighborhood, which will be broken up by its construction. This contradicts the city's goal of hanging onto its middle-class residents—as if they weren't leaving fast enough already! The planning director was at the meeting where the final site was chosen; they tried to exclude him, but he heard about it via the grapevine and practically barged in. But there was nothing he could do. The developer made an appallingly unprofessional presentation of what he wanted to do with the site. The director of urban development doesn't know anything about planning policy, so it sounded good to him. He approved it, making all kinds of horrible concessions without knowing what the consequences would be, and that was that. The planning director didn't have the heart to even get involved; he saw he couldn't change anybody's mind. He left, with a gut response of disgust.

Another community planner related the political obstacles she faced in getting a large wooded area in her community developed in the way desired by the residents. The site was being bid on by a developer whose proposed housing plans were highly unpopular in the community. The planner herself felt that the developer's project would be "horrible," a "rape of a uniquely beautiful site." As discussed earlier, she and the community residents were working to get the department of education to adopt the site for a regional high school, to "save" it from the developer. However, she told us sadly:

It's a real question whether the mayor and his operating agencies think the planning department has any role at all to play in this decision. We've gotten the word that the developer involved is a major contributor to the mayor's campaign fund, and that's how come the decision to let him go ahead with his project was made. We aren't going to have a major effect on the decision directly. The only way we could influence it is if the mayor can be made to feel he has to compromise between the developer and his money on the one hand and the possible loss of votes from angry residents on the other.

Another community planner complained bitterly:

The established power structure is my biggest problem in working for the community's welfare. There are nine men who run this city, and they determine what gets done, particularly by the operating agencies. I've felt the effect of this in my district. Three blocks of it lie between the CBD [central business district] and a large urban renewal project area. I've been going to community meetings to plan for these three blocks; we've been talking about making them residential, or even using it for a park. All of a sudden, word started coming down that the Nuts & Bolts Company, the Chamber of Commerce, and Buymore Department Store all wanted those three blocks used for CBD purposes. The project director of my community task force told me he overheard five men high in the power structure having lunch with the director of urban development. They told him not to let those blocks go residential because they didn't want blacks downtown. It's still hanging in the balance, shaping up for a real fight. I'm hoping that the pressure on the city council from the power structure can be outweighed by pressure from community residents.

Combined, these four basic contradictions lead expansionary community planners to interpret their mission as one of confounding the departments of public works, urban renewal, housing, education, parks and recreation, and so on. As one community planner put it enthusiastically, "We're out to undermine the operating agencies. We're trying to force them to disperse their operations into the neighborhood." He added with some satisfaction, "Most of the other departments of the city are all worked up over area planning. They don't like it. They say we're stirring up the neighborhood and putting sawdust in the wheels of progress. When we hear that, we know we're getting somewhere!"

Ten

Tempting the Fates:
The Problem of Bureaucratic
Backlash

At this point, we must step back and examine what happens when community planners try to put their expansionist ideas into practice. How do they fare when they invade the turf of the operating agencies, which wait like bureaucratic Goliaths—bigger, more powerful, and far better armed with the administrative weapons of seniority, formal authority, and informal links to the city's power structure? The community planners are, after all, relatively young, usually new to the city's bureaucratic system, isolated and low in status even within their own department, and both formally and informally expected to adhere to encapsulated planning. Under these conditions, what form does their expansionism take?

Direct Confrontation

It seems reasonable to expect that community planners
would avoid direct confrontation—a form of administrative
insurgency—in favor of more covert forms of conflict, taking discretion to be the better part of valor. But this is not always the case. Some direct confrontations are forced on the
planner. For instance, when a community planner engages
community residents in drawing up a plan for their neighborhood, the plan naturally focuses on the services and facilities
the residents consider most problematic; this pushes the planner across the invisible line guarding the jurisdiction of the
operating agencies. Discovery of the "trespass" by the personnel of the operating agencies can mean an open outbreak of
hostilities, as in this case:

> I have continual problems with other city agencies that
> are jealous of their own power. This came clear with my
> back-alley project, which the streets department felt was
> an infringement of their authority. I had to be terribly
> cautious in dealing with that department; it was a person-
> ality thing. They're dead set against what community
> planners are doing. What happened was, I'd been work-
> ing with the community residents in my area on a plan
> to clear the trash out of their backyards and alleys and
> use the land for recreational purposes. But it turns out
> that the streets department considers this a problem of
> solid waste disposal—their province—and they really
> resented us making plans for their trash. I happened to
> mention to a guy in the streets department that I was
> working on the trash problem in back alleys, and he just
> exploded. He started yelling at me "What do you mean,
> the trash problem in back alleys? Our department takes
> care of that!" I replied very seriously, "We're all in it
> now. Haven't you heard about the mayor's WAR ON
> DIRT?" It was a pretty snappy comeback, but that's
> about all I can do: become witty, sarcastic, and cynical.

> The head of the streets department has all the power.
> Other city departments around here can put us commu-
> nity planners down in real ways. It's not just comments
> on our long hair; they can really block us.

In working out their area plans the community planners frequently request information from the operating agencies concerning their services and facilities. This simple contact often
flares up into bitter confrontation because some of the data
that planners ask for are political dynamite. For instance,
they seek information about the school system that could be
used to blast the department of education for dragging its feet
on racial integration, information from the building department that could be used to charge laxity and favoritism in
code enforcement, information from urban renewal that
could reveal shortcomings in the implementation of its relocation programs. Administrators in some operating agencies,
fearful (with good reason) that information given to community planners may be leaked to the public or the press, take
offense at even being asked to give out such data. Planners
need the information, so they persist; the personnel of the operating agencies grow increasingly exasperated at being pes-
tered for information they have every intention of keeping
secret; and a showdown finally results. One community planner told us:

> About three-fourths of the operating agencies won't give
> me any information. I ask, they refuse. Relations are ter-
> rible. When I do get information, it's either (a) true but
> not useful or (b) useful, but I can't be sure it's true!

Another recounted:

> I ran into a real hornet's nest in the building department
> shortly after I came here. I wanted to see the ordinance
> and maps that were in effect in the 1950s and early 1960s
> in my area. The information wasn't politically sensitive

or anything; in fact, it was utterly harmless. I just wanted to see it. A fellow in graphics took me down to see a guy in the building department who knew about these maps. I started asking him questions and he answered a few. Then suddenly he blew up. He dumped all his hostility on me. He screamed, "Get out of here, you son of a bitch. I'm sick of you area planners. I'll be damned if I'll give you any information!" I've come to expect this kind of reaction now, and it's unfortunate, because it makes me reluctant to call on people in other departments for information I need. I know I won't be able to get information from them.

In addition to these unavoidable clashes, some community planners volunteer advice to operating agencies openly even when they anticipate a hostile reception. They argue that their contact with the community has shown them things the operating agencies must be told, whatever the consequences. Like sighted persons trying to warn ill-tempered blind men of an impending disaster, they feel a responsibility that transcends caution and etiquette. A community planner who was notorious in his department for warring openly with operating agencies summed up his reasons this way:

We have a special responsibility because we're the only city agency with people out in the street trying to get feedback from the community residents. As area planners, we're like extrasensory devices. None of the other agencies has any way to get the insight into what's needed. Only we can bring back this information on the people's total experience of living in this city. Because of this we have a vital role to play, whether it's appreciated or not. We have to let the city know what's happening out there.

This sense of responsibility for educating the operating agencies about community sentiments leads some planners to initiate confrontations despite their relatively weak position.

For instance, one community planner we talked to had been openly opposing a site plan developed jointly by the departments of parks, education, and urban development. The plan concerned a school and park complex in this planner's area. For what he considered political reasons, the three operating agencies were proposing to locate the school on one side of a major traffic artery and the park on the other. He pointed out:

> There are serious flaws in their proposal. They'll have to build a bridge across the highway, and the kids in my area don't like the idea of a bridge. They won't use it. So in effect the two facilities won't be linked, even though they look close on a map. It doesn't have to be put together so stupidly. They have plenty of land to do it right if they wanted to. They just don't understand how wrong they are.

His attempts to get the operating agencies to reconsider their site plan grew so troublesome that he was told by two political aides of the urban development director to stay away from the city council meeting when the plan came up for a vote. After much soul searching he reluctantly agreed not to attend, fearing repercussions on the planning department if he "disobeyed." Asked why he had chosen to bring down such wrath on his head by challenging the operating agencies openly, he explained:

> It's just so tough to take, when you see your analyses being dismissed for political reasons. As a district planner, I see more of the situation in the community than anybody in the operating agencies. They're not always right; in fact, as in this case, they may be tragically wrong. The fact that we have had so many problems in the city in the past should show them they need a planner who knows something about how the community feels. The operating agencies don't understand the problems of the city and don't want to. For them, everything is expedi-

ence. But as long as they don't listen, and keep going for poor solutions, the crises of the city will continue. I felt I had to try.

Another planner told us of confronting an operating agency to try to stave off possible violence from an outraged community:

> Medical services are a big issue in my community. I worked with a community task force on designing a health program for the East End. When it was done, we sent it to the health commission and the city manager. The health department exploded. They said the proposal was illegal, infeasible, and don't send any more. A few months later I did some more health planning and sent it on to them. This time the director of the health department called me personally into his office to explain his philosophy. He wouldn't give an inch. His basic objection was over community involvement; he didn't want any citizen participation in health programming for the East End. I tried to explain to him why I was bugging his department. He doesn't know it, but his method of doing things is inflaming the community. The people are talking about bombing the health department because they feel they aren't getting the proper kind of health programming. I'm trying to bring community groups and the health department together before something violent happens. So far my warning hasn't had any effect on the health department, but I can't just give up.

Does direct confrontation produce any significant results? Most community planners say no. In a few instances we found that community planners' unsolicited advice to operating agencies was having some impact on policy, usually where the planning department's management had been willing to throw their weight behind the community planners' suggestions. Occasionally, on the recommendation of planners, experiments in combining facilities administered by different agencies were being tried or a community council was being given a voice in setting hours for a multipurpose center. But since these situations generally involve minor service innovations in areas that pose a credible riot threat, planners tend to interpret them as placatory tokens of responsiveness rather than meaningful ventures into citizen participation by the operating agencies concerned. Planners are convinced that such arrangements, hedged with cautionary phrases such as "subject to budget limitations," will collapse just as soon as the operating agency involved feels pushed further than it expected to go. Examples of such breakdowns crop up frequently enough in the planners' scuttlebutt to indicate a high level of cynicism about operating agencies' voluntary concessions to direct planning intervention in their affairs. Here is a typical story:

> We had a lot of trouble recently. One of the area planners worked out a plan with [the department of] public facilities to let the Model Cities council determine what they wanted for their area's recreation needs. Everybody was pleased with the idea. We thought they'd want a play area, a tot lot or something. Ha! They asked for an Olympic-sized swimming pool! The public facilities people were aghast and said that was too expensive. They backed out. They felt betrayed, and so did the community. We should have known it wouldn't work.

In general, community planners view direct confrontation as a low-yield mode of expansionism as long as the city charter gives the lion's share of formal authority to the operating agencies; covert means of expansionism, they feel, accomplish more with fewer hazards. Each time a community planner comes to this conclusion, of course, the community planning pressure system has produced another administrative guerrilla.

Underground Expansionism

Having decided to pursue their expansionism covertly as administrative guerrillas, community planners' first task is to find a means of sleuthing out the secret information they cannot extract from the operating agencies directly. The planner may try to glean information himself through some subterfuge. For example, the planner may try to disguise his identity, as in this case:

> I called the metropolitan district commission and asked them about their policies on using some of the land in their reserve area to deal with the community's school problems. Before giving me any information, they asked who I was. I decided not to identify myself. If they knew I was the community planner in their reserve area, it would raise more problems than it would solve. No one knew I was making this call. I didn't want to complicate the planning director's problems by looking like a spy. So I let them think I was just an interested citizen.

Or the planner may disarmingly conceal his motives for seeking information, hoping to relax the guard of the operating agencies' staff:

> I have a problem with an urban renewal project in my district, Old Fishmarket. A number of interesting old buildings, reasonably sound community landmarks, are slated to come down. The housing department doesn't want to reclaim any old buildings for residential use—too expensive, they say. They're utterly insensitive; they don't care if it's a loss to the community. I've been given the forms to fill out—our department "reviews" the proposal—but it's a farce because I don't have the information I'd need to revise the plan. And if housing thinks I'm after information for purposes of revising their plan, they won't give it to me. What I'm going to do is

go around to people in the various operating agencies involved and say I need more information in order to fill
out the forms. Maybe once I get my hands on more complete data, I can figure out a way to save those old buildings.

Since this kind of personal artful dodging is relatively ineffective, the administrative guerrillas also try to establish an
interagency underground based on ties with staff members in
the operating agencies themselves. Fortunately for the planners' purposes, the operating agencies are far from mono-
lithic. Many of them are experiencing internal revolts, reorganization drives on the part of junior staff members, and
factionalism over policy issues somewhat analogous to the
"old planning" versus "new planning" split described for the
planning department in Chapter Seven. For instance, a planner told us:

> The director of public facilities is openly hostile and jeal-
> ous of the planning department. I mean openly; he tells
> off planners in public—even Joe, the director—using
> the foulest possible language. But there are members of
> his staff that are on our side. They feel our department
> should do the planning for public facilities. They even
> went to see him as a group to voice concern about the
> lack of communication between the planning department
> and public facilities. This gives us hope, and we keep nib-
> bling away.

In this yeasty context, community planners usually can find
enough secret allies to serve as a useful informer system, or as
one planner put it, a "spy network." Once established, the interagency underground becomes the foundation of an administrative guerrilla's expansionist activities. Here a planner describes how part of his underground works:

> The public relations director over in the department of
> public facilities gives me information, covers up for my

community activities, and tells me how we can shoot
down their director and get him to reverse his stands. I
call this guy up daily.

The interagency underground also provides a vehicle
through which the community planner can smuggle ideas and
information into the operating agencies without having them
stigmatized by their origin in the planning department. This
procedure eases the way for such innovations as the operating
agencies' experiments (albeit token) in multiuse facilities and
limited citizen participation discussed earlier.

Armed with inside information and a means of lessening resistance in the operating agencies, the administrative guerrilla
can then go on to utilize his community underground. As discussed in Chapter Five, pressure from mobilized community
groups is the administrative guerrilla's prime weapon against
the operating agencies. Through the tactics we described
earlier—"gratitude traps," the "democratic blitz," and the
"symbolic holocaust"—the planner stages battlefield encounters between his community's residents and the operating agencies, in which the operating agencies are sometimes
forced to alter their policies. This covert strategy, by far the
most popular and successful mode of expansionism among
community planners, allows the planner to borrow political
muscle from his community residents. Bolstered by their double underground, the planners may in rare cases even channel
their expansionism into administrative insurgency, in the form
of a public crusade against the operating agencies.

Containment and Camouflage

How does the planning department management react to the
community planners' clashes with operating agencies? The
answer is complex. Not all of the administrators we talked to

are themselves happy with the department's encapsulated role in city government. Those on the middle levels of management particularly sometimes sound almost as expansionary as the community planners. We found many planning administrators speaking of the operating agencies as "the enemy forces," and telling us proudly of "battles" and "wearing down the opposition." This associate director's expansionary sentiments, for instance, would seem to put him on the community planners' side:

> We're bound to get into the hair of operating agencies. They see our suggestions as getting in their way. They think we should be restricted to physical planning. When we put out a plan for the kind of health services the city should have recently, that got them upset. They only wanted sites from us. But their view is short range and operational, not comprehensive; they can't do general planning. They're concerned with efficiency, not coordination and relating their programs to the larger problems of the city. If we don't get into doing the general planning for them, it won't get done. In the long run we will have to get into the operating budget. I see planning in the future as having to get into PPBS [Program Planning and Budgeting Systems, a scheme for coordinating and evaluating the activities of operating agencies]. The basic problems of the city are social, not physical. We have to get into unemployment problems, job training, and so on—not just site selection for industry. We have to get into crime prevention. Even in housing, there are a lot of nonphysical aspects that we as planners should be dealing with. We'll have a lot of conflict, but we're gradually moving into more PPBS work with operating agencies.

Despite this high-level sympathy for expansionism, we also found in every planning department we visited a deep sense of apprehension about community planners' hostile encounters with the operating agencies. Planning department administrators tend to feel that their own expansionism is "responsible" and that of the community planners "irresponsible." The administrators see themselves as agency loyalists, whose career interests and professional accomplishments are linked to the fate of the department. They stop their expansionism short of jeopardizing the department's budget and informal influence with the city's executive office. They take pains to cover their tracks and conciliate as they go along. The volatile group of young planners that make up the community planning staff, on the other hand, cannot be counted on to show such a fine sense of discretion. For most of them, community service takes precedence over the security of the planning department they are so loosely attached to. As one administrator told us in dismay, "When the chips are down, district planners seem perfectly willing to get the department in trouble." From the administrators' point of view, this kind of reckless expansionism is intolerably dangerous for the planning department. Therefore community planners must be restrained.

As we saw in Chapter Eight, however, the planning department's controls over the community planning staff are too weak to deter them from attacking the operating agencies. "Control by training," even when temporarily effective, almost invariably gives way in the face of community pressure to make such attacks. "Control by inertia," even if ultimately successful in thwarting the community planner's expansionism, fails to prevent his attacks. And "operational controls" tend to have the effect not of blocking the community planners' expansionism but rather of shifting it from direct confrontation to more covert forms of expansionism less hazardous to the department. In the departments we observed, operational control efforts centered on two general policies, *containment* and *camouflage*. In effect, although few administrators we talked to thought of it in this light, both policies are designed to encourage administrative guerrilla tactics.

The aim of *containment*, favored by "old planning" administrators unsympathetic or fearful toward expansionism, is to minimize the community planners' contacts with operating agencies. By this policy, official interagency contacts are restricted to those who can be trusted not to endanger the department with reckless action. For reasons of containment, for instance, community planners may find themselves barred from important meetings even when the subject under discussion is the community planner's own project. Here is one such case:

> I've been spending all my time for the last three weeks on outlining a position on a piece of land in my area, 30 acres zoned for high-rise housing. A developer wants to put up 1200 units. But my community has a greater need for schools, and in their interests the land should be used for three school sites. Especially since few of them could afford this housing developer's rents and wouldn't benefit from the housing he would build, but might have to absorb kids from the new housing into their already overcrowded schools! It's been great working out a plan for this. It's the kind of thing I came here to do. But I haven't had any meetings with the department of public facilities. The chief of the community planning section did this. Even though I'm most familiar with the problem, I'm a step below and not supposed to speak for the department. Last night there was a meeting in my community with people from some operating agencies and politicians from the city council. I was told not to go. The planning director was afraid they would attack me as a member of planning and I wouldn't say the right things.

Similarly, community planners may be restrained from establishing official links with other agencies' personnel even on a volunteer basis, as in this case:

I've been trying to make the city more aware of ecological issues. I started a group of people—planners here in the department—as an ecological task force. We met at my place. I was chairman. I started making contact with other agencies underground and started talking with a research scientist in an operating agency. His job had to do with air pollution management, and it turned out that he had been trying without success to contact people in the planning department for a year and a half. That convinced me that coordination was the most important issue. People in different agencies weren't talking to one another. I wrote some memos to the planning director and associate director asking that some staff time be allotted for people from the ecological task force to interview people from other agencies and concerned community groups. This was immediately ruled out. It seems they had been getting nervous ever since our group got started. I was told that only senior staff, section chiefs or higher, could make initial contacts with operating agencies. I was an "unknown quantity" and could not represent the city planning department to other agencies. I was withdrawn from the ecological task force.

Formal banishment from the ecological task force of course did not prevent this planner from pursuing his project. He simply went deeper underground as an administrative guerrilla and concealed his subsequent information exchanges with other agencies' personnel and with community groups. To understand why such an outcome satisfies the planning department management, we must recall that the goal of controlling the community planners is to protect the planning department, not the other agencies. Planning administrators only wish to avoid having the community planners' expansionism laid at the planning department's doorstep. Thus driving them underground is all that is necessary.

Unfortunately for the administrators, as we mentioned before, enforcing the operational controls that go into a policy of containment carries a high price when applied to a mobile staff. This point was painfully apparent in one department we visited, where containment efforts included strict mail censorship. The planning director, bent on restricting interagency contacts to the "proper channels" at any cost, enlisted the department's secretaries as informers to enforce the policy of censorship. His system worked this way:

> I control all incoming and outgoing mail. All mail gets opened and reviewed. Betty, my secretary, goes through all the mail and brings anything odd to my attention. Everything that goes out gets checked. Anyone who writes a memo going outside the department is to put it in the box for review. Copies of all in-house memos are sent to me as well. If any of the outgoing mail doesn't bear my countersignature, it's sent to me to be signed. If a letter is sealed so it can't be checked, we tear it up. I haven't had to do this often, but I have done it. People try to get around the rule by hand-carrying mail, but I find out. The secretaries let me know. The other day Alice tried to get something out without me seeing it; she told the secretary not to send it to me. But I was informed, and stopped it.

Most of the community planners in this department dodged the censorship simply by typing their own letters to evade secretarial surveillance and exchanging information secretly with their unauthorized contacts in other agencies. Some avoided using their office telephones for fear someone might be listening in on another extension; when they wanted to make unauthorized calls, they used the pay phones down the hall. However, such ill will was bred by the distrust and professional disrespect implied in censorship that the containment policy itself became the focus of administrative guerrilla activity.

At the time we visited this department, a group of incensed

community planners was holding secret evening meetings to
plot methods of subverting the censorship. One of the ring-
leaders (the "Alice" of the preceding quote), at whose apartment the meetings were taking place, told us that she had
reached the point of insurgency over the containment issue:

> I've been censored, told to speak softly, seen my propos-
> als watered down to the point where I won't take it any
> more. Like the housing thing I did. I was forced to water
> it down so that it came out vague and innocuous. The
> original was really good—hard hitting and useful. So I
> disregarded orders not to show it to anybody. I gave it to
> people in some business and industry groups for com-
> ment. I also took it around to some other departments.
> The director found out. He was pretty unhappy about
> if—said I'd better not do it again. I smiled a big nasty
> smile and told him I didn't need to circulate it any more
> because I'd already shown it to everyone I could think
> of! We really had a falling out over it. I'm so disgusted
> that I'd rather take these risks even if I lose my job.
> There's always the chance I may succeed in influencing
> something for the better; that means a lot more to me
> than kissing ass around this department. I can always get
> a job somewhere else if I have to.

Turnover in the community planning staff was higher here
than in any other planning department we contacted—the
price of controlling a highly mobile staff. In trying for total
containment, the department's managers succeeded in transforming some of the community planners from open expan-
sionists to devious administrative guerrillas. But this was accomplished at the cost of driving out some of the most
talented community planners, those who could most readily
get jobs elsewhere.

In the policy of *camouflage*, undertaken by planning administrators more sympathetic toward expansionism (or less
willing to pay the high turnover price of containment), community planning activities that antagonize the operating agen-

cies are disguised and concealed. Again, as in containment, the community planner is driven underground—but this time with the knowledge and approval of his department's management. Administrators following the camouflage policy tacitly (rarely explicitly) strike a "camouflage bargain" with their community planners: if the community planners will pursue their expansionism covertly and thus avoid embarrassing the department, the department administrators will give them a free hand and cover up for them. In effect, the community planner agrees to act as an administrative guerrilla and the department management agrees to harbor him. Where this policy predominates, we find planning administrators and senior staff deflecting and absorbing pressure from disgruntled operating agencies without passing it on directly to the community planners whose activities are responsible. "Hell yes, there's pressure from the operating agencies because of my work," grinned one community planner who was regarded by admiring work mates as his department's most accomplished administrative guerrilla. "The phone is jumping off the director's desk! But he takes care of it for me. My only problem is building enough community counterpressure to keep my plans from getting cut down in the council." Another community planner told how a middle-level administrator camouflaged him more thoroughly than the director was willing to:

> Ronald, my immediate supervisor, takes care of any flak with the director. The director gets all the fire from the operating agencies whose toes we step on, and he sometimes gets nervous. But Ronald insulates us. He doesn't like anyone hassling us. He says to us, "You have to be building your pile of coal out in the community; you can't get involved in this internal politics stuff."

These two operational control policies, containment and camouflage, always occur in combination in a department.

The policy most favored by the director sets the basic tone, but individual administrators within the department— associate directors, assistant directors, and section chiefs— differ enough to provide a counterpoint. Thus even in the most containment-oriented department we visited (the one with mail censorship), we were told by a community planner:

> After a while you know there are certain individuals in the administration that will block certain kinds of recommendations and actions, and others who will push what you're doing or help you do it indirectly. So you know to go through certain individuals and go around others.

Similarly, even in the most camouflage-oriented department in the study, new or "untrustworthy" community planners were contained until they convinced the director or some other administrative sponsor that their guerrilla skills merited camouflage.

In addition, both policies occur side by side because the administration's willingness to camouflage has definite limits. When a community planner drifts too close for comfort to open expansionism in the form of direct confrontations with operating agencies, his administrative protectors may demand that he retreat further underground, with the implied threat of containment if he fails to cooperate. For example, a middle-level administrator remarked:

> Area planners and people in the operating agencies turn each other off in direct contacts. I hear complaints, especially from the streets department, about how a new area planner is coming in and advising them what to do. The new area planners don't know any better yet. This kind of thing makes the engineers in streets yell bloody murder. Guys in other departments come to some of us they know because we've been here a long time, like them. They come up and say, "What is it with that crazy area

planner?" When a guy from another department comes to me, I try to soothe his hurt feelings and explain the approach of the area planner in a way that doesn't threaten him. Then later I caution the area planner about giving other departments the idea that we are trying to run their show. They can't come out in the open like that.

One particularly energetic administrative guerrilla told us of how the planning director held him to his "camouflage bargain" when his underground activities became too visible. This planner had successfully used his double underground to mobilize political opposition to a pet project of the department of public works, a parkway connector between two superhighways. He had leaked secret information gained from his interagency underground, publicized "public secrets" like the time and place of hearings on the parkway, and schooled the protesting citizens in the most effective demands to make. With his help, community groups were able to force modifications in the DPW's proposed design for the parkway. When the DPW later attempted to disregard the agreed-on design and quietly widened the proposed right of way by an additional 20 feet, the community planner was ready again. Under his guidance, the community demanded the second public hearing they were legally entitled to in order to debate the new proposal, swamped their councilmen with protests, and forced the DPW to revert to the original plan. Unused to such alert and well-informed community opposition, DPW administrators set about identifying the source of their problems through their own interagency underground. Once they fixed the blame, they pressured the planning director to contain his troublesome community planner who was "interfering with street construction." Reportedly, the director of the DPW phoned the planning director with instructions to "call off your dogs, or else." So the planning director called

the offending community planner in for a war council. The
community planner told us:

> The DPW began to see me as their big problem, which
> of course I was. They called up the director about it, and
> complained that I had encouraged a mail drive against
> them. They accused me of writing the letter. This wasn't
> exactly true, but I was present when it was written and
> did encourage its writing. The director was afraid I was
> getting too obvious. He reminded me that the planning
> department could get its budget cut, and that since he
> was giving me time and resources to organize the com-
> munity, I had a responsibility to do it in a way that
> wouldn't hurt the department. He suggested that I sit
> back and take it easy, and let the people fight it. That's
> what I was doing anyway, so I guess what he was really
> saying was that I should cover my tracks better.

When a community planner working in a camouflage-oriented department takes up the banner of administrative insurgency in defense of his community, the planning department's policy shifts to all-out containment. If containment
proves impossible, the planner is dropped from the staff, for
department administrators feel they cannot countenance such
dangerous activity. If the administrative insurgent's civil service status protects him from being fired, he will be systematically denied promotions, raises, access to department meetings and department resources, and in general encouraged to
leave on his own. For this reason, as we have seen, administrative insurgency is undertaken only rarely, in extreme situations and by planners indifferent to the threat of being fired
or forced to resign. Most administrative guerrillas keep their
covert expansionism well under cover in containment-oriented departments, or they keep the "camouflage bargain" in
camouflage-oriented departments. Testing the limits but staying within them, they channel their efforts into ever more
creative administrative guerrilla tactics.

Bureaucratic Backlash

Now we must turn to a bitter irony. It would seem that administrative guerrilla tactics serve the individual community planner well, especially in a camouflage-oriented planning department. The planner's use of the double underground allows him to win expansionist victories over the operating agencies and deliver benefits to his community's residents at a level out of his reach by any other means available without structural changes in the city administrative system. But the cumulative effect of individual planners' successes may well doom the community planning program. No matter how well individual administrative guerrillas cover their tracks, there is no way they can hide the consequences of their work. As long as their victories remain sporadic and their prizes small, and only a few administrative guerrillas operate in a small number of communities, they can escape detection or pose as a relatively limited annoyance if discovered. The city administrators may reason that some community pressure is to be expected, and that having it channeled and controlled by members of the planning staff is beneficial. But as the community planning staff grows larger and busier, and community skirmishes against the city's operating agencies begin to draw blood (or rather, funds), community planners are regarded with an ever more jaundiced eye. It becomes obvious that rather than aiding the city in placating its inflamed populace, community planners are masterminding the citizens' attacks. Faced with limited resources to meet the citizens' unlimited and escalating demands, the alarmed city government reacts. It calls a halt to the community planning experiment.

Does this dismal outcome inevitably befall community planning programs that begin to realize the disruptive potential implicit in this type of planning? Our observations indicate that the answer is probably yes. We found a direct relationship: the greater the number of active administrative guerrillas in a planning department's community planning program, the more talk we heard about threatened cuts in the department's budget. In the three departments we visited where the community planning program was relatively new or small in staff, many planners glowingly described the city executive's enthusiasm for the experiment. As we moved to departments with larger community planning staffs including many active administrative guerrillas, apprehension began to creep into planners' remarks about the city executive. After exulting over a recent triumph by his community "troops," a planner in one such department told us, "There's a rumor that the district planning budget is going to be cut." In another department, a camouflage-oriented associate planning director confided, "Area planners must do more than just physical planning, but we have to be awfully careful. Things are getting tense. It might kill area planning if we do too much."

One department we visited had gone over the brink; its community planning program had been abolished. From a peak of thirteen full-time staff positions devoted to community planning the previous year, this department's program had been cut down to two staff members working on a single community project (located in the area with the highest riot potential). Most of the former community planners were still around, reassigned to other duties. When asked what had happened, they all gave basically the same answer: community planning had been stopped because the growing number of successful administrative guerrilla actions had rendered the program intolerable to the city government. Here are some of their comments:

> The city general management service was responsible for the budget cut that killed community planning. They were given the word by the city council to limit our department's involvement with the community, because we

were stirring up the people. The people were becoming aware of their problems. We turned the community on. We showed them they could petition and get changes. The city council was being swamped by demands for planning assistance, and also for new facilities, better housing, and so on. This city is hurting, it has no money. So the council felt, since they didn't have the money to deal with the problems people wanted solved, they better at least cut out this community planning stuff that was getting people so excited.

Community planning got shot down here because it was creating activist groups which were being staffed by city employees—us, that is. We caused controversy between the public and the city; we created turmoil. The city administration didn't go along with this. The people started making demands for meetings with the mayor and council, and started asking the operating agencies questions about their policies on everything from parks to welfare. The mayor and council felt we were feeding the community people these questions concerning social problems. Of course, we were doing exactly that! We talked to the people about physical and social planning of their communities, and then they carried their demands to the council and mayor. The city couldn't meet their needs, so they shot us down instead.

Two years ago, when faced with community pressure, the council believed that the way to reduce this pressure was to give the people some community planning service. This worked great for two years; it stalled the community while they worked out their plans with us. Now the two years are over and the community is saying, "OK, here's our plan. Implement it." The city is horrified. They say, "We have no money, we just had a strike, we can't do it. . . ." Now that we aren't helping them stall anymore, we're a threat. So all community planning has been stopped.

The planning director of this department gave us his own version of the demise of community planning, with much the same interpretation:

When we were forced to taper off the program, it was really going well. For the first time community people were seeing the light on how to improve their own communities. With the support of citizens' groups, I went to the city council for a larger appropriation and more staff to expand our community planning work. The council didn't want to vote down my request because so many of their constituents wanted planning service, but they stalled around. The new budget came and went and still my request wasn't acted on. I finally got the message. The city manager resented the role community planners were taking in dealing with citizens, encouraging them to demand services to improve their community when he, the city manager, ended up having to refuse the services. He told me he resented it. Knowing this, I knew I'd never get my expansion of community planning, because that's exactly what you get from community planning: people wanting more city services. Let's say it's a crummy-looking neighborhood with not enough garbage collection, broken up streets, lousy lighting, poor code enforcement. They know it won't ever get better till they get services, and community planners tell them how to go about pressuring the city. That's just what the city manager didn't want. It was a losing cause, so I gave up.

The director went on to point out that if he had not "voluntarily" cut back on community planning, the planning department would have faced absorption into the department of urban development. In his view this would have destroyed all pretense to professional autonomy of the planning department, so he chose to sacrifice community planning instead. Shortly after he cut back the community planning program, all threatening proposals for combining planning and urban development were dropped.

Clearly shaken by the collapse of community planning, one planner told us that the planning department's general influence in city government had been heavily damaged by its involvement in the community:

> Our department has been squeezed out of actual planning
> work. The urban development department and outside
> consultants do the planning now. This policy has come
> down from the city power structure; they don't want a
> semiindependent agency doing the planning. It shows a
> lack of respect for the planning staff here, and also fear.
> They're scared that our staff is too radical, too young.
> They're afraid the planning director has brought in a
> bunch of advocate planners. The consultants they
> brought in for the East End are wasting a lot of money
> and alienating the community. The community groups
> we've been working with there backed us; the people
> want us to do the planning. The planning director
> pleaded with the city manager to let our department do
> the planning for the East End. He actually made a formal
> motion to the city council and the city manager. It was
> ignored.

In effect, this planner implied, the planning department had
lost its "insider" status in city government by becoming too
closely identified with citizens. He observed sadly, "Neighborhood groups still come to us, asking for help. But we're
barred from using official staff time to work with them. We
excuse ourselves by telling them we don't have enough staff,
but it's really to keep the budget from being diminished further."

Thus it seems that the adaptation forced upon planners by
the community planning pressure system becomes, ultimately,
self-limiting. Without structural changes in the organization
of city government, administrative guerrilla efforts can be
effective only in small doses. When such activity reaches a
critical mass in a planning department, the community planning program that gives rise to it is crushed.

FIVE

THE PLANNER
AND HIS ROLE

Eleven

The Deeper Disillusionment:
Psychological Responses of
Community Planners to Their Work

We now turn from community planners' battlegrounds to the men and women who manage the battles. In analyzing their relationships with others—community residents, colleagues in the planning department, staff of other agencies, the city's political leaders—we have caught occasional glimpses of how community planners feel about their work and about themselves. We shall draw these observations together and look deeper to see how the administrative guerrilla role affects those swept into it by the community planning pressure system.

The community planners we talked to are a mixed group, some new and just moving into an administrative guerrilla role, some old hands who have operated underground for several years, a few trying desperately to evade the pressures forcing them in this direction. But in their varied experience, one fact stands out: planners do not play the administrative guerrilla role for long. As we saw in Chapter Six, the com-

munity planning program has the highest turnover rate of
any section in the planning department. This appears to be
easy to explain because attrition logically should be high
among those for whom role incapacity or role resistance
makes community planning uncomfortable. Moreover, those
whose guerrilla tactics prove totally unsuccessful in winning
benefits for their community residents will lose their community credibility, become frustrated, and leave, further inflat-
ing the turnover rate. As these "misfit" community planners
winnow themselves out of the program, we might expect a
hard core of successful administrative guerrillas to remain.
But this is not the case. We found that the "misfits" commonly transfer out of the community planning program to
some other section of the planning department or switch to
another community within the program. The community
planners who actually leave the planning department for
other cities, other agencies, or other jobs tend to be, surprisingly, not those who *fail* as administrative guerrillas but those
who *succeed*. They typically work in a community planning
program for several years, painstakingly building community
trust and developing their double underground. Using the
guerrilla tactics we have described, they win a series of victories for their communities (interspersed, usually, with defeats), and then they leave. Their nontransferable community
rapport, familiarity with the city bureaucracy, and guerrilla
skills are lost. Their successors must start all over again at
ground level. What motivates these planners to abandon their
efforts at the peak of their effectiveness as administrative
guerrillas? Since success intensifies the pattern, we must look
for explanation to the psychological strains of the role itself.

We saw in Chapter Ten how the administrative guerrilla
role proves self-limiting in an organizational sense, becoming
harder to play successfully as the number of administrative
guerrillas in a planning department increases. For many community planners, a similar self-limiting process seems to take

place on the individual level. As these community planners adopt the administrative guerrilla role, they set into motion forces that undermine their own motivation to continue in the role. The more successful they become as administrative guerrillas, the more troubled they grow about the direction their work is taking. Eventually, usually within two or three years, their psychological distress outweighs the satisfactions of administrative guerrilla activity, and they leave. In effect, the role contains a built-in self-destruct mechanism. Out of the varied concerns and doubts the community planners reported to us, three "complaint clusters" emerge as the primary pathways to the administrative guerrilla's ultimate rejection of his role: (1) the escalating demands of the role; (2) the imbalance between effort and achievement; and (3) the high risk of disillusionment about the meaning of success.

Escalating Demands: "You Get Used Up"

As an informal position of opportunity growing out of a diffuse, loosely structured organizational context, the administrative guerrilla role lacks clear limits. The administrative guerrilla embraces a goal, a total commitment to improving his community, rather than a clearly defined job with set duties and hours. This is the strength of the role; in no other way could the cooperation and trust of a skeptical, hostile community be secured. But the lack of role limits imposes a crushing personal burden on the planner. He cannot avail himself of the rituals of withdrawal used by professionals in more limited roles to protect their "off-duty" privacy— unlisted home telephone numbers, vacations, refusal to attend evening meetings, leaving job worries at the office. In the eyes of his community residents, he has no right to make himself inaccessible or devote time to his own leisure as long as he professes to be their advocate. An active administrative guerrilla literally works around the clock; he is always on emergency call.

Many of the community planners we spoke to relish the high level of personal involvement at first. This feature of the work, some told us, is what originally attracted them to the program. But this sentiment is expressed most strongly by those just breaking into the administrative guerrilla role, those who are still sheltered by the temporary role limits imposed by their unfamiliarity with the city's bureaucracy and the initial distrust of their community residents. As they settle more thoroughly into the role, these temporary limits begin to fade away. The more the planner deals with the city bureaucracy, the more opportunities he sees for pulling strings, creating interagency underground contacts, a bit of intrigue here, some subtle persuasion there, just the right community pressure on this or that operating agency—an endless series of time-consuming underground efforts which, once recognized, seem obligatory. Similarly, the more trust the planner builds in the community, the more the residents rely on him and the more their demands on his time proliferate— lengthy strategy meetings, midnight telephone calls, consultations, speaking engagements, and so on, without limit. The planner cannot shrink from this growing tide of obligations without jeopardizing his credibility as an administrative guerrilla. Eventually, as the demands on his time and energy escalate, the planner begins to think about withdrawing from the administrative guerrilla role in the interests of personal survival.

In addition, some of the initial satisfactions of the role begin to pall. Some told us that the effort of talking and plotting with community residents, so exhilarating at first, later became exhausting. One remarked sadly:

> You know, in this job the people you meet generally hate you. They assume you work for the rich, for big busi-

ness. They call you a lackey, a rights grabber. You always have to be proving you're on their side, and after a while it gets to you. Many times I've thought of giving the whole thing up and never working as a city planner again.

Another said simply, "I'm getting tired of working with people. It takes too much out of you."

Planners who were being called upon to go more and more frequently into high crime areas told us of their increasing apprehensions about the physical hazards of their work. For instance, one planner said:

> I've begun to realize how dangerous it is to be an area planner. I didn't used to worry about it, but by now I've seen so much violence in my area that I've become convinced the danger is real. I won't randomly walk around in West Oldtown like I did at first.

Another confided:

> The other night I was coming out of a community meeting near a high drug traffic area. A group of women from the meeting insisted on walking me to the trolley stop. Once I would have laughed at this, but no more. I was damn glad they were with me.

One planner who had been repeatedly accosted on the street and had her apartment burglarized twice said, "It's wearing me down. I want to stay but the city is getting unbearable." Another sighed, "If only I could grow my vegetables and breathe some fresh air for a change! Everything in the city is growing sicker. I think my work is important, but it's a horrible experience for me."

Eventually, successful administrative guerrillas reach a breaking point at which their physical and emotional stamina or the tolerance of their families gives way before the escalating demands of the role. One planner who had asked to be transferred out of community planning into another section of the planning department said:

> When I got so involved in the black ghetto here, I went to night meetings almost every night and often didn't get home until 1:00 in the morning. My husband put his foot down. He was worried about my safety, and wanted me home in the evenings. It was interfering with our lives too much. I felt guilty about deserting my district, but I had to move out of the program.

Another planner who was leaving the department for a teaching job in a small town told us:

> I've got to leave. For one thing, I never see my wife any more. I really like her, and it's not tolerable that we don't have any time together. Also, I've gotten to feel alienated from my community. For a while nothing could have gotten me to leave them, but you get burnt out. My health's about gone. I have insomnia. I have ulcers. I have to go—I'm burnt out, I've served my purpose, I just don't care anymore.

The Effort-Achievement Gap: "What's Your Frustration Threshold?"

A second corrosive feature of the administrative guerrilla role eats like slow acid into the planner's motivation: the frustrating gap between effort expended and success achieved. In the initial phase of the role—the heady process of winning community trust, setting up the double underground and mobilizing community pressure—an administrative guerrilla enjoys a certain temporary insulation from the frustration that later comes to dog his work. In this first task, the construction of a machine to pry loose city services and facil-

ities for his area, his energy investment does bear a relationship to his results. But once he sets his machine into motion,
his success must be gauged by a different measure: the benefits he can win for his community.

At this point the link between effort and achievement gives
way, for the ultimate outcome of guerrilla campaigns depends
more on the vagaries of city politics than on the planner's
own energy input. Hard work on the planner's part is a necessary but not sufficient condition for success. He must work
just as hard on the projects that fail as on those that succeed,
never knowing which will be which. Since defeats typically
outnumber victories for even the most skillful administrative
guerrillas, the planners playing this role quickly accumulate
more experience in frustration than fulfillment. The longer
they stay in the role, the greater their exposure to frustration.
Some come almost to expect it, even while maintaining their
high energy input:

> I want to see a 235d [federally funded] housing pro-
> gram in South Oldtown. I'll struggle, I'll hassle, I'll try
> everything to get it. This kind of thing takes fantastic ef-
> fort. But I know chances are I won't get it; or if I do, it
> won't work right.

A tone resembling battle fatigue creeps into their comments
about their work:

> This isn't something you could keep on doing if you
> weren't almost fanatically dedicated; the job has too
> many heartaches and too few rewards.

> Area planning hits highs and lows. Mostly lows. Some-
> times you just feel like giving up.

For the typical administrative guerrilla, the frustration eventually becomes unbearable. As one put it:

> It's not that I'm becoming disillusioned. Hell, I was a
> cynic when I started. But what I find at the moment is
> that my personal stamina is not up to withstanding the
> level of frustration that I knew I'd have to withstand. I
> understand it and expect it, but I just can't take it much
> longer. Nobody can take it indefinitely. That's why when
> people ask me about going into community planning, I
> always ask them, "What's your frustration threshold?"

The remarks of community planners who have tallied up
lengthy personal records of all-out efforts which came to
nothing reflect increasing alienation from their present role.
Many talk of relocating in another city, another job, even another country, in order to reestablish a link between effort
and achievement. These comments are typical:

> I'm not beaten. Right now I may be disenchanted because
> things are so frustrating in this job, but I still expect to
> put big things through. I want to accomplish something,
> especially in housing. But if I can't do it here, then I'll go
> elsewhere, to some other planning department or a con-
> sulting firm.

> I'm afflicted with the do-good disease. I must do it or I
> wouldn't be happy. I have to feel socially useful, and I'm
> not socially useful here. If I stay here much longer, I'd be
> deluding myself. It's becoming an impossible situation
> here. The center of action isn't here, but in politics.

Frustration is, in fact, the most common explanation community planners offer for the high turnover rate in their program. Many of those who were leaving explained that they
had simply been worn down by chronic disappointment. We
found one departing community planner busily redecorating
his new apartment, located with pointed symbolism in the
path of a proposed highway he had been unable to block as
an administrative guerrilla. He was leaving the planning department to work for a private community service organization. "If I could have produced as a community planner," he

said, "I'd still be there. I just got too frustrated to stay." Another community planner who was leaving to work as a planning consultant to a South American government told us, "Not being able to do anything, I'd feel like a fink if I stayed." Many community planners told us sadly of watching the exodus of their friends in the program, as one by one they reached their "frustration threshold." One said:

> All my best friends have left the community planning program. Six of the seven guys that were here when I came have left. They wanted to get closer to implementation and felt they were beating their heads against the wall here. Two went over to Model Cities, others are working with community groups. You get a lot of community planners leaving because they're disgusted and tired of being frustrated.

In another city a community planner, his own alienation growing daily, told us:

> I'm depressed about the whole thing. The people who could have done something about planning and its archaic attitudes are leaving. Guys who have been here for two years are leaving just when they could do something about it. Zap—they're gone. They're fed up with the inefficiency and lack of accomplishment. The longer you are in area planning, the more you see what needs to be done and how to do it. But you also find out more about the limits and constraints that make it impossible to do anything. Finally you can't stand it any more. First two people leave, then three more—then suddenly it becomes a wave of resignations.

Disillusionment with Success: "Pushing Deck Chairs around on the Titanic"

Ironically, the very victories sought so determinedly and at such high personal cost by administrative guerrillas are themselves a third feature rendering the role unbearable after a few years. At first any victory is sweet for the administrative guerrilla. But many gradually come to feel uneasy about the nature of the victories they win.

Administrative guerrillas frequently express ambivalence about the *politicality* of their successes. Although repulsed by the fusty irrelevance of apolitical "old" planning traditions, they would still like to think of themselves as professional planners rather than politicians. This is not merely a matter of vanity; many told us they feel a moral commitment to use their training and special planning skills in what they see as a desperate struggle to save the cities. But in the administrative guerrilla role, they find themselves forced to consider political expediency first and rational planning second, if at all. For instance, we were told by a dismayed community planner, "I don't perform a planning function at all in my area. I just serve as an information liaison and help them hustle things through various city agencies." Another observed, "There's no point in assisting the community to make up a real plan. They've got to take an extreme stand in order to have enough ground left for compromise with the decision makers. Planning gets drowned in the politics of it." "Schizophrenic" is a term we heard over and over from planners describing their struggle to retain rationality and objectivity while acting as administrative guerrillas. One planner summed up the dilemma this way:

> Planners should inject themselves into political situations more than they do now. They have to; otherwise getting their plans implemented depends on the whim of politicians. But there's great risk in doing so. The planner's "thing," his special contribution, is the rational approach —the ability to sit back and look at problems objectively. You impair this sort of thing if you get too involved. If planners start fighting politically on behalf of the people, they could lose it. This could happen to me

in West Slum. I could lose my ability to look at things
rationally if I start taking issue with the department of
public works or something. I'm willing to take the risk.
At this point in time planners must risk their rationality.
The only way to have any impact nowadays is to be
more activist, to make noise. Planners need to stir up the
issues; but if they go all the way, they won't be planners
any more.

Among the more active administrative guerrillas, we found
chagrin, almost outrage, that the profession of planning fails
to provide a way out of this dilemma so that they can work
effectively for their communities without relinquishing their
professional status. Quite a few denounce the profession as
fraudulent; here are some typical remarks:

> Planning has so little legal basis; it's all a game, a game of
> persuasion.

> There's so little evaluation of what has been done in
> planning. There are so few principles of planning. A
> planner is analogous to a doctor of sick urban areas, but a
> doctor of 5000 years ago! It's pathetic how little we
> know about what we are doing.

> This isn't a profession. It's a racket!

With their image of what constitutes planning coming un-
glued, many administrative guerrillas symbolically resign
from the profession, refusing to identify themselves as planners. Despite their formal degrees in planning, they claim to
be architects, artists, philosophers, public servants. They
speak about dropping out of the profession entirely to teach,
paint, write, or to "become an apprentice to a guitar maker"
or "maybe go on an archeological dig in Turkey." One planner with a particularly outstanding academic background in
planning told us:

> I'd like to do something less intellectual, like be a garage mechanic, a tradesman, or operate a small business. Whatever I do, I want to do it well. And I know that what I'm doing now, I can't ever do well.

Another, the most active administrative guerrilla in his department, said soberly:

> I expected planning to be more scientific than it is, something where your recommendations and conclusions would have some rational foundation and make some sense. They make such a big spiel about the profession, it misleads you. We're supposed to be able to deliver more than the nonplanner. But now that I've seen how much of it is bullshit, I don't think planning has the tools to deliver very much. Planning doesn't have a methodology. I don't think I'll be a planner much longer. I don't know where I'll go, though. Maybe back into the Peace Corps. Maybe there's something for me in New Towns. I really don't know what I'm going to do.

In the anomie reflected in these remarks, we can glimpse the abyss of personal anguish that lies behind the administrative guerrillas' high turnover rate.

Planners also report qualms about the *conservatism* of their successes as administrative guerrillas. Many originally gravitated to the community planning program because they thought it offered a vehicle for their equalitarian, humanistic, change-oriented values. They expected to champion the cause of underdog groups—racial minorities, the poor, the politically impotent. Once they become advocates for a particular neighborhood, however, these values begin to turn upside down. The community groups the planner works with usually equate upgrading of the neighborhood with exclusion: whites want to keep out blacks, blacks want to keep out poorer blacks, poor blacks want to keep out transients. Unable to assure his community of compensating tradeoffs and support services to ease the potentially blighting impact of these unwanted groups, the planner uncomfortably finds his own efforts drifting in the direction of neighborhood protection. His successes, when they come, may be won at the expense of the very underdog groups he originally defined as his primary clients. The moral confusion many successful administrative guerrillas feel, particularly when issues of race are involved, shows up clearly in their remarks. Here is a typical agonizing situation:

> I've been in contact with another new organization in my area, encouraging them to take on planning activities of their own. They want to do this. It looks like a winner; they've incorporated and want to get into the housing business. I'm giving them guidance and technical advice, and I've said I'd help them with problems they might run into from city hall. One thing, though: this is basically a neighborhood protection group. They want to maintain a high standard by keeping out undesirables. They have a point. I mean, irresponsible transients do hurt a neighborhood. They don't keep up the property. This group wants to keep their area attractive, have strong code enforcement, prevent division of buildings into rooming houses that would bring in migrants and have a blighting effect. They say it's not racial, that they want to keep poor white migrants out too. But since the area borders on the Model Cities area, it's pretty clear who they have in mind. I'm trying to keep this from becoming a racial issue. I encouraged them to speak out for open occupancy. Somehow I don't think they will.

To their dismay, planners are called upon to plot guerrilla campaigns for purposes of excluding "undesirables," as in this case:

> The people in my area don't want any scattered site public housing. Their argument against it is that they don't want undesirables in the neighborhood. Each housing unit is to cost $30,000. This really burns them up. They

say, "Why should those drunks and welfare chiselers get those $30,000 houses, when we work and pay taxes and can't afford anything half that good?" I'm torn myself. I've tried to explain to my people that a racist policy— that's what it boils down to—is to their detriment. On the other hand, I'd like to see the neighborhood stabilized and I'd favor other types of low-cost housing programs rather than public housing. At any rate, after finding out about the program from me, our people came out and protested it. I advised them. They've been so effective that even though it's the mayor's pet program and backed by the redevelopment authority, it hasn't been able to get off the ground for over a year. My people have a back-up strategy in case they lose: they'll all put their names on the waiting list so that this community's poorer residents can be first and keep others out. They got this idea from me too; I thought it would help them accept the program in case they lose. Otherwise they might blow the houses up. I don't like helping with this kind of thing, but it'll be worse if I don't.

Some queasily offer explanations for their advocacy of exclusionary policies, never sounding totally convinced themselves:

I wouldn't want to be responsible for putting black families in Bluecollar Hills and then have them be attacked by the whites there. The white gangs would terrorize black families. There could be bloodshed. I don't think too many black families want in anyway. They're going to the next area over, Transitionville. . . . Actually, I don't believe that blacks want to get out of the ghetto any more. They want their own community. The blacks will be better off in the ghetto if the Model Cities program works. Once it's funded up, they'll get better services there than if they moved into a white low-income area like mine.

My own feeling is that blacks shouldn't be in this area. Ethnic Valley will survive only if one ethnic group lives there. The community can survive only if the people

have common interests, common problems, similar economic levels, and a sense of unity. If a lot of blacks move
in, the Italians here will all move out. This is an attitude
I've formed since working with a community leader here.
I was very moved by him, his feeling for his people.
Many of them are first generation. I used to think, two or
three years ago, that integrated housing could be made to
work anywhere. Now I've come to see that Ethnic Valley is an exception to the rule.

For a few administrative guerrillas, the very act of winning
physical facilities for their neighborhoods comes to seem antithetical to their equalitarian values and thus morally repre-
hensible. As one planner put it:

What do I say to my people when I know that our area
needs more recreation equipment but another area needs
it more? How can I feel good about getting them a playground when a poorer area needs three schools?

For many planners, this gulf between equalitarian values and
the conservatism of community advocacy turns their pride in
success to ashes. The more successful they grow as administrative guerrillas, the mose insupportable the role becomes.

Most undermining of all is a growing sense of gloom and
impending catastrophe that forces many administrative guerrillas to recognize the basic *triviality* of their successes. As
one planner explained:

I spent my first year here getting disillusioned because I
couldn't get all the projects I planned implemented. But
that was a sophomoric reaction. I spent my second year
really getting disillusioned, in a deeper sense. I found out
that planners do get some things implemented, but began
to recognize how insignificant the projects themselves
are. We need massive institutional changes, not a tot lot
here and there. Projects are irrelevant. I got a project
through: four schools for my area. But it's no good. I can

see that I underestimated the continuing need for more
schools and everything else in my area. The schools I got
will be finished in three years; by that time they'll need
more schools. It'll just be the same problem again. Getting these schools didn't help that much. The physical act
of building a building isn't the answer anyway. Schools
aren't the same thing as education. Reading levels will
still go down. There still won't be jobs for the graduates.

With an air of hopelessness, planners told us they feel powerless to give their communities what they really need. With
the basic patterns of city growth set by private developers,
the city government's policies determined irrationally, and
the whole urban system rapidly running out of money for
basic services, the needed solutions seem to lie beyond anything community planners can do. Voicing a sentiment
echoed by many others, a planner asked, "What's the point
of it all, unless you can change our ridiculous national priorities and get some money out of Washington?" Some, like this
planner, told us they felt like pawns in a political con game:

The whole issue of advocacy in the community planning
program was used by the federal government as a device
to keep the peace without real commitment on the part
of the federal government. If urban renewal and Model
Cities aren't enough to keep the ghetto cool, they figured,
let's have one more program. Let's have another biscuit
thrown out. Anyone with eyes can see that advocacy
planning isn't any gift of power to the people as long as
the economics and politics of the city lie outside of community control. How can you plan with resources somebody else owns? How can blacks in the inner city plan,
when the people who own the resources of the city live
out in the suburbs? I think even the lousy schools are
part of the plot. Kids are coming out of high school not
able to read and write because those in power have a
vested interest in limiting the education of people in the
inner city. And us, the community planners, we're supposed to help keep the lid on.

For administrative guerrillas at this point of disillusionment, success at winning project-level benefits for their communities is like salt in a wound, an irritating reminder of a larger pain. The images they use to describe the city—dying organisms, sinking ships, disintegrating machines—make it clear how futile their guerrilla efforts have come to seem to them. "We're just holding the city together prior to its eventual collapse," one said, "just plugging the holes as they keep getting bigger." Another likened planning to plastering "band-aid type programs on a city stricken with cancer." Said another, "What we do is surrealistic. It's like pushing deck chairs around on the Titanic." One even remarked, "The best way to do something about the city's problems is to speed up the inevitable collapse." Many spoke soberly of their fears of riots, shoot-outs between the community and the police, growing unemployment, the spread of drugs and drug-related crime. "Maybe cities *should* die!" one said, adding, "I said this at a meeting of area planners and they all treated me as if I had finally seen the light. We all know area planning is making only minimal impact on the urban environment."

We talked to some administrative guerrillas who were leaving because disillusionment had finally rendered their successes totally meaningless. The emotional numbness of their remarks gives some indication of the crushing psychological burden of the administrative guerrilla role:

> One reason it's best that I'm leaving is my pessimism and its effect on the rest of the community planners. My wife and I used to have open house for the guys here. It was great, we all sat around talking about our schemes and dreams. But now my effect on everybody else has gotten to be negative. I feel that society is absolutely mad now. To me the future is a horrible prospect. Lots of middle-class technicians are dropping out these days. Their reasons are probably like mine. What difference does it make?

It's not that I'm afraid of having nothing to show for my
work. I'll be leaving because I'm frustrated with my own
lack of commitment. No one has any any more. No one
seems to either give leadership or create a philosophy
that could give others inspiration and charisma. The task
is so enormous. We need to remake society, and make
the city into a temple for human behavior. Not just survive. My God, I feel alienated.

Defending the Self

Despite their disappointment with planning, departing community planners seem unlikely to abandon permanently
the profession in which they have invested so much time and
energy. In their talk of leaving, even the most exhausted administrative guerrillas give the impression that after a period
of recuperation, they hope to find some way to apply their
planning skills in community service again. "When I go, I'm
not going to do *anything* for three months," one said, "but
then I'll probably go back to the grind in another department." Another told us he dreamed of taking an extended vacation, then doing community planning as a volunteer consultant on a part-time basis. "I'll paint in the mornings," he
said, "and in the afternoons I'll be a planner." One leaving to
teach said he thought of his new job as convalescence but
added that since he could combine this with economic development planning on an Indian reservation near his new location, "I can still keep up some planning activity."

It seems that, although driven out of their present positions
by the strains of administrative guerrilla effort, these planners
anticipate eventually finding another niche in the planning
profession. Accordingly, they must rationalize their present
intolerable role in a way that preserves both their self-respect
and their respect for future planning activities. Many administrative guerrillas we talked to were in the process of formu-

lating a two-layered argument to separate themselves and their future planning roles from the community planning positions they would soon be fleeing. On the first level, this common argument involves redefinition of community planning goals so as to escape a sense of personal failure; on the second level, the attribution of failure to specific rather than general obstacles so as to maintain hope for more success in future planning positions.

Redefinition of Goals.   Unable to point to tangible improvements in their areas, administrative guerrillas can shore up their self-esteem by redefining their goal to match their primary accomplishment: the organization and education of community pressure groups. As one planner explained:

> My work is something special to me, but I've had to learn to live with uncertainty and frustration. To get by, you have to redefine what you mean by success in planning. Sometimes I view my work as a success where others might not. To have community people try to get their requests processed, even if they lose, is a kind of success. Sure, you might still like to see something material happen; but looking at success in this broader way helps.

Another told us:

> I'm one of those people who wants to see results. But I define results in my own way, in terms of my concept of process. To me, community commitment to do something about their problems can be seen as a result. Very often physical results of the community's plan are less important than the process of making the plan itself, the meaning it has for the people involved. The fun of it all is in the making, not in the product itself. The important part of community planning is involvement of the people in the planning process.

According to some, mobilization of the community is the administrative guerrilla's *only* task. Once this is accomplished, the planner himself becomes redundant and serves his community best by leaving. "Of course I won't stay here," said a highly talented administrative guerrilla who took this position. "My job is to set up organizations and then go. I just keep circulating." Another planner who was leaving the department claimed:

> It's functional that I leave my community now. They don't need me any more. They know the names of city officials and politicians, who to call, how to put the pressure on. They don't need me to bring them downtown any more. They're mature as a political group now and it's time for me to phase out. If they want another district planner, I say they're just chickening out. They can take care of themselves now.

With this rationalization, the administrative guerrilla can take leave of his community "troops" in good conscience, not as a general deserting in the face of defeat but rather as a technical adviser whose training job is done.

Particularization of Obstacles.   With most of their efforts blocked, community planners can still nourish hopes for success in anticipated planning roles elsewhere by pinning the blame for their current frustrations at least partly on local conditions. Even among the administrative guerrillas most pessimistic about the utility of American planning and the ultimate survival of American society, we often found a lingering faith that they could somehow accomplish more with a change of organizational and political scenery.

Some claimed the city they were working in was uniquely resistant to community planning because of its traditions or political and economic makeup, the implication being that community planning would prove easier in other cities. For instance, planners talked about the conservative atmosphere of their cities. "This is a blue-collar town," one said, "New ideas have a hard time here." Another remarked snidely, "The people in this city have a plantation mentality. They call it 'The Land of Easy Living.' If I can accomplish anything in this place, I say 'Hallelujah!'" The city's power structure frequently came under fire. For instance, a planner remarked, "Very few good people go into politics in this city. It's left to hoodlums. It's full of dirty money. The idea of planning here is almost ridiculous."

Some praised the "efficiency" of private consulting firms in contrast to the red tape of their current positions. Other, taking the opposite view, told us they planned to try another city planning department rather than a private firm, because in a private firm their creativity and social service concerns would be stifled.

Others argued that the poor relationship of their planning department to the rest of the city government was to blame for the frustration of community planning. No matter what the current arrangement, they were convinced that some alternative would prove more workable. Planners in independent planning departments recommended mergers with operating agencies such as the housing department or finance or urban renewal. "We ought to have a combined department like in Port City, with planning and urban renewal in one redevelopment authority," argued one planner. "That way we'd be more involved in implementation." But in the very city with the combined department so admired by this planner, other community planners told us they longed for a separate planning department. One said, "We're just an appendage to the rest of the redevelopment authority. We get treated like a bunch of dodoes." Some planners in departments responsible to a planning commission advocated abolition of the commission system so that planners would work directly as the mayor's staff. "We should be the right hand of the mayor, close to him, because that's where the power is," we were told. But in departments directly under the mayor, we found planners complaining about being used for political chores and pressured to show loyalty to the mayor's administration; here planners wished for a buffering planning commission.

Some planners traced their problems to the planning director and praised directors in other cities, whose approach, they felt, created a better climate for community planning. One told us:

> It's the fault of the director that we're such a rubber stamp, powerless, useless agency here. He has acknowledged in coffee breaks how weak he's been. I'd say that Chutzpah's planning department in History City is where the action is.

But in History City, this "dynamic" director was utterly despised by many of the community planning staff, who castigated him for sanctioning all the policies they detested most —superhighways through the city, mass clearance in the ghetto without adequate relocation programs, and concentration of planning effort on the central business district instead of residential communities. They would happily have traded him for a "weaker" director who was less "inhuman" and "piglike."

We need not try here to assess the relative validity of these planners' conflicting visions of the most favorable conditions for their work. Objective truth or falsity is irrelevant to the psychological functions such beliefs play. As long as the community planner can feel that somewhere the grass is greener, he can keep intact his motivation for anticipated planning positions in a future "better situation."

Community Planning and the
Problem of Role Volatility

The psychological strains we have described are hardly unique to administrative guerrillas in community planning programs. In this respect, community planning resembles other social service efforts that immerse the staff of bureaucracies in community contact work. We can, for example, find parallels in many religious or quasi-religious programs —missionary work, priests involved in community organization, the work of the Friends Service Committee, Saul Alinsky's Industrial Areas Foundation, and so on. Although such programs afford stable careers to some, they expose large numbers of individuals to a pattern of contradictory demands, somewhat analogous to the community planning pressure system, which renders their roles unbearable for more than a few years. Service occupations such as social work and public health work, both characterized by high turnover among those with most community contact, also subject many individuals to pressures impossible to tolerate indefinitely. Organizations working for reform in civil rights, consumer protection, and legal aid experience similar high turnover among their paid staff of community contact workers. And of course the federally funded social service efforts undertaken in the 1960s—such as VISTA, the Peace Corps, and the now defunct Community Action Program—involved many persons in stressful roles almost identical to those assumed by community planners.

All of these social service programs appeal to idealism, particularly among youth. To varying degrees, all are characterized by vagueness or ambiguity of goals and loose organizational structures that allow for positions of opportunity in which individuals doing community contact work structure their own roles. As we saw in analyzing community planning, the two factors together—idealism coupled with positions of opportunity—lead individuals to fashion for themselves unusually taxing roles. They find personal demands escalating past the point of tolerability, the disparity between effort and achievement becoming unbearably frustrating, and the satisfactions of success paling before the enormity of their self-defined tasks. These are what might be called *volatile roles*. Once actualized, they self-destruct, quickly driving the role occupant to the breaking point of psychological strain and thereby forcing him out of the role. At the same time, they maintain high appeal to new recruits eager to combine their idealism with a position of opportunity. Thus high turnover is structured into the very fabric of volatile roles.

Obviously, volatile roles do not lend themselves well to stable careers. They demand a degree of fever-pitch dedication so destructive to personal life and emotional tranquility that most occupants of such roles can put in only a temporary stint. How this fact is interpreted, however, varies considerably. In the older social service programs which sometimes give rise to volatile roles, such as the priesthood and social work, participation is considered to be part of a career. Legitimized protective role limits and rituals of withdrawal from excessive role demands being available to participants, their acceptance of volatile roles is viewed by their employers as voluntary and somewhat abnormal. Those who choose to extend their work into volatile roles, when they finally reach the breaking point and leave, are considered dropouts, casualties. Under these circumstances, occupants of volatile roles may feel a sense of personal inadequacy. On the organizational level, the high turnover rate among participants taking on volatile roles is a puzzling problem to the parent bureaucracy.

At the other extreme lie some of the newer social service programs we have mentioned, such as VISTA and the Peace

Corps. These programs require entry into volatile roles by their participants, providing them no protective role limits or rituals of withdrawal. However, they have also formalized the high turnover rates inherent in volatile roles. Their participants sign up for a specified period of community contact work short enough so that they usually come to the end of their contracts before reaching the breaking point at which they would have left anyway. Both they and the bureaucracy they work for define involvement in the program not as a career in itself but as an interruption or postponement of the participant's career. Thus no stigma of personal failure or inadequacy attends the participants' departure, and their organizational sponsors consider the high turnover rates a normal, predictable feature of the program.

To the confusion of all concerned, community planning combines inconsistent elements of these two extremes. Community planners enjoy none of the protective role limits and rituals of withdrawal available to those in older "career" social service programs. They are forced more or less involuntarily by the community planning pressure system into volatile roles much like those of VISTA or Peace Corps volunteers. Yet neither they nor the bureaucracy that sponsors the program fully acknowledge the implications of this situation. The planning department's management and older staff interpret the high turnover rate in the program as a sign of community planners' irresponsibility and lack of commitment to the city and their work. Community planners themselves, despite their rationalizations, seem unable to suppress guilt feelings about their inability to withstand the psychological strains of their volatile roles indefinitely. Caught in the middle, the community planners suffer doubly the burdens of role volatility: they are forced into a role that threatens to destroy them, and then they are blamed for not being indestructible.

SIX

CONCLUSIONS

Twelve

Community Planning:

A Necessary Step Backward

In the preceding chapters we have analyzed community planning on a number of levels. One focus has been the organizational forms that experimental community planning programs are taking in major American cities. We have also tried to convey a sense of the poignant intermingling of determination, despair, euphoria, and frustration felt by many of the men and women who work as community planners. The numerous organizational processes and behavior patterns we have discussed vary, in ways we have tried to make clear, among individual planning departments and among individual planners; but out of the variations, a general picture of the community planning experiment emerges. The basic outlines of this composite picture bear review at this point.

Community planning is a child of the contemporary urban crisis. As American cities grow more troubled, city planning departments face attacks on their traditional methods and role from all sides. These attacks come from intellectuals within the planning profession, from mobilized citizens' groups demanding community control, from political leaders frantic over the civil unrest and physical decay of the city's inner core, from private advocate planners championing the interests of particular communities, and even from some of the planning department's own staff members who strive for more direct involvement in urban problems and their solutions. Although a variety of innovative forms of planning are currently being debated within the planning profession, city planning departments faced with this challenge have gravitated to the one alternative that appears most feasible within their limited budgets and authority: decentralization of city planning. Many planning departments in large cities are answering their critics by launching experimental community planning programs in which individual members of the department's staff are assigned to work with the residents of a specific community on that area's planning-related problems.

The new community planning and traditional city planning are, it would seem, incompatible from the outset because of two basic differences in the planning assumptions on which the two approaches are based. First, community planning relocates the planner's accountability. Traditional planning has been organized as an *elite council* in which decision making is limited to a relatively small group of insiders (political officials and influential businessmen to whom advice is offered by city planners), with the planners isolated from their nominal clients (the citizenry at large). Community planning, on the other hand, requires that planning be organized as an *arena council* in which decision making becomes an open forum, with the planner and his constituency of community residents ranged against the traditional elite group in cases of interest conflict.

Second, community planning redefines the planner's sphere of activity. Traditionally, the planning department has restricted its planning efforts to a small part of the city's development: physical land use, mainly as it concerns the expenditure of public funds. This narrowness, partly a matter of preference and partly forced on the planning department by its marginal political influence and weak mandate, leads the department to assume a role of *encapsulation* in city government. Organizationally, the department adapts itself to a division of labor which allocates programming of services, as well as important controls over private land use, to the city's operating agencies. Community planning, which directs the planner's concern to the total quality of life in a specific community, cannot pour itself into this narrow mold. Too many of the community's basic problems are social in nature or in other ways lie outside the encapsulated planning department's jurisdiction. Community planning, in other words, assumes a role of *expansionism* in which the planner addresses his planning skills to the broad spectrum of community needs and problems even though this takes him outside the traditional confines of city planning.

Some of the other innovations being tried on an experimental basis by a few planning departments (for example, Program Planning and Budgeting Systems, or PPBS) are based on assumptions equally at odds with the traditional city planning approach, yet they yield little conflict because their assumptions are rarely carried into action. Designers of community planning programs seem to expect their creation to follow a similar course. Community planning is intended to serve the planning department symbolically, through its existence rather than its operation. It is usually envisioned as a way to get its parent bureaucracy, the planning department, off the hook by demonstrating the department's relevance and sensitivity to both city politicians and city residents. The disruptive potential of the new program may be considered, but it is not taken seriously. Usually no conflict is anticipated. The new program makes its debut with no one quite sure what it is supposed to do but all vaguely convinced it's a good idea.

As the new community planning programs begin to operate, however, it becomes clear that this experiment is destined to cause trouble. To the alarm of planning administrators, community planning staff members show an unforeseen vigor and ingenuity in translating the potentially disruptive assumptions of their assignment into action. The reasons are threefold.

The first explanation lies in the way the community planning program is staffed. Community planning positions are filled disproportionately with young, socially concerned, highly talented planners trained in the orientation we have called *"new" planning*. As opposed to those of the planning department's staff whose training inclines them to *"old" planning*, these young planners have stretched their definition of professional city planning to include citizen participation, social planning, short-term projects, and political activism to get plans implemented. The arena-council, expansionist assumptions of community planning are far more compatible with their training and professional self-image than are the elite-council, encapsulated assumptions of traditional city planning. For them, community planning is not just a job but part of an ideological battle against a planning Establishment they feel has proven itself irrelevant to the city's most urgent problems. Thus the new program starts with a staff unusually determined to be disruptive if they see their social concerns being blocked by the department's traditional approach.

Second, the community planning program is organized in a way that gives planners extreme latitude in their work roles in the new program. Released from direct supervision and relatively unaccountable for any clearly defined product, the community planners find themselves in *positions of opportunity*, free to channel their efforts in directions of their own choosing without the approval or even the knowledge of their administrative superiors. Thus the new program provides its staff with unusual opportunities to pursue disruptive courses of action.

Third and most important, the community planning program exposes its staff members directly to the community, stripping away the protective insulation enjoyed by the rest of the planning staff and enmeshing them in a network of social dynamics that virtually forces them into disruptive actions. The key problem for the community planner is that to be successful in his assignment of planning with citizen participation, he must develop rapport with the residents of his community. If the residents ignore or distrust him, he has failed in his own eyes and in the eyes of his administrative superiors. However, building such rapport proves impossible without putting the community planning program's arena-council, expansionist assumptions into practice. For instance, the community residents are usually suspicious and hostile to city government officials. To overcome this crippling "city hall image," the planner must dissassociate his personal identity from that of the planning department. To be effective, he must demonstrate a credible transfer of allegiance from the city to his community. This drives him outside the framework of elite-council planning into the role of an arena-council community advocate. Besides demonstrating allegiance, he must also prove his serviceability to community residents before they will work with him. Unable to deliver any positive benefits for his community because the planning department lacks direct control of resources and has no formal role in the programming of city services, the planner can only offer to aid the community in pressuring those who do administer city resources and services—the city's political officials and operating agencies. This pushes him into rejecting planning encapsulation in favor of aggressive expansionism. Thus the community contact aspect of the new program puts the community planner in a double bind: to carry out his assignment, he must engage in actions viewed as disruptive by his superiors.

Inevitably, the community planner finds himself ringed by a pattern of contradictory demands we have termed the *community planning pressure system*. On the one hand, he is led by his own inclinations and pressured by the dynamics of his community contact work to follow out the arena-council, expansionist assumptions of community planning. On the other hand, he is pressured by his immediate employers in the planning department to conform to the department's elite-council, encapsulated planning traditions. This clash of expectations takes place in a highly charged bureaucratic context, with operating agencies jealously resisting the community planner's slightest encroachment on their traditional jurisdictions and political officials casting a jaundiced eye on community planners whose actions threaten to embarrass the city government.

Taking advantage of their positions of opportunity, community planners resolve the contradictions of the community planning pressure system by fashioning for themselves an unanticipated role, becoming what we have called *administrative guerrillas*. They go underground within the bureaucracy that employs them, responding covertly to pressures from the community while seeming to work within the limits of traditional planning.

Guerrilla activity centers around the major resource at the community planner's disposal: information. Planners playing the administrative guerrilla role develop a *double underground* to glean and dispense inside information about developments affecting their communities. Through an interagency underground of carefully cultivated informers working in operating agencies and other sections of the planning department, the community planner keeps abreast of both inside information and "public secrets" of interest to his constituency. This information is judiciously leaked to the planner's community underground so that residents can anticipate the city's moves and further their community's interests through methods such as the "gratitude trap," the "democratic blitz," and the "symbolic holocaust." The same tactics are used to protect the community against outside threats such as interstate highways routed through areas the residents wish to see preserved for other uses.

In the course of constructing his double underground and mobilizing his community "troops" for political action, the community planner usually finds himself shifting his energies from planning to community organization and education in political strategies. In effect, his goal is displaced so that instead of creating a community plan, he begins to center his efforts on community advocacy, working to develop greater citizen access and influence in city government.

Of course, many others besides community planners can and do serve as community advocates—in particular, elected representatives. However, as we have seen, a vast difference exists between the consequences of *political enfranchisement* (the kind of advocate service offered by elected representatives) and *bureaucratic enfranchisement* (the kind of advocate service offered by community planners). The issue is not one of access to policy making but rather access to policy implementation. The immediate concerns of community residents often have little to do with legislative action. They involve the procedures of administrative agencies: how the zoning and building codes are enforced, whether trash gets collected on schedule, the opening and closing hours for recreational facilities, whether a street is designated for one-way traffic, where the new school or park gets located, what goes on in the schools, whether the police walk their beats or use patrol cars, how strictly welfare eligibility is checked, and so on.

The operating agencies controlling these procedures resist penetration and their activities are enormously complicated.

Most political representatives simply lack the time, inclination, and expertise to monitor the city's administrative machinery on a daily basis on behalf of their constituencies. Moreover, political concerns may deter elected city officials from antagonizing the powerful heads of operating agencies by intervening directly in administrative procedures. Other kinds of community advocates (such as privately employed or volunteer planners, social workers, clergymen, community leaders of various kinds, Model Cities personnel, and VISTA workers) also generally lack access to and understanding of the details of the operating agencies' activities.

Thus while community planners are not the only advocates for community residents, they are uniquely situated to offer bureaucratic enfranchisement—being knowledgeable, strategically placed to gather information inside the bureaucracy, granted the necessary time by virtue of their job assignment, and able to avoid retaliation (at least temporarily) by means of clandestine administrative guerrilla tactics. The fact that the community planners are in a sense "betraying" the city administration by becoming undercover advocates further enhances their credibility with community groups, since these groups generally work in terms of a conflict model of city-community relations and harbor dark suspicions about the possible cooptation of advocates who seem to run no risks for the community's sake. In turning for help to administrative guerrillas in the community planning program, the citizens are seeking an informal bureaucratic enfranchisement which has been denied them formally, and which they have not been able to get from their other community advocates.

Not all community planners adopt the administrative guerrilla role. Those we have called *role resisters* refuse on principle to depart from the department's traditional planning approach even in the face of extreme community pressure to do so. Although not necessarily insensitive to their communities' broader problems, the role resisters adhere to the "old" planning emphasis on long-range physical planning and departmental traditions of elite-council encapsulation. They reject involvement with citizen participation, political activism, and social planning as unprofessional. Basically opposed to the community planning program's stated objectives of decentralization and citizen participation, these planners find their work so stressful that they avoid community contact whenever possible and talk frequently of transferring out of community planning into some other section of the planning department.

In addition to the role resisters, other community planners fail to adopt the administrative guerrilla role due to *role incapacity*. They wish to act as administrative guerrillas but lack the necessary interpersonal skills or suffer an unlucky accident (such as a "premature delivery failure") that irrevocably impairs their rapport or credibility with the residents in their community. Many successful administrative guerrillas report experiencing an awkward period of role incapacity early in their community planning work. Guerrilla skills seem to be acquired by a trial and error process, with the planner learning from mistakes in his first community and then managing his intended role more effectively in a new community. Thus role incapacity may represent a temporary phase in a community planner's movement into the administrative guerrilla role.

Since more than three-quarters of the community planners we encountered were active administrative guerrillas and since this role appeared among the community planners in every planning department we visited, we feel convinced the role is no aberration or accident that can be eliminated from community planning programs in their present institutional context. Rather, this role is an intrinsic part of the new programs—the predictable outcome of the community planning pressure system.

Development of the administrative guerrilla role, however, represents an adaptation to the contradictions confronting the community planner, not a stable resolution of these contradictions. Tensions still inevitably arise. For one thing, the administrative guerrilla's "cover" within his own department is far from perfect. Some of his colleagues in the planning department, becoming aware of the administrative guerrillas' covert political activism and community advocacy, react with the utmost hostility and antagonism to the direction the community planning program is taking. Polarization develops between the "new" planning oriented staff of the experimental program and the proponents of "old" planning working in other sections of the department. The widening gulf is further accentuated by the two factions' extreme differences in personal style, background, and work attitudes. As community planning gathers momentum, the problems of coordinating the community planning program with the traditional activities of its parent bureaucracy grow increasingly acute.

Sociological theories on the life cycle of innovations in bureaucracies suggest that such a troublesome experiment is likely to be quickly suppressed or modified by its parent bureaucracy. The community planning program, however, escapes this fate because of the unusual organizational characteristics of the planning department, which we have labeled a *counter-irrational bureaucracy*. To survive and protect its interests in the irrational context of city politics, the planning department has been forced to develop an equally irrational internal structure. For instance, to compensate for low salaries the department uses professional autonomy as a reward even though this means renouncing rational hierarchy and supervision. In response to the department's politically determined budget, the planning director tries to strengthen his position by responding rapidly to informational requests from political officials even if this leaves the planning staff's work schedule in shambles. In the effort to enhance its weak advisory role in city policy making, the department overextends itself with innumerable new projects and programs, hoping that one may unexpectedly capture the imagination of a powerful political sponsor. The chaotic internal organization that results from these counter-irrational adaptations renders innovations such as community planning less efficient and elegant than they might be in a more rational organizational setting. But at the same time, a counter-irrational bureaucracy like the planning department lacks the controls—advancement, hierarchical access to information, supervision, scheduled production expectations—usually employed to keep deviant staff members in line in bureaucracies. Thus the organizational chaos resulting from counter-irrationality shelters disruptive innovations like community planning and allows them to survive intact and even flourish despite the threat they pose to the parent bureaucracy's traditional mode of operation.

The planning department's management does not easily give up the attempt to control administrative guerrillas in the community planning program. Indeed, elaborate systems of *controls by training* and *operational controls* are devised to socialize or coerce the program's staff into compliance with the department's traditional approach. The effectiveness of such controls is limited, however, by the unusually high potential for job mobility among community planners. Young, highly qualified, and usually uninterested in making a permanent career in the city planning department, community planners whose activities are successfully restrained by the department's controls will simply depart for positions of greater freedom and opportunity in some other agency or city. The planning department's management faces a dilemma: curbing administrative guerrillas through direct controls means driving the most talented and creative staff members out of the experimental program. As we have noted, the community planning experiment holds great symbolic signifi-

cance for the department, constituting its major answer to
the critics of city planning. The thought of mediocritizing
such an important new program's staff gives pause even to
the most apprehensive and control-minded of department
managers. Thus the management falls back on an indirect
form of control, *control by inertia*. That is, the department
simply refuses to budge from its traditional elite-council encapsulated stance in its official presentation of department
recommendations, ignoring the contrary recommendations
and reports submitted by community planners. Far more effectively than direct controls, this approach circumscribes and
isolates the community planner's operations. However free
the individual administrative guerrilla may be to pursue his
arena-council expansionism on a personal level, he cannot
push his department into taking a broader and more politically active role in city government.

Nevertheless, the community planners' individual administrative guerrilla efforts inevitably bring them—and through
them, the planning department—into conflict with powerful figures in the city's bureaucracy. Specifically, the community planning pressure system sets planners on a collision
course with the city's operating agencies. Community planners are initially pushed into involving themselves in the affairs of the operating agencies by three factors: (1) their acceptance of *total* rather than *segmental* responsibility for their
communities' well-being, which demands an expansionist
approach; (2) the unrelenting pressure for expansionism from
their communities' residents, who are far more concerned
with plan implementation and the quality of city services
provided by operating agencies than with the abstract benefits of encapsulated planning; and (3) the complicated administrative machinery usually set up for federal community development grants, which forces community planners to
depart from the planning department's traditional encapsulated role.

Once planners begin to interest themselves actively in the relations between their communities and the operating agencies, their commitment to expansionism becomes both irreversible and self-accelerating. The more they learn about how the activities of operating agencies affect their communities, the more they are convinced of the meaninglessness of encapsulated planning and the urgency of expanding the planning effort into other city agencies' jurisdictions. To the many community planners who view their work as vocation rather than employment, opposition to the operating agencies acquires the moral overtones of a "just war." By resisting expansionism and thus thwarting the planners' fervent commitment to community service, the operating agencies come to seem not merely administrative obstacles but forces of evil. This sense of outrage, apparent in the rhetoric of community planners' verbal attacks on the operating agencies, lends moral force to the expansionism generated by the community planning pressure system. The planners feel their possibilities for gaining voluntary cooperation from the operating agencies are slim because of basic structural differences in the two groups' mandate and orientation, involving contradictions in their definition of goals, perceptions of work parameters, criteria for success, and reference groups. Therefore, as community planners move into the administrative guerrilla role, they increasingly range themselves against the city's operating agencies and choose these agencies as the target on which to unleash their community "troops."

At first, the depredations of community planners on the sovereignty of operating agencies are sporadic and well concealed. If at all possible, administrative guerrillas avoid direct confrontations as a dangerous and low-yield mode of expansionism, preferring to work covertly through their double undergrounds. In this way they hope to dodge both the wrath of antagonized operating agency personnel and attempts at control by worried or unsympathetic superiors in the planning department. As more community planners join the program and move into the administrative guerrilla role, however, concealment proves increasingly difficult. However skillfully individual planners maintain their cover, the nature of their work is revealed by its consequences: a change in the level of the citizen apathy, disorganization, and ignorance which has traditionally insulated city government from the grievances of city residents.

Political officials and particularly the personnel of operating agencies begin to notice a proliferation of unusually active community groups making unaccustomed demands, suddenly showing an unnerving skill in maneuvering through the protective red tape that previously deterred citizens from utilizing their formal democratic options. Citizens begin to seem suspiciously privy to the inside information that previously gave the advantage of surprise or the protection of secrecy to the city's decision-making elite. Since the demands of citizens' groups exceed the city's financial capacity to respond, even those in city government who are sympathetic to citizen participation in policy making find this surge of citizen pressure intolerable. Personnel in the operating agencies, typically opposed in principle to any community control, explode with indignation at this challenge to their autonomy. Even though some of this citizen pressure may be unrelated to the efforts of community planners, the community planning program is quickly identified as the source of the "trouble."

By this time, some of the administrative guerrillas in the program have had enough accidental or unavoidable open clashes with operating agencies to make their presence known. Moreover, some administrative guerrillas may have moved into *administrative insurgency*, dropping their cover entirely and publicly attacking the city administration in a kind of suicide mission to save their community from some serious impending threat that cannot be fought by subtle methods. Powerful figures in the city administration begin to feel they are harboring among their employees a group of disloyal agitators who irresponsibly run around leaking privileged information and stirring up the citizens. In effect, they conclude that the community planning experiment, intended to ease tensions rather than aggravate them, has backfired. A *bureaucratic backlash* builds, its object to abolish community planning.

In response to this backlash, the management of the planning department may try to defend its experimental program, through *containment* if the planning director is personally committed to elite-council encapsulated planning and through *camouflage* if he is personally sympathetic to the arena-council expansionist assumptions of community planning. Both defenses fail, containment because the planning department lacks effective controls over its community planners and camouflage because there is no way to disguise the consequences of the community planners' administrative guerrilla efforts no matter how well hidden the community planners themselves may be. Once a critical mass of administrative guerrilla activity is reached, the program inevitably provokes counterattacks from outside the department, particularly from the operating agencies. Ironically, it seems that through its very success, the community planning program creates the condition for its own suppression by external pressures on its parent bureaucracy. The planning department that sponsors community planning, due to its own marginal position in city government, cannot resist indefinitely a strong bureaucratic backlash. Eventually, it can be forced—by threats of budget cuts and injury to its advisory role—to discontinue the community planning program. Thus the community planning experiment may be, in an organizational sense, self-limiting.

Community planning is also self-limiting on a social psychological level for the individuals who participate in it. The extraordinarily high turnover rate among those acting as administrative guerrillas indicates that many planners find this role tolerable only for a relatively short period. Administrative guerrillas complain of a high level of stress traceable to features inherent in the role. First, the personal demands on the planner's time, energy, and emotional commitment steadily escalate because the guerrilla role fails to provide the clear role limits and rituals of role withdrawal available to most professionals. Second, the characteristically wide gap between effort expended and achievements attained exposes the planner to an ever-increasing accumulation of frustration and disappointment which wears down his commitment to the role. Third, the satisfactions of the role often sour because the administrative guerrilla's successes are inconsistent with his broader value commitments and self-image. For instance, many administrative guerrillas express deep ambivalence about the politicality of their work, feeling they are abandoning their training in planning skills entirely in favor of political activism in which they are basically amateurs. They are disturbed by the conservatism—in some cases, the racism —of the demands their community residents wish to see implemented. And many find themselves increasingly alienated from their work by a growing recognition of the triviality of their victories, virtually meaningless when measured against the magnitude of the urban problems they confront.

After two or three years of exposure to these stresses, the typical administrative guerrilla will reach a breaking point of exhaustion, frustration, and disillusionment and will drop out of the program, partially protecting his self-esteem with one of several common rationalizations for leaving. The departing planner takes his painfully developed, nontransferrable community rapport and guerrilla skills with him. His place in the community planning program will be taken by a fresh planner, who will typically be molded by the community planning pressure system into a new administrative guerrilla. Because of this systematic rapid turnover, we have termed the position of administrative guerrilla a *volatile role:* one that self-destructs once it is actualized, quickly driving out the role occupant. In this respect, community planning resembles other social service programs such as religious service work, social work, civil rights organizations, VISTA, and the Peace Corps. All of these programs attract young and idealistic recruits, many of whom—like the administrative guerrillas in the community planning program—drop out after a few years of intense involvement.

The common feature in these programs appears to be that they combine idealism with positions of opportunity, thus allowing a large proportion of their staff to fashion volatile roles for themselves. Many such programs have made some organizational accommodation to their high level of role volatility. For instance, in some of the older service programs (such as social work), role limits and rituals of role withdrawal are available to those in the program who wish to avoid taking on a volatile role or perhaps wish to take a respite from their volatile role while still remaining with the program. In some of the newer programs (like VISTA), the high turnover intrinsic in volatile roles is institutionalized and role occupants are expected—even required—to leave after a specified period. Tragically for the community planners' self-esteem, role volatility in community planning is so far neither easily avoidable nor clearly recognized for what it is. Forced into a role which cannot be borne for long, the community planner often is blamed by others and by himself for desertion and irresponsibility when he leaves. The emotional burden of community planning for individuals who enter it would be considerably lightened if it were recognized that the program imposes a volatile role on most of its staff, preventing them from making the job a permanent career. Without this recognition, many community planners enter the program expecting a long plane ride and find themselves instead on a roller coaster, caught up in a rush of exhilarating, all-consuming frantic motion that quickly runs its course and leaves them unexpectedly earthbound, shakily wondering what happened.

The Future of Community Planning

What lies ahead for the community planning experiment? Is it, as some believe, a passing fad doomed to bring about its own demise and fade from the city planning scene? We believe not. The concerns and pressures that originally give rise to community planning programs do not disappear with the suppression of the community planning experiment—quite the contrary. The city government still writhes on the horns of the same dilemma: how to stay within the limits of its pitifully inadequate resources and still somehow cope with growing urban decay, unrest, and the draining away of the city's economic lifeblood to the suburbs. Barring an unforeseen massive influx of funds, decentralization of planning will remain one of the most attractive options available to the city government as an inexpensive pacificatory symbol of its concern for city residents.

Similarly, pressure for community planning from within the profession of city planning seems unlikely to slacken, as more and more young planners gain exposure to "new" planning in the course of their training. The "new" planning orientation—encompassing political activism, expansion into social planning, and commitment to arena-council citizen participation—could of course be channeled into a number of alternative innovative approaches to city planning. However, without a major reorganization of the power relationships presently obtaining between the planning department and other parts of the city's administrative machinery, it seems likely that decentralization in the form of community planning will remain the outlet most feasible for "new" planning enthusiasts within the planning department. Pressure for the perpetuation of community planning also comes from higher levels of government, since community planning or something approximating it remains a requirement of a number of federally funded urban development programs.

Perhaps most important, the community organization and mobilization encouraged by the program during its existence assures a continuing clamor for bureaucratic enfranchisement from community groups. Where community residents have become familiar with the planning department's potential for providing community advocates, they will constitute a lobby for the restoration of community planning. As conditions worsen in their communities, it seems likely that greater numbers of citizens' groups will demand assistance from the city on a decentralized basis, formally asking for planning aid and informally trying to secure the services of an administrative guerrilla.

Because of these strong pressures from multiple sources, the suppression of the community planning experiment seems unlikely to be permanent. We predict that after a dormant period, the crushed community planning programs will reappear in altered form, perhaps under a different name, with a new set of controls designed to contain their staff more effectively than before. The reactivated community planning pressure system will again force the new community planners into evasion of these controls, generating a new crop of administrative guerrillas. Once the critical mass of guerrilla activity is reached, the program may again succumb to a bureaucratic backlash—only to be resurrected later as the cycle begins anew. Despite its apparent precariousness, this innovation seems fated to be with us until major changes take place in the financing of cities, the mandate of planning departments, the nature of professional training in city planning, or the level of citizen grievances. The community planning experiment is not a fad, but a movement—the predictable outcome of pressures that drive irresistibly, with a kind of tortured tropism, toward the most immediate "solution" to recurring and fundamental urban problems.

Any assessment of what the community planning experiment will mean for urban development and the profession of city planning in America must, at this early stage of the movement, be tentative. Our analysis of community planning suggests that the movement is in many ways irreconcilable with rational urban planning and development. Some problems that plague community planning are too serious to be shrugged off. For instance, meaningful decentralization of city planning requires a degree of community consciousness and organization on the part of community residents that rarely if ever characterizes urban populations in this country. The few identifiable "communities" that do exist in our cities are not the kind appropriate for planning units, being small and usually lacking in consensus on their boundaries, development priorities, and legitimate representatives. In the absence of population collectivities with clear social and geographical boundaries, decentralized planning must involve the creation of planning units arbitrarily designated as communities despite their heterogeneity and lack of cohesion. The troubled efforts of the community planners we interviewed to create a community where none existed before by heightening community consciousness, organizing the residents, and singling out parts of the present or potential resident population as the "true community" while ignoring others only underscore this problem. It is hard to see how decentralized arena-council planning can be made to operate successfully without the benefit of preexisting communities.

An even more serious question grows out of the inevitable conflict between interests of the city population as a whole and the interests of smaller collectivities of city residents. Rational and equitable allocation of city resources and services, let alone the benefits and costs of private urban development, seems unlikely to emerge from a free-for-all of small units

each seeking to maximize its individual share. Weakly organized communities or those lacking aggressive administrative
guerrillas will continue to lose out despite their urgent needs.
As we have seen, some of the most successful community
planners are deeply distressed by the Darwinian implications
of their own efforts. One thoughtful community planner put
the problem succinctly: "Without structural changes in
United States society, we can only heighten participatory democracy and add to the number of self-seeking groups. This
organizes the debate, not the results. It's a policy of 'Screw
thy neighbor.'" Parochialism, irrationality, and insensitivity
to all arguments of relative need are part and parcel of community planning. In this sense, we must interpret community
planning as a step backward from the ideal of a humane kind
of city planning more sensitive to equity than to power.

However, the existence of these persistent and undeniable
problems does not in itself demonstrate the undesirability of
the community planning movement. Community planning
cannot be extricated from its social context: a nation suffering
the rapid and bitter breakdown of whatever value consensus
it may have had in the past. Decentralization in any social
system that lacks value integration must necessarily increase
internal conflict, but conflict is not a self-evident dysfunction
in such a system. Where basic priorities and values are themselves at issue, the amplification of previously unheard grievances will seem dysfunctional from the perspective of those in
privileged positions, but highly functional to those who are
disadvantaged.

So it is with community planning. The planning alternative
to the parochial pluralism of the community planning movement is not an abstract ideal of humanistic rationality. Rather
it is the traditional elite-council planning that has catered to
commercial, institutional, and industrial interests, virtually ignoring the needs of city residents. This ordering of priorities
does not necessarily result from conspiracy and corruption on

the part of a tightly organized, insensitive power elite. Indeed, in most of the cities we visited, a more pluralistic model of shifting alliances and coalitions among overlapping and sometimes conflicting power factions (some quite sympathetic to citizen needs) seems to fit better with our observations. However, the details of the city's power structure are overshadowed by its economic plight. Whether the city's power structure is unified or fragmented, the policies issuing from city hall have a similar urgent aim: maintaining the economic viability of the city.

Given the present institutional context of city government, this concern inevitably implies greater responsiveness to the large public and private institutions whose economic contribution is felt to be important to the city (business, industry, hospitals, universities, civic centers and stadiums, and the highway and parking systems to serve them). Correspondingly, it means less responsiveness to the city's residents, whose economic contribution as individuals is viewed as negligible—whether they be black or white, and regardless of their income level. We saw citizens' groups of all types registering concern over inadequate city services, unwanted developments in their neighborhoods, or displacement by highways, institutional expansion, and urban renewal. These groups had greater or lesser access to and influence on their local government, depending on their own characteristics and the particular city involved. Certainly the cities differed in the way the chief executive and other city officials regarded citizen demands. But overall, even in the most receptive cities, the interests of residents were given lower priority than those of the commercial, civic, institutional, and industrial organizations they found themselves in conflict with— especially on the issue of land use.

Since the definition of city needs reflected in past city plans and policies is so inimical to their own interests, community residents understandably distrust centralized city planning. From their limited perspective, decentralized planning is far preferable, even though it may increase conflict and retard rational urban development. Community planning appeals to them because it offers a way to protect their communities from an otherwise impenetrable bureaucracy that has systematically victimized city residents, sometimes reluctantly but with ominous consistency.

It is our belief that neither centralized nor decentralized city planning can function rationally and humanely without basic social changes. Both are hamstrung by "missing factors"—missing money, missing institutions to cope with the balkanization of metropolitan areas into scores of autonomous administrative units, missing authority and legitimacy for the concept of planning, even missing faith that the decline of America's cities can be halted. As long as city planning means dispiritedly juggling meager resources in a zero-sum allocation game, someone must lose—and badly. Decentralized community planning (where it is effective at all) will necessarily be bitter, narrow, and selfish, as residents of each community try to make sure they are not the losers. And centralized planning (where it is effective at all) cannot help but be autocratic, responsive to economic power, and insensitive to the needs of community residents, as concern for the city's economic viability dictates.

If some of the missing factors were supplied, features of the community planning movement might be incorporated into centralized city planning in such a way as to satisfy community residents' claim to bureaucratic enfranchisement formally rather than informally. We can envision, for instance, a system of "tradeoff planning" in which communities might be encouraged to assume the burden of serving a city-wide need in order to secure some equivalent special benefit for their own community (over and above normal services) by way of compensation. Formal mechanisms for the dispensation of information and redress of grievances—say, by an ombudsman system—could be established to render the general services that community planners are now called on to provide as administrative guerrillas. Greater formal veto powers over planning decisions could be extended to the neighborhoods affected, replacing the informal veto powers now secured by guerrilla tactics; an arbitration procedure might be added to deal with the difficult stalemates that often result from guerrilla-inspired community vetoes. Planning control could be extended over the city's operating agencies to assure more rational delivery of services, with mandatory consultation with community residents and easily accessible grievance machinery. Similarly, increased planning control over private developers could force greater responsiveness to community demands in this area. Centralized city planning with such broadened scope and formalized citizen inputs could perhaps in time discard its reputation as a tool of giant business and government organizations and be seen as a means of enhancing the general welfare.

In the meantime, the community planning movement offers the best hope of bureaucratic enfranchisement to city residents whose interests have been dangerously and unjustly ignored by traditional city planning. With its flaws and shortcomings, community planning represents a step backward from what planning must someday become if it is to guide urban development constructively. However, this form of planning must be measured not only against ideals but against the available alternatives. Amputation of a crushed limb may seem to injure a person further, but it can be necessary for his ultimate survival. Heightened solidarity in racial minorities may seem an escalation of race consciousness, yet it may be necessary to create the conditions for equality and a true end to racism. In the same way, community planning seems a step backward in the advancement toward meaningful city planning. But in the strained and uncertain social environment of urban America in the 1970s, the step backward is necessary.

Appendix A

The Interview Schedule

A. *The Organization of the Planner's Work*

1. What is your rank and present position in the agency?

   (a) How long have you held this job?

2. What does your job consist of—what do you do?

   (a) How do you get your work assignments?
   (b) What happens to your reports?
   (c) How are they evaluated? How do you know if you're doing a good job or not?

3. Has the job changed much since you first came on?

4. What are the main problems you run into in doing the job the way you think it should be done?

5. Which of the other departments of city government give you the most trouble?

(a) Should the functions of any of the other city departments be transferred or more closely coordinated with the planning department?

6. What rules or regulations, written and unwritten, are you expected to follow?

7. Why did you leave your last position?

8. Why did you decide to take a job with this agency?

(a) What were you promised?
(b) What did you expect?

9. Did things turn out the way you hoped they would?

10. What are your chances for advancement in the agency?

11. Since you've been working here, have you ever been offered a position in:
(a) another planning department
(b) a state agency
(c) a federal agency
(d) a university
(e) a private business

12. Would you consider taking a job with any of these departments or firms?

(a) How would you feel about working for an (urban) (suburban) planning agency?

13. How many of your colleagues have left this agency since you started working here?

(a) Why did they leave?
(b) Where did they go?

B. *Planners' Role Orientations and Their Transformations*

14. What kind of work did you expect planning to be at the time you were graduated from college?

15. What was your first planning job?

   (a) Where and when?
   (b) How'd you like it?
   (c) Was it what you expected? (Brief job history)

16. Do you feel your previous training prepared you for the work you're doing now, overprepared you, led you to expect something different?

17. What kind of work in planning do you prefer to do? Why?

   (a) What size of unit?
   (b) What kinds of projects?

18. What does planning mean to you?

19. Do you think plans are relevant or irrelevant to city development?

20. Do you think of yourself as a professional?

   (a) What does being a professional planner mean to you?
   (b) How would you define it?

21. Do you look upon your work as a job, one that has its rewards but still basically a job—or do you see it as something very special, like a calling?

22. Many young planners expect to plan and help implement a large number of projects when they leave school. But after a few years of actually working in the planning field, they become increasingly uncertain of how much they will accomplish during their professional careers.

   Do you agree or disagree? Please comment.

23. Do you see yourself as:

   (a) a technician—one who does his own assigned work and prefers to stay out of other people's business
   (b) an independent intellectual—one who formulates and

presses his own views on basic policy issues even if
others disagree

(c)   a broker—one who works out compromises between
the community and the city, or between contending
forces in the government or the agency

(d)   an advocate—one who represents a certain group of
people in the community, particularly a deprived minority group

(e)   a regionalist—one who is dedicated to advancing the
development of regional planning and regional government

24.   If you were choosing a career over again, what profession
or occupation would you choose?

C.   The Role of Planning in the Decision-Making Process

25.   What do you think is the function of the planning agency
in this city?

26.   How much influence do you think you have on the decisions of city officials?

(a)   Can you give me some examples?
(b)   In what way do you influence decisions?

27.   What do you think is the planner's proper role in the city's
decision-making process?

28.   What additional powers should the planning department
have?

29.   Do you think planners should have architectural review, or
site review only?

30.   Is your work affected by political pressure to modify your
professional views?

(a)   What do you do about it?

31. Some writers say planners have become so dependent on the good will of the city manager and city council that they cease to do any real planning and spend their time in doing housekeeping chores for the city officials.

Do you agree or disagree? Please comment.

D. *Involvement in Policy Issues*

32. What controversial issues has the planning agency been involved in recently?

33. What do you think are the most crucial policy issues facing your department?

34. What do you think your department should be doing for the city that it is not doing now?

    (a) Is there anything it should be doing faster?

35. Have there been any formal or informal discussions among you and your colleagues about basic city planning policy issues?

    (a) (If no) Why no discussion?
    (b) (If yes) What were they?

36. Why do you think planners tend to refrain from getting involved with the basic planning policies of their agency and city government?

37. Have you ever had a serious or basic difference of opinion over a planning issue with anyone in the agency?

    (a) Or with anyone in the community?

38. What would you do if the director or city officials rejected what you believed to be the best program or solution to a problem?

39. Under what conditions would you resign in protest from this agency?

E. *The Planner's Stand on Current Controversies*

   40. Do you feel planners should concern themselves with social as well as physical aspects of city development?

   41. Many academic planners seem to feel that regional or metropolitan planning is a necessary condition for meeting the urban crisis, yet many practicing planners are unenthusiastic or opposed to these types of planning. Why do you think this is so?

   42. What role should the residents play in the planning and rehabilitation of their neighborhoods?

        (a) How much authority should they have?

   43. What do you think of the HUD requirements of citizen participation?

   44. Can you think of a time when you were torn between responding to the demands of residents in a section of the city and the politics of your agency?

   45. What part do you think advocate planning should play in the planning process?

   46. In your experience, which interest groups are most likely to oppose proposals made by the planning agency?

   47. What kind of reasons do people give when they oppose the agency's proposals?

   48. Has there ever been a time you didn't understand the reasons of those who opposed a project or proposal you supported?

   49. Has the composition of interest group pressure changed over the years?

        (a) Is it more or less an asset?

   50. What contacts do you have with the leaders of the city's minority groups?

51. Who do you think benefits most from the work of your department?

52. Planners have been accused of being too concerned with improving the central business district, to the point of neglecting the deterioration and shortage in housing.

    Do you agree or disagree? Please comment.

53. Urban renewal and the highway programs have been bitterly attacked on the grounds that these programs have been insensitive to the needs of the poor and members of minority groups in particular. Do you think that city planners are in any way responsible for these programs and the negative consequences that have flowed from them?

    (a) Do you think planners abdicated their professional responsibilities to minorities and the poor?
    (b) Should they have acted differently?
    (c) Are planners, you and the other members of your department in particular, acting differently now?

F. *For Agency Director Only*

54. Could you furnish me with a table of organization and job descriptions of the positions in the table and those not given? I'd like to know also:

    (a) The number of employees in each of these positions and the number of vacancies for each of these positions.
    (b) The range of salaries for professional staff people in your department.
    (c) Something about your in-service training program, if any.
    (d) Do you generally promote from within the agency or seek planners for higher positions from outside the agency?
    (e) Could you describe the typical career pattern for the planners in your agency?

55. Could you draw up a list of all the powers the agency has been legally granted and also a list of all the prerogatives or

informal planning powers the planning agency has acquired over time as a matter of custom?

56. Does this agency have high or low turnover?

   (a) Could you give me the actual numbers for those hired and leaving during the past year?
   (b) Which of the planners in your department are planning to leave?

57. How did you first make contact with the planners you've hired?

   (a) Have you had trouble filling vacancies? If so, why?
   (b) What has your agency done in response to the shortage?

58. What do you look for in hiring staff for your department?

   (a) What do you think about hiring planners fresh out of graduate school?

59. How do you evaluate the work of the members of your staff?

   (a) What criteria or measures of efficiency or of quality do you use?

60. How often do you have staff meetings?

   (a) Do you have any other kind of scheduled meetings between you and the agency staff?

61. Whose advice do you take most seriously in forming policies for the agency? (Both in and out of the agency)

62. Have you ever had a serious difference of opinion with:

   (a) members of your staff
   (b) city manager
   (c) councilman
   (d) mayor
   (e) members of the community

(f) federal official
(g) state official

63. Do you feel you get enough cooperation from top city officials?

64. What kind of proposals does the city administration seem most receptive to?

(a) Does timing make any difference?

65. Do you expect the budget for your department to go through next year as requested?

(a) Has it increased over the years, or decreased?
(b) How much more do you think you should be getting over what you're getting now?

67. Does the city government, or does the planning agency itself, ever call in outside planning consultants?

Appendix B

Background Data Sheet

G. Background Data

68. Date of birth: _____

69. Where raised: _____

70. Marital status: M__ Sing__ D__ Sep__ W__

71. Does your spouse work? no__yes (occupation)_____

72. Education:

	name	location	yrs	degree	major	minor
high school						
college						
grad school						
other						

73. Association membership:
Professional—   Social and political _____
AIP: yes__yrs__no__   _____ yrs__

357

ASPO: yes__yrs __no__   _____yrs __
others: _____ yrs__   _____yrs __
          _____yrs__   _____yrs __

74. Professional activity:
     Do   you   attend   professional   meetings?   yes__how
     often_____no__
     Have you ever submitted a paper for the association meet-
     ing?
     yes__no__how many____when_____
     Have you ever read a paper at the association meeting?
     yes__no__how many____when_____
     Have you ever submitted a paper for a professional publi-
     cation in your field?
     yes__no__how many____when_____
     which_____
     Have you ever published a paper in a professional journal?
     yes__no__how many____when_____
     which_____
     Do you subscribe to any professional publications?
     yes__no__
     which: JAIP____ASPO yearbook____others_____

75. Religion:
     Prot____Cath____Jewish____other_____none_____

76. Would you please tell me the primary occupation of the
     following relatives, even if retired or deceased:
     Father_____
     Father-in-law_____
     Brothers_____
     Brothers-in-law_____
     Sons_____

77. Please indicate your individual income range:
     _____below $9,000   _____$14,000–15,000
     _____$9,000–10,000   _____$15,000–20,000
     _____$10,000–11,000   _____$20,000–25,000
     _____$11,000–12,000   _____$25,000–30,000
     _____$12,000–13,000   _____$30,000 or over
     _____$13,000–14,000

78. Political affiliation:————————————————————————

JOB HISTORY

Agency / Concern	Job Title(s)	Years	Very Satisfied			Very Dissatisfied	
			1	2	3	4	5

Bibliography

Abrams, Charles. *The City Is the Frontier*. New York: Harper Colophon Books, 1965.

Altshuler, Alan. *The City Planning Process*. Ithaca, N.Y.: Cornell University Press, 1965.

Bailey, F. G. "Decisions by Consensus in Councils and Committees." *Political Systems and the Distribution of Power*. Edited by Michael Banton. London: Tavistock Press, 1966.

Baron, Harold M. "Black Powerlessness in Chicago." *Majority & Minority*. Edited by Norman R. Yetman and C. Hoy Steele. Boston: Allyn and Bacon, 1971.

Bensman, Joseph, and Arthur Vidich. "Social Theory in Field Research." *Sociology on Trial*. Edited by Maurice Stein and Arthur Vidich. Englewood Cliffs, N.J.: Prentice-Hall, 1963.

Blau, Peter. *Dynamics of Bureaucracy*. Chicago: University of Chicago Press, 1955.

Building the American City: Report of the National Commission on Urban Problems (Douglas Report). New York: Praeger, 1969.

Chinoy, Ely. *Automobile Workers and the American Dream*. Garden City, N.Y.: Doubleday, 1955.

Clark, Burton R. "Organizational Adaptation and Precarious Values." *Complex Organizations*. Edited by Amitai Etzioni. New York: Holt, Rinehart and Winston, 1961.

Davidoff, Paul. "Advocacy and Pluralism in Planning." *Journal of the American Institute of Planners*, XXXI (1965), 331–338.

————, and Thomas Reiner. "A Choice Theory of Planning." *Journal of the American Institute of Planners*, XXV (1959), 108.

Downs, Anthony. *Inside Bureaucracy*. Boston: Little, Brown and Company, 1967.

Dyckman, John W. "What Makes Planners Plan?" *Journal of the American Institute of Planners*, XXVII (1961), 162–167.

Eldredge, H. Wentworth. "Toward a National Policy for Planning the Environment." *Urban Planning in Transition*. Edited by Ernest Erber. New York: Grossman, 1970.

Ewald, William R., Jr. "National Planning Cannot Wait for an Elite." *Urban Planning in Transition*. Edited by Ernest Erber. New York: Grossman, 1970.

Fagin, Henry. "Advancing the 'State of the Art.'" *Urban Planning in Transition*. Edited by Ernest Erber. New York: Grossman, 1970.

Fellman, Gordon. "Neighborhood Protest of an Urban Highway." *Journal of the American Institute of Planners*, XXXIV (1969), 118–122.

Fried, Joseph P. *Housing Crisis U.S.A.* New York: Praeger, 1971.

Frieden, Bernard J. "Toward Equality of Urban Opportunity." *Journal of the American Institute of Planners*, XXXI (1965), 320–330.

Gans, Herbert J. *People and Plans: Essays on Urban Problems and Solutions*. New York: Basic Books, 1968.

————. "The Failure of Urban Renewal: A Critique and Some Proposals." *Urban Renewal: People, Politics and Planning*. Edited by Jewel Bellush and Murry Hausknecht. Garden City, N.Y.: Anchor Books, 1967.

————. *The Urban Villagers*. New York: The Free Press, 1962.

Gouldner, Alvin W. "Metaphysical Pathos and the Theory of Bureaucracy." *Complex Organizations*. Edited by Amitai Etzioni. New York: Holt, Rinehart and Winston, 1961.

————. *Patterns of Industrial Bureaucracy*. Glencoe, Ill.: The Free Press, 1954.

Hansen, Niles M. *Rural Poverty and the Urban Crisis: A Strategy for Regional Development.* Bloomington: Indiana University Press, 1970.

Heikoff, Joseph M. "The Planning Profession in Search of Itself." *Planning 1964, Yearbook of the American Society of Planning Officials.* Chicago: ASPO, 1964.

Hollander, Theodore E. "How Encompassing Can the Profession Be?" *Urban Planning in Transition.* Edited by Ernest Erber. New York: Grossman, 1970.

Howard, John T. "City Planning as a Social Movement." *Planning and the Urban Community.* Edited by Harvey S. Perloff. Pittsburgh: University of Pittsburgh Press, 1961.

Lewis, Peter, A. "The Uncertain Future of the Planning Profession." *Urban Planning in Transition.* Edited by Ernest Erber. New York: Grossman, 1970.

Liebow, Elliot. *Tally's Corner.* Boston: Little, Brown and Company, 1967.

Lipset, Seymour M. "Bureaucracy and Social Reform." *Complex Organizations.* Edited by Amitai Etzioni. New York: Holt, Rinehart and Winston, 1961.

Mauro, John T. Speech reprinted in *Planning 1968, Yearbook of the American Society of Planning Officials.* Chicago: ASPO, 1968.

Merton, Robert K. *Social Theory and Social Structure.* Glencoe, Ill.: The Free Press, 1957.

Michels, Robert. *Political Parties.* Glencoe, Ill.: The Free Press, 1949.

Mills, C. Wright. *White Collar.* New York: Oxford University Press, 1951.

Powledge, Fred. *Model City.* New York: Simon and Schuster, 1970.

Rabinowitz, Francine F. *City Politics and Planning.* New York: Atherton Press, 1969.

Raymond, George M., Malcolm D. Rivkin, and Herbert J. Gans. "Urban Renewal: Controversy." *Urban Renewal: People, Politics and Planning.* Edited by Jewel Bellush and Murry Hausknecht. Garden City, N.Y.: Anchor Books, 1967.

Report of the National Advisory Committee on Civil Disorders (Kerner Report). Washington, D.C.: Government Printing Office, 1968, Vols. I and II.

Reps, John W. "The Future of American Planning." *Planning 1967, Yearbook of the American Society of Planning Officials.* Chicago: ASPO, 1967.

Safford, Walter W., and Joyce Ladner. "Comprehensive Planning and Racism." *Journal of the American Institute of Planners*, *XXXV* (1969), 68–74.

Scott, Mel. *American City Planning Since 1890*. Berkeley: University of California Press, 1969.

Seeley, John R. "What Is Planning? Definition and Strategy." *Journal of the American Institute of Planners*, *XXVIII* (1962), 92–93.

Segoe, Ladislas. "The Planning Profession: Its Progress and Some Problems." *Planning 1964, Yearbook of the American Society of Planning Officials*. Chicago: ASPO, 1964.

Selznick, Philip. *Leadership in Administration*. Evanston, Ill.: Row Peterson, 1957.

———. *TVA and the Grass Roots*. New York: Harper & Row, 1949.

Stollman, Israel. Speech reprinted in *Planning 1968, Yearbook of the American Society of Planning Officials*. Chicago: ASPO, 1968.

Vidich, Arthur J., Joseph Bensman, and Maurice R. Stein, Eds. *Reflections on Community Studies*. New York: Harper & Row, Harper Torchbook edition, 1971.

Wheaton, William L. C., and Margaret F. Wheaton. "Identifying the Public Interest: Values and Goals," with accompanying comments by C. David Loeks and Charles R. Ross. *Urban Planning in Transition*. Edited by Ernest Erber. New York: Grossman, 1970.

Whyte, William Foote. *Street Corner Society*. Chicago: University of Chicago Press, 1955.

Wilensky, Harold L. *Intellectuals in Labor Unions*. Glencoe, Ill.: The Free Press, 1956.

Williams, Robert L. "The Planner and His Profession." *Planning 1964, Yearbook of the American Society of Planning Officials*. Chicago: ASPO, 1964.

Index